Leslie

Fen Farming Family

Putting You in the Picture

To Elspeth

Best Wishes
Lesley & Paddy

Lesley Goad

"In life we don't remember days,
We remember moments"

Copyright 2014 Lesley Goad

First published in 2014 by

Milton Contact Ltd

A CIP catalogue record for this book is available from

The British Library

ISBN: 978-0-9929289-0-2

**Part of the proceeds from the sale of this book will go
towards research into Parkinson's Disease in memory
of Sarah (Sally) Goad.**

Image on back cover: Dion Gallichan Photography

Printed in United Kingdom

Milton Contact Ltd

3 Hall End, Milton, Cambridge, UK

CB24 6AQ

www.miltoncontact.co.uk

Fulfilment

Deep in the pool of life all wonders sleep,
　　Yet at a touch are summoned to disport,
Full-sensed and yielding gaily to the will
That lures them from the silence and the gloom.

Like winking bubbles in a glass they rise,
All iridescent, leaping to be free
And every moment changing their design;
A destiny in every random gleam.

So butterflies are born to brave the air,
As pastel poplars grace the flowing breeze;
As dolphins arc and dive in ecstasy
And children run upon sands in glee.

But for the burning genius of the sun,
The pale moon's Cupid glance upon the earth
And every rhythm pulsed from farther space,
Creation's sweet fulfilment had not come.

When memory's eye looks down the aisles of Time,
Let golden dreams dissolve the mists of grief:
When, in the shadow and the light, the years
Will wake and pass in beauty, one by one.

Like daffodils the young friends dance again;
Love's roses linger in the summer dusk;
Glowing the harvest where ripe wisdom dwell
And innocent December's quiet farewell.

Ted Ellis 1909-1986
Norfolk Naturalist, Author and Friend.

Dedication

A gift to my husband Paddy Goad

With Love from Lesley

"So long as men can breathe, and eyes can see
So long lives this, and this gives life to thee."

William Shakespeare
Sonnet 18

Contents

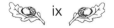

Millway 'Goadfest' garden, 2012

Musical Goads: Paddy singing with Martin on guitar

'GOADFEST' 2012

My husband Paddy and I decided to have a family get together at our home, 'Millway' Stretham, Cambridgeshire, and after a lot of planning we set upon Sunday July 8th 2012.

We sent out invitations with our 2011 Christmas cards and waited for the right responses from his two brothers, six cousins and their families, all sharing descent from Great Grandfather James Stuart Goad and Mary Jane Jacobs-Goad.

Full of enthusiasm Paddy and I started planning the details, a hog-roast lunch was ordered for all, so we decided to hire a marquee, tables and chairs, knowing how inclement English summers can be.

As it turned out, 2012 was the wettest spring/summer since records began, flooding occurring constantly in various parts of Britain.

The day before we erected extra tents as a precaution, but still hoping the weather would be kind to us. After a momentous deluge and downpour the night before, Sunday happily stayed dry for us – all generations meeting and mingling in our garden, the sun even shone for us.

There was lots of talking, laughter and bonding with individual families who rarely meet, travelling from Cambridgeshire, Derbyshire, Hampshire, Leicestershire, Lincolnshire, London, Norfolk, Scotland, Suffolk and Yorkshire.

Music was provided by Paddy's brother Martin and friends. Having once been part of the 1980s band 'The Look' and having then appeared on the BBC Show 'Top of the Pops' playing their hit, 'I am the Beat'.

All the musical generations of Goads then sang their "party pieces", a good fun day was had by all, and a group photograph was taken for posterity.

I had prepared a sketchy 'Family Tree' for the occasion, with a few interesting photographs of the past I had selected for interest; our cousins brought their favourites too, along with their memories. Happily reminiscing together we discovered how little we knew of our previous generations, and all this uncertainty proved to be the catalyst to me writing this family story.

Lots of gaps in our family tree! Lots of questions we asked, and we found lots needing to be answered!

The little knowledge I had gathered Paddy asked me to write down for clarity, and to also fulfil his and the family's curiosity of the unknown Goad farming heritage.

After many interesting, emotional and exciting months of researching and writing it has become what you see here today.

Our successful family day was christened by the younger generation as "Goadfest" and hopefully in the future there will be many more

Thank You to all the family for helping make the day so special.

Goadfest 2012

'Goadfest' 2012, Sunday July 8th

Family Attended

Paddy Goad
Patrick Goad
Vanessa Goad
Thomas Goad
George Goad
Grace Goad
Sarah Goad
Helen Goad

Lesley Bettinson-Smith-Goad
Mark Smith   Paul Smith
Octavia Smith   Antonia Smith
Max Casey   Scarlett Smith
Elsa Smith   Luca Smith
Thea Smith

Martin Goad
Kate Goad
Polly Goad
Alice Goad

John Howes
Derek Fullerton

Christopher Goad
Carol Goad
Yen Han Goad
Jane Goad Godfry
Paul Godfry
Susan Godfry
Hannah Godfry
Poppy Goad
Paul

Richard Goad
Pauline Goad
Nick Goad
Cathryn Goad
Laura Goad
Jamie Goad
Ben Goad
Jason Goad
Kerry Goad
Liza Jane Goad
Ted Owen Goad

Cathryn Goad Haylock
David Haylock
Emma Haylock
Ben Haylock
Sinead

David Marchant
Sally Marchant
Georgina Marchant
Christopher
Louise Marchant

Timothy Marchant
Jax Marchant
Alison Marchant
Simon Marchant
Romy Marchant
Calvin Marchant

Gillian Goad Johnson
Darren Johnson
Hannah Johnson
Joanne Blazey
Andrew Blazey

James Goad
Fiona Goad

Goad Brothers and Cousins

Photograph Left to Right

Christopher Goad – Paddy Goad – John Howes
Timothy Marchant – Gillian Goad-Johnson – Richard Goad
Cathryn Goad-Haylock – Martin Goad – David Marchant

Also remembering our two absent cousins and cousin-in-law:

Robert Goad (1941 – 2010)   John Goad (1952 – 2003)
Robert Johnson (1944 – 2004)

Putting You in the Picture

Our Goad family ancestors

Introduction

'Putting You in the Picture'

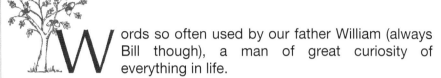

Words so often used by our father William (always Bill though), a man of great curiosity of everything in life.

This started as a project to put Paddy, my husband, 'In the picture'; to find his unknown ancestors and his family farming heritage.

Previously, all family knowledge had ended at Great Grandfather James Stuart Goad and with mysteries!

I was lucky enough to have a basic 'Goad Tree' started by Paddy's late cousin John, given to me by his sister Cathryn Goad-Haylock, plus past letters from James Stuart Goad's cousin in Canada, lent to me by Gillian Goad-Johnson, John and Cathryn's sister.

I also had some new and exciting information from a long lost cousin, John Howes.

Life is all about love stories and creating families, every generation has the same lives to cope with, birth, marriage and death and all that comes between. Only the circumstances of their time, age and its conformities will decide how it will all 'pan out'.

So, with my basic computer skills and with boundless enthusiasm I started on my journey, wherever it would take me and I finally clicked on to Ancestry.co.uk.

I have found tales to tell of disappearances, clothes on river banks, strange meetings and a suspected bigamous marriage; of a military Indian heritage completely unknown to the family, and with many lives touching great events in history: The

English Civil War, The Relief of Lucknow, The Charge of the Light Brigade, the dawn of nursing at the Royal London Hospital, WWI and our G.C. Naval hero of WWII, and his bravery when on destroyers in the Arctic convoys.

But I also discovered the simple joys of a rural farming life in the Cambridgeshire Fens, its changes through the centuries, and the interesting everyday characters whom we share our genes with. I have found tragedy and smiles in our past, and sometimes been on an emotional journey. Trying to bring a family to life of the past two centuries is a mammoth task, understanding their actions and relationships and evolving the character of and for them.

My research has taken me to many continents; from India, with X2 Great Grandfather William Trickett Reilly Goad, to America with Stuart Goad, our Great Uncle and Canada with Berry Wayman Tibbitt, Great Grandfather James Stuart Goad's, cousin, to experience their 19th century stories. All to link up with the Goad family descendants of today.

It has been a journey of many words, of patience and excitement, happiness and sadness for ancestors' lives that I have touched. Feeling empathy and understanding of the situations they have found themselves in. Gazing at the photographs and having a feeling of recognition the more you understand their lives.

A family tree is like a patchwork quilt of many shades, patterns and colours, as are people. Some stand out in their actions, others are of personal importance, each life has its own significance.

We are trailing a thread, linking the lives of our families, until we feel we have a sense of our own existence. I have gathered the threads of some of our farming and other ancestors, giving them shape and colour, trying to create a picture of our past generations – all the dark and light of their lives, their sadness and joys, which unknowingly have become a part of us today; to feel our heritage, and to become closer as a family, which consequently enables us to continue and to 'Be'; and with this knowledge, to feel secure in a kind of immortality.

I am just Goad by name by being married to Patrick John Goad (always Paddy though).

I have tried to 'Paint a Picture' in words, of a few family members whom I have grown to admire and love the more I found out about them and I hope after reading my efforts and thoughts, you will feel I have done justice to those gone before.

I hope you get as much pleasure from meeting them as I have had from finding them for you all.

Goad-Jacobs

What's in a Name?

Since the beginning of time people have been known by their name, usually linked to them by association to a trade or as a 'son of ', our surname groups us into families.

When born we all inherit our fathers name, a woman after marriage, usually takes her husband's name, thus becoming part of another 'clan' group.

This is the reason for this book, to fulfil our curiosity of our ancestors and their lives and to research and find the beginning of our 20th century family farming heritage.

All this will hopefully give us a sense of belonging and a cultural identity.

Our tribal name Goad, which is of old English origin, is not common and has links to land and cattle. On old land surveying maps a goad was the equivalent measurement of 1 old rood or todays ¼ of an acre. Also, when driving cattle, the spiked stick used by drovers was known as a goad. In the English language dictionary to 'goad' someone, is to stimulate someone into action, derived from the use of this ancient stick.

It appears land and cattle are in our ancient roots or maybe just a good stick!

By our great grandfather James Stuart Goad marrying Mary Jane Jacobs in 1882, she brought to the present day Goads a Jewish heritage of surprising interest.

Jacobs was a name chosen by many Jews when they decided to 'anglicise' their lives.

Their religion defines the Jewish nation and for this they have been persecuted all over Europe for generations, many fleeing to Britain for safety. The largest influx to Britain began in the early 17th century, although Cambridge has the earliest record of a large Jewish community in the 11th century.

For survival, they tried to integrate with the local people by changing their distinctive dress and the sound of their ethnic names, as these helped to give away their cultural identity.

The name Jacob or Jacobs was a frequent choice for a new beginning.

Jacob was the name of the Father of the twelve tribes of Israel in The Bible, so this made him important to all Jews, Israel being the 'Motherland' of the Jewish people, so consequently, an obvious popular first choice when taking a new name.

In 1902 a British law was passed, that to change your name and to become a naturalised British citizen, your new name had to be advertised in the daily newspaper.

In the first few years hundreds of thousands had been declared, mostly of Jewish decent because of the constant 'pogroms' taking place all over Europe at that time.

Hence so many of us today have these Jewish roots.

Judaism is Matriarchal, so their inheritance follows the female bloodline.

Our own family named Jacobs, when following back our direct grandfathers, takes us to a William Jacobs, born 1605, a farm labourer living in Brinkley, Cambridgeshire.

His descendants over the centuries had integrated fully into the Christian population, but still retaining the tradition of their Jewish names, shown by our own Stretham ancestor x3 Great Grandfather Meshach Jacobs and his two brothers, Shadrach and Abednego, although they were not practising Jews.

Many of Jewish heritage who do not observe any Jewish customs, will still honour the day of 'Yom Kippur'. The day of Jewish atonement celebrated in the month of September. The most important Jewish holiday, it is the day for forgiveness and the renewing of the soul, commemorating the day Moses received the Ten Commandments from God. Also the giving and receiving of His forgiveness to the people of Israel, for making and worshipping the Idol of the Golden Calf, when being led from Egypt by Moses on their forty year journey through the desert, back to their homeland Israel.

It is a day of fasting and prayer.

A prayer spoken still in most of the synagogues on this day today, is quite significant:

"Every man has a name given to him by the hills,
Given him by his walls.
Every man has a name given to him by the stars,
Given to him by his neighbours.
Every man has a name given to him by his sins
And given to him by his longings.
Every man has a name given to him by those who hate him
And given to him by his love!"

A 'New Name' for them is a 'New Story' in a 'New Land'.

How important our name is to us all!

Map

Cambridgeshire, 19th – 20th Century Goad World

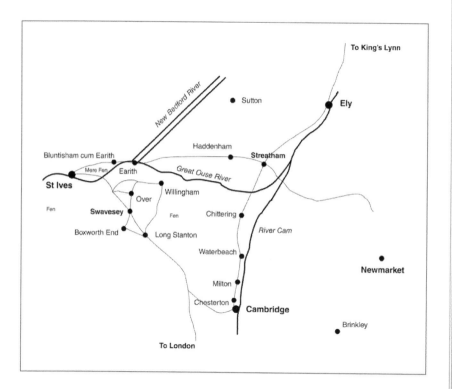

19th and 20th Century Goad World Cambridgeshire, England

Places named are all mentioned in the text

Chapter One

Sarah Curtis-Overton Marshall

1807 – 1884

'A MOTHER OF US ALL'

| Thomas Overton 1805 - Unkn. b. Norwich | m (1) 1826 | Sarah Curtis 1807 - 1884 b. Longstanton | m (2) | William Marshall 1787 - 1870 b. St. Ives |

Thomas Overton m (1) **Sarah Curtis** m (2) William
1805 - Unkn. 1826 1807 - 1884 Marshall
b. Norwich b. Longstanton 1787 - 1870
b. St. Ives

Elizabeth m. **William**
1827 - Unkn. 1858? **Trickett**
b. Norwich **Reilly Goad**
1836 - Unkn.
b. Calcutta, India

James Stuart Goad
1859 - 1928
b. Middlesex, London

Family Tree for Sarah Curtis -Overton Marshall 1807 – 1884

William and Sarah Marshall with their Family

This photograph was sent from Canada by her daughter Phoebe Marshall-Tibbitt's descendants. She was their X3 Great Grandmother too.

Sarah Curtis-Overton /Marshall

1807 – 1884   'A Mother of Us All'

Westminster, London, 1780.

In 1780, John and Mary Worley took their baby daughter to be christened Elizabeth.

She had been born on April 18th, it was now May 8th and the curate would be expecting them. They were part of the household of Sir Thomas Dingley Hatton.

It was the beginning of the London social season and it would be Harvest before they all went back to the country Manor in Longstanton, Cambridgeshire, when every hand would be needed on the land.

The Hatton family had been landowners in Longstanton since before the reign of Elizabeth 1st. Sir Thomas was descended from from Sir Christopher Hatton, the Queens Lord Chancellor. He was the patron of Sir Francis Drake, the second explorer to circumnavigate the world in 1580. Naming his ship in which he sailed 'The Golden Hind' as a tribute to the golden hind on the Hatton Family crest.

John and Mary's family had a long history on the Longstanton estate. Elizabeth grew up there, becoming a dairymaid at the 'Big' house, producing wonderful butter and cheeses.

In 1807 she married William Curtis, a local man, who also worked on the estate.

William and Elizabeth's daughter was born on December 5th, early, or so she said! But they were living in a time where it was quite normal to have a baby on the way before exchanging wedding vows!

The baby was 'our' Sarah. She flourished in the country air. She was bright, pretty and hard-working. By the time she was twelve she was living at the 'Big House'.

In this age, servants were chosen from the promising children of the humbler households on the estate. Sarah was now helping The Lady Hatton with her children, although little more than a child herself.

Every 'Season' she went to the London House as part of the big household of the family. Until one day she met a young man there from Norwich, Norfolk.

Thomas Overton, in London to make his 'fortune', and he swept Sarah off her feet!

They were duly married in St. Leonard's Church, Shoreditch, London.

Their friends Thomas and Elizabeth White were their witnesses; they left their marks in the register, with an X, just as Sarah and Thomas also did. She was nineteen and surprisingly illiterate!

It was December 31st 1826.

Sarah then had to leave the employment of the Hatton family and she and Thomas resided in rooms in Shoreditch. Their daughter Elizabeth duly arrived in 1827, born when visiting Thomas's home city of Norwich and then, when back in Shoreditch, London in 1828, their son William was born, both children named after Sarah's parents back home in Cambridgeshire.

But by the summer of that year she too was back home, living with them again in Longstanton, supposedly a widow!

Her husband, Thomas Overton had disappeared, being presumed drowned. His clothes having been found folded on the bank of the River Thames.

What a terrible event for her to cope with at such a young age, now left alone to bring up two young babies, one child for each year of her marriage.

She was now back working again on the Hatton estate, this time as a dairy maid like her mother.

But Sarah soon formed an attachment with an old friend of her father's called William Marshall, a newly widowed 'pig-jobber' from Bluntisham-cum-Earith, a village nearby. Although twenty years her senior, they were married on December 29th 1829 at St Michael's Longstanton, her village church.

Sarah was a survivor, she knew how to look after a house and home and she had found someone to take care of her. William also recognised all this in her, it suited them both.

They settled happily in Bluntisham to married life with their ready-made families. Their first son, John Curtis, came along in 1830, Emma 1833, Joseph 1834. By the time James William 1841 and Phoebe 1846, arrived, they had moved to the nearby village of Swavesey, their family now completed.

Other babies didn't survive, but Sarah always did her best for them, William worked hard for them all too. He was also a dairyman, making and selling cheeses, the family skills Sarah had known from a child.

In the 1851 census William Marshall and John Curtis, his son, who was now twenty years old, were taking cheeses to London to sell. They stayed with friends at 20 Norris Street, in the parish of St. Leonard's, Shoreditch, which is strangely enough the same area Sarah had lived when married to Thomas Overton.

Sarah and Thomas's daughter Elizabeth Overton is now living in London too, working in a house at Hanover Square, Mayfair. Significantly the census tells us there is a family of Goads living on that street too!

The threads of our future lives are intertwining! But that is Elizabeth's story later!

Sarah's first son William Overton, when young, had been sent to Swavesey to attend school. Living at Boxworth End with his aunt, his mother Sarah's sister, her family name being Hepher (Hepher, a name connected to Goad's in this family story for many generations).

Sarah must have believed boys should be educated. Times were changing. William, age 23 in 1851, had become an Engine Fireman, now married to Selina and living in Woodstone, Huntingdon. The railway had come to Cambridgeshire in 1847.

By 1861 they were living in Wisbech St. Peter, William now an Engine Driver, proudly being part of the dawn of the 'Railway Age'.

He and Selina have two daughters, Emma Elizabeth and Selina.

In 1871 he is still driving the Engines and has added a son William to his family.

Berry Wayman Tibbitt, his nephew (his sister Phoebe's son) wrote in his letters from Canada of often seeing him on the trains between King's Lynn and Cambridge, when he was a boy.

William's hard work and education gave him success. Sadly he died in 1880 at the age of fifty three, at Wisbech St. Mary, but one would like to think of this as a success story and the pride of his mother Sarah.

In 1861 Sarah and William Marshall are living at 15 High Street, Swavesey. William is now seventy five, a great age for his time, and still working hard, making cheeses. Living with them now is their son, James William and his wife Sophie, both aged twenty, from King's Lynn. They are helping with the cheese making, Sarah now caring for their baby son Walter, as well as having her other Grandson, two year old James Stuart Goad, her daughter Elizabeth's son, with her as part of the family, along with her teenage daughter Phoebe.

It was at this time in her life Sarah met her supposedly dead husband Thomas Overton while travelling on a train to Liverpool Street station in London, where earlier she had gone to collect her baby grandson James Stuart Goad to take him back to Swavesey to live with her.

An event she kept as a secret until her dying day, when she finally confesses her thoughts and fears to her daughter Phoebe, to then be recorded by her grandson Berry Wayman Tibbitt (See Chapter Three).

At the great age of eighty three, in 1870 William has died and was laid to rest at the cemetery of the local Non-Conformist Chapel in Swavesey. They had had a long and happy union, forty two years of family life, sharing good and bad times. Surely she will miss him!

There is the featured wonderful Marshall Family photograph possibly taken around William's eightieth birthday in 1867. A fine looking man with a bushy white beard.

He and Sarah are sitting, lovingly surrounded by all their family dressed in their Sunday best, the men sporting a buttonhole flower. One can see all the touching bonds. I researched these

Marshall children of theirs and found an interesting, hard-working country family, dairy and cheese products being the main way of earning their living.

Is Phoebe there? Now married to Wayman Tibbitt, I am looking at it and trying to see who is who! Is the lady in black, sitting next to Sarah her elusive daughter Elizabeth, the widow Goad? If so, it would be the only possible picture of her.

Is James Stuart her son there – now at school in Swavesey, aged twelve? He will miss the man who was not only his Grandfather but had been to him like a father too.

Sarah is now sixty five, and on the census is classed as a Dairywoman.

Still working hard!

Sarah is now a grand seventy five, still working; the 1881census says she is now a cheese-maker. She is still caring for her family; James William, now forty, her youngest son is with her, Sophie his wife having died in 1880. Sarah has the care of their young son Albert age four, young Walter has grown up and left. But James William is now blind and unable to make cheeses, so is now dependant on his family. How sad! What a worry and responsibility for Sarah, still busily working at her age.

James Stuart Goad, aged twenty one, has now gone to live with his Aunt Emma Marshall-Hepher and her husband Edward, him belonging to the large local family of Hephers from Swavesey. They are now living at 95 Duck Lane, Haddenham, cheese-making and dealing and keeping a market garden there. Son Arthur (22) is a wheelwright, daughter Emma (16) working in the market garden with her father and daughter Selina (13) and son Marshall (11) are still pupils at Haddenham school. Their cousin James Stuart is helping his uncle as a cheese-maker and dealer in the tradition of his late Grandfather William Marshall.

Sarah sadly dies in 1884 aged seventy eight. But not before she had seen her grandson James Stuart become a farmer in his own right, taking the tenancy of The Dairy Farm, in Swavesey High Street, and married to Mary Jane Jacobs of Stretham.

How proud she must have been of him.

Uncle Edward Hepher's sign

Latterly she had become frail, the years of hard physical work had taken its toll on her, and she had gone to stay at the nearby village of Willingham with her daughter Phoebe, now a widow, who cared for her until the end.

Her death certificate states, 'Cause of Death – Decay of Nature'. What wonderful Victorian language to describe her condition of simply 'old age'.

Berry Tibbitt who was twelve at the time and Phoebe's son, writes of his Grandmother Sarah's deathbed confessions, which occurred at this time. All relevant to our future family destiny, to be written about and analysed later.

How do we see Sarah's life? Considering the times she lived in.

One can imagine the changes she had seen, from the turn of the 19th century to its almost close. Life had been hard, but they had no grand expectations, just the warmth of family around to help each other. She seemed a caring wife, mother and grandmother and very hard-working, able to mix with all levels of society, successful as a nanny to the wealthy when she was young. She had bravely overcome the trauma of her first marriage to Thomas Overton and subsequent widowhood.

Her love for all her children and grandchildren seemed such a big part of her life, with her second husband always beside her, the marriage of Sarah and William's of over forty years seems to have been a good, happy and loving one. A true Matriarch of her time.

She left a family legacy of love, confessions, mysteries and stories for another generation to solve.

Finally there is the wonderful portrait photograph of Sarah sent to us from the Canada cousins. She is sitting quite ladylike, with her arm resting on a table. She is wearing her Sunday best, a beautiful shiny black dress, and with braids and lace in her hair. But you can see the evidence of her life of hard work by her gnarled hands, showing in a stark silhouette, while resting on her dark skirt.

What is she thinking?   Oh, Sarah! If only you could speak!

Sarah Curtis Overton Marshall

Sarah Curtis Overton/Marshall: Working in the Old Farmhouse Kitchen

I turned and
Caught a glimpse of your shadow
Cast from years before.
And I knew you!
I had felt you watching me
In an unknown space of time we met,
Our two lives touching briefly,
The same?
You with your endless toil and struggle!
Me?
It seems nothing changes!

Lesley Goad

I wrote this poem whilst working as a cook/housekeeper at Temple Garth, an old mediaeval farmhouse in Lincolnshire, in the early 1990s.

The house and old kitchen was still as an 18th/19th century farmhouse, decorated as having been left in a time warp, nothing modern to be seen. A wonderful space full of the atmosphere of the past and its inhabitants lives.

It seemed just right for inclusion here; its words and feelings sounding like an echo from the past. And so appropriate while writing this book, with my thoughts now so full of the lives of our four woman farming ancestors – Sarah, Elizabeth, Phoebe and Mary Jane.

Me – I had probably just spent a hard day waxing and polishing the old flagstone floors and let my fertile imagination get the better of me in the late afternoon twilight!

Chapter Two

Phoebe Marshall Tibbitt 1847 – 1890

'Mother of Our Canadian Cousins'

Sarah Curtis Overton   m (2)   William
1807 - 1884   1829   Marshall
b. Longstanton   1787 - 1870
                               b. St. Ives

Elizabeth   Phoebe Marshall-Tibbitt
1827 - Unkn.   1847 - 1890
b. Norwich   b. Swavesey

James Stuart Goad
1859 - 1928
b. Middlesex, London

Family Tree for Phoebe Marshall -Tibbitt 1847 – 1890

Phoebe Marshall-Tibbitt

Phoebe Marshall -Tibbitt 1847-1890 - 'Mother of Our Canadian Cousins'

Firstly you may ask: Why am I writing about a woman who is not of the Goad family – very distantly related to us today?

What is her importance in the overall picture?

As I researched our Great Grandfather James Stuart Goad's life I found Phoebe there, from his very birth and she appears to be such a big part of his life throughout it.

Elizabeth, James Stuart's mother was her half-sister, Phoebe being the last child of Sarah and William Marshall, pig-jobber, dairy-man, cheese-dealer and Sarah's second husband.

Phoebe was one of the important three / four mother figures who cared for James Stuart throughout his life. We first see her as a teenager, living with Elizabeth Goad and caring for her nephew James Stuart Goad as a baby. Also it was her son Berry Wayman Tibbitt and his sister Ella, (James Stuart's cousins), who emigrated to Canada in 1892 and whose letters written in his nineties, to his young Goad cousin, in the 1960s, (James Stuart Goad's Great Granddaughter Gillian), that have given us so many 19th century memories. A contact of an amazing span of time (to be written of later).

So without Phoebe's link, our story would be so much more of surmise than an actual account of real people.

Phoebe was the fifth and last surviving child of Sarah and William Marshall. She was born in 1847 in the Cambridgeshire village of Swavesey. She had one older sister Emma and three elder brothers, John Curtis, Joseph and James William. She also had two older half siblings, Elizabeth and William Overton – Sarah's first family, which William raised as his own from when they were no more than babies.

She, like Elizabeth and Emma before her, helped her mother at home and in the dairy – learning the skills of butter and cheese making, for those to later be sold at local markets by her father

William, and brother, John Curtis. They also took produce to the London markets, transport being easier now the railway had come to Swavesey in 1847, the year she had been born.

In 1861 her eldest sister, Elizabeth, was widowed and left London to live in King's Lynn, Norfolk. Phoebe aged 14 went with her there to help look after baby James Stuart and the shop that Elizabeth had in the St. Margaret's area of town. The reason Elizabeth probably chose to go and make a home in King's Lynn could be that it was familiar to her, as her half-brother, James William, was living and working there and married to a local woman Sophie, with whom he had a baby son Walter.

Being a young widow with a small baby in the moralistic Victorian times she was living in, it would be easier to be in a town where she was a stranger.   Less questions to be answered!

But after a few years Sarah and William needed them all to help back in Swavesey.

William was now over seventy years old, he was still making cheeses for a living. The life of work never ended in these late Victorian days, there were no pensions for the elderly.

John Curtis had married and gone to Leicester with his family. Joseph too had married and left home for London. James William was a good cheese maker and Phoebe could help her mother in the dairy too.

Elizabeth became housekeeper for the largest land-owning farmer in Swavesey, a William Carter.

Phoebe took James Stuart to live with his grandparents.

These events are all borne out by the 1871 census.

Phoebe was a pretty dark-haired girl, as she appears in her photograph. Now back home, working hard helping with family dairy and cheese making, she began walking out with a local dairyman, Berry Wayman Tibbitt from the nearby village of Willingham, Cambridgeshire.

In 1868 while the family were visiting London, Phoebe and Berry Wayman married in St. Simeon Zealots Church, Morpeth Street, Tower Hamlets, Bethnel Green; the area of London which they visited regularly to sell cheeses and produce at the markets.

She was his second wife; his first wife Anne and child having died in childbirth three years previously. A common event of their time, childbirth still being very precarious for a woman.

Berry Wayman and Phoebe settled to married life living in Willingham, Cambridgeshire, a village a few miles from her mother and father in Swavesey. They set up home in a small cottage at 123, Church Street. Phoebe continued to make her special cream cheeses working beside her husband.

In 1870 her father William Marshall died at the grand old age of eighty three, a loving, hard-working, good father, happily her mother had James William, Sophie and Baby Albert with her for comfort and support.

Their son Berry Wayman was born in 1872, Berry and Phoebe giving him the two traditional Tibbitt family names. Two years later daughter Ella came along. Life was very busy and both had to work hard to make a living for the little family. Unhappily in 1876 her husband Berry Wayman got sick and died of kidney and heart problems. His death certificate said, "due to his excessive alcohol drinking!" This left Phoebe a widow at the young age of thirty, with Berry only four and Ella just two years old.

Excessive drinking of alcohol was common at this time. Most homes brewed their own beer, the first weak brewing being for women and children. English ale being the preferred traditional drink for generations, regarded as a health safeguard owing to the erratic quality of local water supplies. It was normal for there to be an ale house on the corner of every street. But the nineteenth century saw the beginning of the temperance movement, owing to society's concern of the poverty alcohol drinking caused in working families.

Phoebe continued as a cheese maker, making ends meet, keeping the little family together. The only other options were to live off the Parish as a pauper or the workhouse; these no-one readily accepted in their lives. Luckily she had a family around her for support and her husband Berry had left them a legacy of £388.4s.2d, strangely not going to probate until 1884 when his father, the village butcher, died. But enough to help pay the bills, and give a feeling of security.

Berry and Ella attended Willingham village school and when they were old enough they too learned the family craft of the dairy. Sarah, her mother, was now looking after her brother James William who was now blind, also his young son Albert, aged 4, as his wife Sophie had died in 1880. Nephew James Stuart has gone to live with her sister Emma and family at Haddenham, Cambridgeshire (1881census).

In 1884 when Berry was just twelve and Ella ten, their Grandmother Sarah's health failed and she came to live with them at Willingham. Phoebe nursed her mother, who had sickened and was unable to care for herself. Towards her end, Sarah's mind wandered over her past life, thinking of events she had tried to forget. Anxious thoughts of her first husband, Thomas Overton and how he had suddenly disappeared, and was believed dead. His clothes then being found by the bank of the River Thames! And of in later years when she had seen him again, alive!

At the time of getting ready to face her God, it explains her dying fears that she had not really been married to William, a man with a Non-Conformist Baptist faith, the dear good man she had lived with for over forty years. These thoughts were all preying on her dying mind. She talked of Elizabeth, her strange life, of Captain Goad, James Stuart's father, her love for James Stuart and all the previously unspoken events which had surrounded her life.

Phoebe and Berry comforted her and listened to her stories, which Berry later wrote down as 'confessions'. Letters we have to this day, written by him, which I have called 'Grandmother Sarah's Deathbed Confessions' (See next chapter).

What a sad time and what an effect and impression it must have made on her twelve year old grandson Berry.

Sarah dies aged seventy eight, a long, loving, hard-working life; giving all to her family. Her death certificate says, 'Cause of Death – Decay of Nature'. Just old age!

A 'Lady' of her time, she had fulfilled her destiny well. Truly a loved family Matriarch – to be greatly missed!

It was now Christmas 1890, Phoebe hadn't been feeling well; she had a pain in her chest and found it difficult to breathe at times. December had been a bitter cold month. The sharp easterly winds blowing, unstopped by the flat stark fen landscape. There had been large snowfalls and temperatures were low. The River Ouse levels at Earith were icy and perfect for the traditional holiday fen skating races.

It was Friday December 26th, they had had the family Christmas Day festivities the day before, although still dairy chores to do, but when finished, as it was 'Boxing Day', Berry and Ella went off fen skating with their friends, to enjoy some holiday fun.

While they were out Phoebe sat dozing by her fire, her big shawl wrapped around her to keep warm in the draughty cottage. She got up, poker in her hand, to attend the stew pot lodged by the fire for their supper and dizzily fell, her shawl falling into the hot flames. Her clothes then catching alight with terrible consequences.

Below is a copy of the local newspaper, The Cambridge News account:

Shocking Death of a Widow

Friday January 2nd 1891 Willingham

"A sad accident occurred last Friday to Mrs. Wayman Tibbitt, widow of Berry Wayman Tibbitt, dairyman. On the day named her two children left her at home in her usual health and while they were skating on the Ouse a message reached them to the effect that their mother had been burnt to death in her home. The County Coroner, Mr. W. C. Palmer held an inquest on Saturday, when Henry Robinson, carpenter of Willingham, deposed that on Friday last his attention was called to the house of the deceased. He went in and found one of the rooms full of smoke and subsequently discovered the deceased lying on her back with her head in the fireplace, she appeared quite dead. There was a saucepan on the fireplace and the poker in the fire. Dr. Lewis of Willingham said he had attended the deceased all her life. "She was suffering from consumption and heart disease". He made a post-mortem examination and gave

the cause of death as asphyxia, caused by the smoke and flames, which arose from the burning clothes. A verdict in accordance with the medical evidence was returned"

Such a sad day for Berry, eighteen, and Ella, sixteen; left alone to cope with life on their own. What a terrible way to lose a loved one. One can hardly imagine their sorrow and pain but the family did their best to help, all grieving in their own way.

The census of 1891 sees Berry, 19, Head of House, living with Ella, 17, occupation given as dairyman and dairywoman.

They are still living in the cottage where their mother Phoebe had died at 123, Church Street, Willingham. Her will went to probate in 1891 and was administered by Arthur Hepher of Haddenham (her sister Emma's eldest son) his cousin, Berry, being under the legal age. Her estate was £37-9s-6d. A small amount now left from husband Berry Wayman's will.

But by late 1901 they had moved on, probably finding the memories too painful to be still living in Willingham.

We know Ella marries, Harry Read, a Devon man and they emigrated to Canada for a new life. Berry is on the Chicago, Illinois census in 1904 with his new wife Fanny Haslett and their two children. In 1910 the census finds the little family in Emmerson, Manitoba, finally to settle in Victoria, British Colombia.

They had five sons, one being called Harry Read Tibbitt after his sister Ella's husband. One would like to think Berry and Ella were close as brother and sister all their lives, a support to one another in the new country they had adopted, I think Berry and Fanny calling their son Harry Read confirms this thought and that they were making a fresh start away from all the painful memories of Church Street, Willingham, Cambridgeshire.

Berry even though he was far away in Canada, and communication was only by letter, always thought of his Goad cousins living in Swavesey. James Stuart and Mary Jane had been by their side throughout the time of Phoebe's death. Berry's later sparse letters to their next generations after their deaths speaks for itself. He wrote to their daughter Mabel Goad Ashby at Waterbeach, granddaughter Molly Goad-Marchant when she was at Hill Farm and lastly Mary's great granddaughter, Gillian Goad-Johnson when she was a teenager.

He was hungry for news of his family left behind in England. It is to him we owe the 'Goad Memories' in his letters. He obviously felt the need to pass them on!

As he was only twelve years old at the time of his Grandmother Sarah's death, it must have been his mother Phoebe, who impressed the importance of the information on him. I have later printed these letters and written a personal conclusion.

Berry's great granddaughter Joanne Robb contacted Darren Johnson, Gillian-Goad-Johnson's son, in 2005 when he was researching online, sending him a letter of Berry's she found with his belongings in 1967 after he had died.

Berry and Phoebe are such an important link to today's story of how we see the past. Berry especially for his determination to pass on the past, realising its importance to future generations in linking their lives to us today.

All this brings our X2 Great Aunt Phoebe with her son Berry, into a 130 year circle from the 19th century, to tell us her important story and its significance to our 21st Goad family of today.

One joy is the photograph of Phoebe, sent to us by her Canadian family of today, enabling us to see the beautiful likeness of a significant ancestor.

She is touching our lives through the years; her immortality of a kind.

Church Street, Willingham, Cambridgeshire

Chapter Three

Berry Wayman Tibbitt 1872 – 1967

'Keeper of Secrets'

Elizabeth Overton-Goad	Phoebe Marshall		Berry Wayman Tibbitt
1827 - Unkn.	1847 - 1890	m	1831 - 1876
b. Norwich	b. Swavesey	1868	b. Willingham

James Stuart Goad
1859 - 1928
b. Middlesex, London

Berry
Wayman
Tibbitt
1872 - 1967
b. Willingham

Family Tree for Berry Wayman Tibbitt 1872-1967

Berry Wayman Tibbitt as a young man

Thoughts and Extracts from Nine Letters

Sent to Gillian Goad-Johnson by Berry Wayman Tibbitt.
Written between 1964 and 1966.

Berry Wayman Tibbitt and Gillian Goad-Johnson exchanged letters for three years before his death in 1967. When it began he was ninety two years old, she was just sixteen.

Berry had received a Cambridge Independent newspaper, forwarded to him by an English friend now living in California, USA.

It was August 1964, and Gillian's photograph was on the front page, as she had been chosen to be Ely's Annual Hospital Beauty Queen for that year. She was the elder daughter of John Stuart Goad (Jack) of Hill Farm, Stretham, Cambridgeshire.

In Berry's words, *"He took a flying chance she was related to his cousin James Stuart Goad who married Mary Jane Jacobs of Stretham,"* and wrote to her.

He says, *"For many years I have been trying to obtain news of the Goad family."*

He was *"Highly delighted"* to receive a reply from Gillian, confirming that James Stuart was her Great Grandfather and, *"Highly tickled"* to hear from her.

He wrote nine letters, between August 1964 and October 1966; all with snippets of his life in them. He says, *"My hobby is genealogy and always find my thoughts going back to my first twenty years in England."*

Twice he mentions 'the skeleton in the closet'.

The third letter contained what I call 'The Letters of Confessions and Secrets'; the words of his dying Grandmother Sarah Curtis Overton-Marshall and of her thoughts of her daughter Elizabeth Overton-Goad. These I have researched and printed in the next chapter.

In the 'confessions' postscript, he leaves the question to Gillian as to whether he is doing the right thing in disclosing these facts!

"I write of your family skeleton in the closet and wondering whether if it is wise to send it, I believe it is only known by me. Could I leave it with you?"

Fifty years later Berry has given me help in solving the puzzle of Elizabeth and William Trickett Goad's life together and Sarah's too. Helping me put the pieces together for a clearer picture of their lives and personalities.

In Berry's letters he promised, *"Nubs of news"*.

He was conscious of Gillian's young age. He sent photographs of interest – one of himself, describing himself as *'a grizzled old fossil' and* one of Mabel Goad, Gillian's Great Aunt, dressed so stylishly and sitting in Ryders Farm garden. Him stating, *"The writing on the reverse is that of her Great Grandfather James Stuart, his cousin."* Berry was a man with a true sense of history.

"I know what I write, as an old man, may not be interesting to a youngster, but if you lay them to one side and show them to your grandchildren, they may then become interesting, not so much the subject matter but the thoughts they may arouse!"

Again he says, *"Lay them aside for 50, 60 or 70 years and they may interest you and yours."*

So I enclose a few stories, thoughts and quotes from the past life of Berry Wayman Tibbitt, handed down to us in his letters and which may interest you.

As he so prophetically wrote to Gillian: *"Here is one for the book!"*

Is Berry looking over my shoulder today? As at the end of one of his tales he writes: *"Was that telepathy or mesmerism?"*

Was he psychic?

Did he see and believe this day would come?

So thank you Gillian for keeping Berry's letters safely when receiving them so young, and letting me use them today.

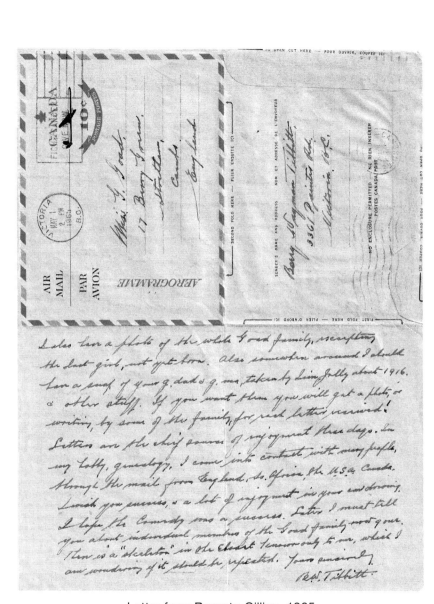

I also have a photo of the whole Goad family, excepting
the last girl, not yet born. Also somewhere around I should
have a snap of your g. dad & g. ma, taken by Jim Jolly about 1916,
& other stuff. If you want them you will get a photo, or
writing, by some of the family, for each letter received!
Letters are the chief source of my enjoyment these days. In
my hobby, genealogy, I come into contact with many people,
through the mail from England, So. Africa, the U.S.A. Canada.
I wish you success, & a lot of enjoyment in your endeavour.
I hope the Comedy was a success. Later I must tell
you about individual members of the Goad family, now & over.
There is a "skeleton" in the Closet known only to me, which I
am wondering if it should be repeated. Yours sincerely,
R.S. Tibbitt.

Letter from Berry to Gillian, 1965

Berry writes, *"When I was last in England (1897) I stayed about four months with the Goads. They (James Stuart and Mary Jane) were the only close family I had left, and your Great Grandmother was fond of me, and wrote regularly. Her last letter was written after the death of her husband (1928) and I believe she died a few weeks later"*, Also, *"As I sit alone in my cottage, with all city amenities, in a Douglas fir forest, so many thoughts arise. I don't know where to begin. I realise you are too young to be interested in the thoughts of an old man, but don't be too interested in a young man for the next few years. I strongly object to early marriages.*

My old Grandma Marshall used to say to my mother, "Now my dears, what is the world coming to. There is no accounting for young folks nowadays. Why when I was a girl we never thought of such things!"

Well Sarah! How very tongue in cheek! You can see the twinkle in her eye! She was nineteen when she married Thomas Overton in 1826.

Were they just words of caring and wisdom in her old age?

Some more Berry memories

"To begin with myself, I was born at Willingham, Cambridgeshire on 18th February 1872. And I am beginning to get old. As I tell the old ladies, "90 is not 19!"

I landed in Montreal in 1892. In 1897 I returned to England to sell property my Grandfather left me. I stayed at Swavesey with the Goads. James's mother and my mother were half-sisters, so I knew all the Goad and Jacobs family well.

While waiting for my probate settlement at Michaelmas, I decided to get a bicycle and join the French Touring Club in Cambridge and ride to Paris. (There were no cars in those days).

I was visiting Lydia Jacobs in Stretham (Mary Jane's younger sister), *and told her of my intention. Her friend Nesta* (the Stretham brewer's daughter), *was there too, and said she would join me and ride as far as London to see her sister. We arranged to meet at noon the next day at Aunt Harvey's home* (Mary Jane's widowed Aunt Rebecca who ran a boarding house at 35, Bridge Street, Cambridge).

Next day I arrived earlier than Nesta, and told Aunt I was riding to Paris.

A few minutes later Nesta came in. Aunt gave us our lunch and concluded it was a "put up job". "Were we running away to get married?" I said, "Nothing of the kind. I had no use for women anyway".

We left about 12:30 and when we got to Royston, Cambridgeshire, it was raining, so I decided it was wiser to take the train. We found we had just missed one, and had to wait two hours.

After a while I became uneasy and started to walk the platform. Finally I went in and told Nesta I felt I had to go back to Swavesey and left.

She thought I had gone crazy!

*I rode as hard as I could. When pushing my bike up Cambridge Castle Hill, I ran into Emmie Hepher (*His cousin, Aunt Emma Marshall Hepher's daughter), *who said her brother Marshall would like to see me. I said I couldn't go there now as I was in a hurry.*

*When I reached the village pub (*Swavesey), *the pedal came off with the hard pedalling. When arriving at the farm, Mary came out of the dairy and said," Thank God! He has answered my prayers." She said," Jim is down with erysipelas"* (An infection from handling pigs).

The Doctor had called and promised to send the medicine on the next train, but it had failed to show up. "Would I go to St Ives to pick it up?"

I turned round, and rode to St Ives and found the medicine had gone! I rode back home, just as crazy, with the bike pedal now in my hand. I could have easily had it fixed in minutes in St Ives!

*So then I took over and ran the dairy business for six weeks until James's recovery, during which they took a two week vacation, having Mary's sister Lydia (*Jacobs) *to run the home and the bunch of kids (*Our Swavesey children).

Was this telepathy or mesmerism? I think the latter!"

I think the first is more likely!

"Words to show the wandering spirit I have always possessed!

> *I lived twenty years in England.*
> *Fourteen years in Chicago.*
> *Three in Manitoba.*
> *Twenty six in Saskatchewan.*
> *Four in Alberta.*
> *Twenty six in Victoria BC.*

In 1903 in Alberta I met and married an Irish redhead called Fanny Hazlett. It was the best day's work I ever did (Lovely sentiment after so long a marriage!).

Since my wife died in 1952, I have lived in a four room cottage, ten miles by road from Victoria. I have four married sons: one, Bill, living about 15 miles away. He says, "No Dad, only 14.4, I measured it!" (Happy banter between father and son)

This son has just retired from the Royal Canadian Air Force as a Flight Lieutenant. The other three boys all have degrees and all doing well.

Oh, yes, I have six grandchildren and six great grandchildren."

When writing he says, "*I promise to send a photograph in reply of every letter you write*". Was this an incentive for Gillian to write? He was just hungry for news from "home", but, sadly, all the people he had known had died.

He couldn't relate to Gillian's father John Stuart's (Jack) generation. In one reply she mentioned her uncle William (Bill) Goad. Berry replied, "*The Will Goad I knew died in 1918*" (James William Goad, 1890-1918 – his cousin, James Stuart's son).

On June 4th 1967, Gillian received a letter from Berry's housekeeper, Mrs. E. Barr, to say that Berry had died peacefully in his sleep on May 6th. She says, "*He was a fine old gentleman, and will be greatly missed by the community. He enjoyed her letters immensely and looked forward to receiving them*".

His lifelong affection for his cousin James Stuart and Mary Jane Goad has led us to these thoughts of him here today, and his memories have helped shape our understanding of our 19th century family.

Berry Wayman Tibbitt

Appendix I: The Family

I too have been writing to Canada, to Berry's great granddaughter, Joanne Robb.

She has sent me the confirmation of my hopes that Berry lived a fulfilling and happy life in Canada and confirmed that Ella and Harry had happily settled and had a family in California.

So in conclusion to this tribute to Berry, I write a little resume of his immortality.

Berry and his family.

Berry Wayman Tibbitt   m.   Fanny Hazlett
1872 – 1967   1881 – 1952
Born Willingham, Cambridgeshire   Born Northern Ireland
Emigrated to Canada 1892.
Married in Alberta 1903

1st son:

Berry Wayman Tibbitt   m.   Charlotte O'Neil Streeter
1904 – 2001   1927   1903 – 2001
They had 2 boys.

2nd son:

John (Jack) Francis   m.   Margaret Wright Glover
1908 – 1993   1940   1903 – 1996
They had one daughter, Frances, the mother of our corresponding cousin, Joanne Robb.

Jack served with the Canadian Militia as a marksman, but a severe eye injury while at competition barred him from serving overseas in WWII.

Jack graduated from the University of Saskatchewan. He was a mining and petroleum geologist. He was employed by The Hudson Bay Oil and Gas Company for 25 years in Calgary.

In 1937, Jack, in the company of an ex-Mountie who spoke Eskimo, made the first trip overland from Churchill, Manitoba, Canada to Arctic Bay on the Northern tip of Baffin Island. They left Churchill on March10th, with an Eskimo dog team escort and after a trip full of adventure and peril arrived at Arctic Bay on July 2nd, carrying mail to that region. An Eastern mining syndicate had commissioned him to investigate reports of gold in that area.

Jack does sound as if he had his father's tenacity and sense of adventure!

3rd son: James Weybourne Tibbitt   1911 – 1925

4th son:

Harry Read Tibbitt	m.	Deana Marie Gilbert
1918 – 1998	1947	1927 – 2009

They had three sons.

Harry served overseas in WWII in the Canadian Air Force.

5th son:

Arthur William (Bill) Tibbitt	m.	Margret Dorothy Caplette
1921 – 2003	1954	1919 – 2012

They had one daughter.

Bill served in the Canadian Air Force during WWII and retired as a Flight Lieutenant in 1964. He was a flight training instructor in Germany at the Canadian Forces Base in Baden-Baden in the 1950s. After retirement Bill lived in Victoria BC, which is the capital of British Columbia, situated on the Isle of Vancouver in the Pacific Ocean.

Berry must have been very proud of the achievements of his four sons, his first generation family in the 'New World'.

After his farming and dairy background in Willingham, Cambridgeshire, England, he had worked his way to being a Postmaster by the end of his working life.

One comment he made to Gillian is that anyone remembering him in England, would have known him as Jack Tibbitt. Was he known as Jack all his life I wonder? Only that one mention in all my research of this fact! Jack is certainly more of an everyday name; Berry Wayman being such unusual christian names, both being the maiden names of his father's grandmothers.

Now through you Joanne, his great granddaughter, we link the threads of your family ties from across the years and Atlantic Ocean to today's Goad family here in England. This fact, I believe, would have made Berry Wayman Tibbitt a very happy man. Perhaps he <u>did</u> foresee that this day would come, and <u>is</u> looking over my shoulder! Fifty years after his last letter, I am now achieving what he strove for all his life.

Photograph of Autumn Leaves Painting

For Berry Wayman Tibbitt and Ella Tibbitt Read

All my life I have painted with brush or pen and in the 1980s I did a series of rainbow collage paintings. This one was a gift to a friend as a memento of her visit to New England, America. It contains a collection of autumn leaves which she brought back with her.

As we know, the rainbow is symbolic of a Promise; the Lily of the Valley flower signifies 'The Return of Happiness'.

So I dedicate this painting along with its symbolism, to the memories and hopes of Berry and Ella, and to the success of their new lives in the 'New World' across the Atlantic Ocean.

Lesley Goad 2013

Appendix II: Confessions, Secrets and Mysteries

Sarah Curtis Overton-Marshall

<u>Deathbed Confession:</u> As heard by her grandson, Berry Wayman Tibbitt, in 1884. It was found in his notes by his great granddaughter, Joanne, after his death in 1967.

<u>1884</u> - *"As my Grandmother (Sarah Curtis) lay dying at our house in Willingham she unfolded the whole story. Elizabeth never married a Capt. Goad.*

James Stuart was son of James Stuart, a barrister, located later I believe in Edinburgh, Scotland. Until the boy was 14, he sent regularly quarterly remittances through the mail. My mother Phoebe cashed several of them. The family name Goad, <u>in my opinion</u> is fictitious.

Apparently the birth was never registered."

Berry Wayman Tibbitt

More Secrets and Mysteries

A letter written by Berry Wayman Tibbitt to Gillian Goad-Johnson before his death in 1967.

He was James Stuart Goad's first cousin.

May 10th 1965

"Perhaps it is inadvisable for me to leave a family secret of which I am perhaps the only possessor. Whether I should divulge it, has me guessing!

My maternal Grandmother was Sarah Curtis b. 05-12-1807, baptised at St. Michaels Church, Long Stanton, Cambridgeshire.

She was Nanny to the children of the Hatton Family at the Manor House, Long Stanton. When they travelled she accompanied them.

Eventually she married William (sic) Overton in London, by whom she had two children, Elizabeth and William.

Elizabeth was reported to have married Capt. Goad an Army Officer and William was an Engine driver on the GER running from Lynn to Cambridge. I saw him many times on the Engine.

Later William (sic) Overton Sr disappeared; his clothes were found upon the banks of the River Thames.

Sarah waited many years before marrying James (sic) Marshall.

The story was given out that Capt. Goad was ordered abroad and there was a baby.

Grandma Marshall undertook to look after this baby. (James Stuart)

As she was leaving Liverpool Street Station with the baby, a man got in the carriage, each recognised the other, neither spoke and he left at the next stop.

It was William (sic) Overton!

The question arises? Was my grandmother's 1st marriage legal or bigamous?

Was the 2nd legal?"

Berry Wayman Tibbitt.

Appendix III: Personal Conclusions after Research

I have been researching Sarah's life and times and have come up with this feasible solution.

Facts

December 31st 1826 – Grandmother Sarah married Thomas Overton at Saint Leonard's Church, Shoreditch, London.

1827 – Elizabeth Overton was born.

1828 – William Overton was born.

1828 – Thomas Overton disappears, his clothes are found on the Thames riverbank, London. No record of his death can be found.

1828 – Sarah takes her young family back home to Longstanton, believing she is a widow.

1828 – A Thomas Overton is again in the marriage register of Saint Leonard's, Shoreditch. This time he is marrying a Jane Riley.

December 29th 1829 – Sarah marries William Marshall at St. Michael's, Longstanton.

30 Years Later 1859 – Sarah meets Thomas Overton while travelling on a train at Liverpool Street Station, London, baby James Stuart in her arms. They recognised each other and, not speaking, part again.

My thoughts

Sarah obviously wouldn't have wanted her life turned upside down by the knowledge of this being public while she was alive. She had built a good new life and family.

But as a God-fearing woman, when she was near to death it would certainly have preyed on her mind. I believe she married William Marshall in good faith – A marriage which lasted 42 years.

Thomas Overton was the bigamist. Perhaps Sarah wasn't his first wife either!

As to all the surmise of Elizabeth's marriage, despite reading Berry's conflicting evidence in his letters, we know William Trickett Goad existed.

We now have the added knowledge of William Trickett Goad's existence from Elizabeth's granddaughter Maud Goad, James Stuart's first born daughter and the mementoes she saved and handed on:

His photograph

- The Times newspaper
- and miniature painting.
- His name is also on James Stuart's marriage certificate in 1882

Four more separate acts of provenance for him:

These new facts have now emerged and hopefully a better conclusion of events has been found.* But perhaps the puzzle will never be truly solved!

However, the facts give us a feasible story.

*See Elizabeth Overton Chapter.

Chapter Four

Elizabeth Overton Goad 1827 – Unknown

'Objects Contain Absent People'

Sarah Curtis
1807 - 1884
b. Longstanton

m (1)
1826

**Thomas
Overton**
1805 - Unkn.
b. Norwich

Elizabeth
1827 - Unkn.
b. Norwich

Family Tree for Elizabeth Overton Goad

Elizabeth Overton Goad's Mementoes

Saved for us by Maud Goad-Hepher

Elizabeth Overton-Goad

'Objects Contain Absent People'

In 1827 Elizabeth Overton was born in the big cathedral city of Norwich, Norfolk, England, home of her father Thomas Overton. It had been, in the Middle Ages the second city to London, owing to the wealthy wool trade with the nearby continent of Europe. Even so young men still went to London for adventure and advancement.

That is where her mother Sarah Curtis and her father Thomas Overton met and married and later where her brother William was born in 1828.

But that same year the children were also taken to Longstanton, Cambridgeshire, to live with their grandparents, William and Elizabeth Curtis, their namesakes. Elizabeth and William were too young and knew nothing of their father Thomas' disappearance and of his clothes found discarded on the Thames riverbank.*

*See Sarah Curtis' Marshall's story.

Elizabeth grew up in Swavesey in Cambridgeshire, along with her brother William, mother Sarah and in the care of their stepfather William Marshall, whom their mother had married in 1829, the only father, so good and kind, that they were to ever know.

She enjoyed helping her mother in the home and when each of her younger brothers and sisters were born loved playing the 'big sister' to them all.

Their living would have been frugal but good, with all the benefits of living in the countryside of vegetables, fruit and milk. Early 19th century agriculture was having a short renaissance at this time. This upbringing will hold Elizabeth in good stead for her future, as, like her mother, she was bright and pretty.

One day there was a knock at the cottage door and Elizabeth saw a tall lady wearing a beautiful dress being ushered in by her mother, Sarah, giving her a curtsey as she spoke.

Elizabeth then realised it was The Lady Hatton, from the nearby village of Longstanton, where her mother had been in service before her marriage.

She had come to ask Sarah for Elizabeth to live and work for her at the Manor House. Who else to help her as she got older but the daughter of a past servant that she and her family had trusted and valued?

So Elizabeth found herself at the age of fourteen learning all the ways of the 'big house'.

She loved being in the grand silk-draped, mirrored rooms, admiring the beautiful ornaments and glittering silver, and helping the housekeeper with her duties.

After a few years of living and travelling between Longstanton and London, with hard work and experience she now became Lady Hatton's maid, taking care of her beautiful dresses and clothes. She learnt how to dress her Lady's hair and care for the many jewels she possessed. Elizabeth blossomed in this environment of wealth and beauty which she had grown to love. Trying always to be there when she was needed and now with time, becoming a friend and confidant to her Mistress and the Hatton family.

She was given gifts and dresses which she remodelled for herself by adding new lace and ribbons. Elizabeth had now become a very confident and beautiful woman, comfortable in mixing in the higher echelons of society.

Their London life followed the Royal Court season from May to August. The first big event being the May Day opening at the Royal Academy, showing there the new paintings exhibited by the celebrity artists of the day – always an exciting beginning to the Season, with Queen Victoria and her husband Albert attending. It was then followed by days of racing, parties, balls, theatre and all the entertainments that London now provided in the three summer months until August – the time when the Queen and her retinue left for their holidays in Balmoral Castle in Scotland and the great landowners went back to their country estates.

The coming of the railways had brought the country people to its capital. Its streets were constantly thronged with busy people. A city full of noise, smoke and crowds, including pickpockets and beggars wearing tattered shawls and clogs, opportunistically roaming the streets; shoppers and workers walking to the newly opened department stores in Regent Street; bankers to the hub of the city in the Bank of England, Threadneedle Street and lawyers and clerks to their work at the Inner Temple. The rich, in their horse drawn carriages and handsome cabs, dashed through the streets to their important destinations. London was now the working hub of the British Empire. England, a country being made wealthy by the great Industrial Revolution, showcased at the Great Exhibition for the people, held at the newly built Crystal Palace in 1851. On land owned by Dukes and Earl's, grand houses were being built on the open green area around Buckingham Palace; streets of large houses placed in squares with big central gardens, homes fit for the growing wealthy middle classes.

This is where Elizabeth called home in 1857, St Georges Square, Mayfair.

One day she was escorting Lady Hatton to a garden party, when later sitting alone quietly under the shade of a big tree, she looked up and saw a young man who regularly visited a house in their street, and he came and spoke to her, recognising her as someone he knew. He introduced himself as William Goad, a cousin of her neighbours, the Goad family in their Square.

They talked, laughed and enjoyed the hours of a summer afternoon, as two young people together.

Elizabeth was lucky in her job, the Lady Hatton was fond of her after the many years they had been together. She, now elderly, attended fewer parties, so Elizabeth found life not quite so busy.

Now it was the magic summer of 1857 for Elizabeth and William.

On her days off she would meet William and they would take walks in The Mall, Hyde Park or Kensington Gardens or just window shop on Regent Street. In the evenings they would attend one of the shows or plays at one of the many theatres at Drury Lane or The Haymarket and of course it was inevitable that they fell in love.

William Trickett Goad had been born in Calcutta, India, his father Charles, now retired and living in Kensington, had been a colonel in The East India Company Army.

William had been sent back to London, England with his elder brother Charles for his education at a boarding school. Sadly, his elder brother had enlisted, fought and died at the Crimean war.

Now William was getting pressure from his father to enlist and help quell the mutiny which was threatening the British in their Indian colony. So, in February 1858, he joined The Duke of Cornwall's Foot Regiment as an Ensign. He came from three generations of soldiers, all serving in India.

His story is told in the next chapter.

Elizabeth kept for all her life the Times newspaper announcement of his enlistment.

Their parting was difficult for them both; William promising to come back to her, Elizabeth sad but proud that William was doing his duty serving his country.

The next year was very difficult for Elizabeth, she continued to work hard, the Lady Hatton valuing her loyalty, was kind and helped her pass the long months. A lady's maid is a very privileged position and they had become good friends by now. Elizabeth was always dependable and very discreet in her work.

Every day she read The Times, always searching for William's whereabouts. She saw reports that he was at the heart of the battles, but thankfully at the year's end in 1858, William came safely back from his Indian 'adventure', and was granted extended leave to recover from the ordeals of the past months, a trial rewarded by a special medal from the Queen.

He and Elizabeth were then married, with Lady Hatton's blessing. She then decided to go back to the country Manor at Longstanton to retire to a quieter life in her latter years.

William and Elizabeth were now lodging in Kensington near his father and mother, Charles and Harriett. The next year Elizabeth gave birth to their son, whom they named after a friend, James Stuart. He was born in late 1859, and everything seemed so happy, William was back with his regiment, although she noticed how, since coming home from India, there were many subtle changes in him.

She couldn't understand why William seemed so secretive, but one day he came to her and told her he would be going away for a while, he had a special job to do and was being sent abroad. He would leave her in the care of their friend, the Scottish barrister James Stuart. She also knew William was an associate of Napoleon 3rd's entourage, as she had overheard him and his friends talking of their escapades into the night after dinner.

In May 1860, to the shock of Elizabeth, she read in the Times Gazette, a notice declaring William Trickett Goad 'Absent without leave' from his regiment.

She had thought he was on an Army mission!

Her friend James Stuart then told Elizabeth of the message from William, expressed to him before he went away, 'that if William never came back from his mission, he should be presumed dead'. She had been left an allowance and James Stuart, his son, was cared for financially until he was a man – the whole situation being much to the disbelief and distress of Elizabeth and almost unbearable to cope with.

Sarah her mother quickly came to London to help and comfort her daughter. After a time of grieving Elizabeth decided to leave London; she felt she couldn't go back to Cambridgeshire to live, so she went to set up home near her brother and sister-in-law James William and Sophie in King's Lynn.

Sarah took baby James Stuart back to Swavesey for a while, but on the way home, sitting opposite her in the railway carriage, she met the man she thought dead, Thomas Overton, her first husband. She had not seen him for thirty years! They never spoke a word, although both recognizing each other, he looked and quickly got out at the next stop.

Another shock for Sarah to cope with, but after great thought, and considering the effect on her and William, she decided to say nothing of the encounter, fearing its consequences to all their lives in the future.

Elizabeth now became Widow Goad, the lady in black. She packed away her beautiful chintz dresses and shawls William had brought back from India as gifts for her – the memories all too painful of their short life of love together. She had the photograph of William taken on their wedding day; he had the one of her with him when he left. She also had The Times newspaper and the miniature of Napoleon 3rd which had previously been given as a gift to William. They were all carefully packed away in a special box.

Like her mother she too was left with secrets and memories and a son to take care of.

From her home in St. Margaret's Square, she opened a shop selling fabrics and ribbons imported from India, which came in through the nearby docks in the city, being a large Norfolk shipping port. Her young sister, Phoebe, had come to live with her, helping her care for James Stuart and delighting to help with the selling of the exotic bright Indian wares in the shop. But their days in King's Lynn were to be short.

Sarah and William Marshall were ageing and soon needed the help of James William and Phoebe with the dairy and cheese making. So they all decided to begin a new life back in Swavesey. Elizabeth took a job as housekeeper for Mr William Carter, the largest land owner and farmer in the village.

She had never come to terms with losing her William and the trauma of his disappearance. She found life difficult and coped by losing herself in hard work.

Phoebe took James Stuart to live with his grandparents and they all settled back into village life in Swavesey.

The years went by; in 1870 her dear stepfather William died – she was so glad to be there for her grieving mother.

She was hard-working and independent, always being known as Widow Goad, always dressed traditionally in black. For Elizabeth, her years 1880 – 1890 were years of heartache and turmoil. The only good thing being her son James Stuart taking the tenancy of The Dairy Farm, High Street, Swavesey and his marriage to Mary Jane Jacobs, a woman from the nearby village of Stretham in 1882. She was glad to be able to help him begin his married life, giving him part of his father's legacy, as James Stuart was a good, hard-working man, and a son to be proud of.

For Elizabeth it was a decade of illness and death for all her Marshall family.

In 1881 her brother William Overton died at fifty three, a brother she was so proud of and of what he had achieved by becoming an EGR Engine driver. He had called his first daughter Emma Elizabeth, after two of his sisters, which shows the closeness and affection they had for each other.

Sister-in-law Sophia, her brother James William's wife also died that year. Poor James William has lost his sight, with the consequence of him having to rely on his seventy year old mother Sarah, who was also caring for his four year old son Albert and still making cheese to support them all.

1884 saw the loss of her dear mother Sarah, the Matriarch of them all. She had reached the grand old age of seventy seven. She had been the one constant in all the families' lives. Nothing would ever be the same again.

Truly the end of an era.

1885 Brother Joseph Marshall died in London.

1886 Brother James William's son Albert died aged nine.

1887 Her dear sister Emma Marshall-Hepher died, she who had also done so much to help her over the years of caring for James Stuart, only fifty years of age.

1888 saw her last two brothers die. John Curtis Marshall in Leicester and blind James William Marshall; his end so tragic, ending life as a village pauper with Elizabeth and Phoebe helping where they could.

But 1890 brought the saddest death of all to her, sweet youngest sister Phoebe. It shook the whole family apart, never to be the same again.*

*See Phoebe's story.

At the age of sixty three, Elizabeth now had no-one of her generation in her family left alive. The big noisy brood of Sarah and William Marshall were all memories in Elizabeth's head.

The one good thing being James Stuart and Mary Jane who were creating their own big noisy brood at Dairy Farm,

Swavesey, to continue on in the family example of Sarah and William, his grandparents.

Strangely, by the 1891 census, we find Elizabeth living in Newmarket, aged sixty four, housekeeper to Henry Bulman, his wife Jane and their five children. He owned a Drapers and Outfitters at York Buildings in the High Street. There were eighteen other people listed on the census as living there too, all in their twenties, presumably all lodging and working above the shop. Obviously a very large department store, poor Elizabeth, it seems more unending hard work for her.!

Why did she leave Swavesey and take on such demanding work in Newmarket at her age?

Was it because of the continual trauma of losing her family, especially Phoebe?

Being in your mid-sixties in the 1890s was a great age to be making new beginnings!

But she had James Stuart! Why had she left him just as he was starting a new family with Mary Jane? She had grandchildren by 1891, four of them. How close was their relationship?

How often did they meet? Her life looks so distant and lonely.

One would like to think even if they hadn't lived together, James Stuart and she would have developed a good mother / son bond! Why did she not go to live on the farm with James Stuart and Mary Jane?

At the age of sixty four surely it was usual to do this at that time! Especially as they had so many children and a dairy farm to run and to have a Grandparent around to help could be a blessing for all.

Maybe she didn't get on with Mary Jane! One has to consider that, Elizabeth showed by her life she was an independent and proud woman by never remarrying, her relationship with William and his loss must have influenced her whole life.

But life is full of unknown hardships in the late 19th century. The last time we see Elizabeth is on a census in 1901. She is seventy four years old, listed as still housekeeping, this time at a 'Subscription' home in Newmarket. Was this a boarding house for workers? I haven't yet discovered its meaning.

She still appears to be working hard and this is the last evidence of her existence.

There are no stories of Elizabeth in the family; previously, no-one knew who great grandfather James Stuart's mother was.

She doesn't appear on any official documents; not Newmarket church records, or archives, death or census records; she just disappears. But where did she go?

It is the early 20th century when good records were kept. Maybe they were lost in a fire or by wartime bombing.

One thought though, we know she gave her granddaughter Maud her mementoes. Maud, knowing their significance, continued to cherish them for so many years.

Thankfully, these were to come to us more than one hundred years later, brought to us by Maud's grandson, John Howes. Thank goodness he cared enough and realised the significance these would have to the Goad family today.

Elizabeth had told James Stuart of his father. In 1882 he declared Williams name and occupation on his marriage certificate to Mary Jane (*William Goad, H. M. Army Officer*). No more is known of Elizabeth, no memories of her exist. I have pieced together her life, trying to find her as a person, painting her and her story for you all. She is Widow Goad all her life officially, she leaves just a shadowy, sad, enigmatic picture for us, and sadly there are no known photographs of her. Our X2 great grandmother Elizabeth Overton-Goad.

James Stuart and Mary Jane's Marriage Certificate. 1882

For Elizabeth

Had I the heavens embroidered cloths,
En wrought with golden and silver light.
The blue and the dim and the dark cloths
Of night and light and the half-light.
I would spread these cloths under your feet;
But I being poor, have only my dreams;
I have spread my dreams under your feet;
Tread softly because you tread on my dreams.

W.B Yeats. 1865 – 1939.

I have dedicated this favourite poem of mine to the life of Elizabeth Overton-Goad. She cherishing her few mementoes of her time with William Trickett Goad.

A photograph of the mementoes is at the beginning of the chapter.

A significant copy of The Times, dated Saturday February 13th 1858. The day he enlisted as an Ensign in 32nd Foot Regiment Duke of Cornwall Infantry.

The miniature painting, to us is of an unknown man. After thorough research I believe it to be Napoleon 3rd, Emperor of the French at this time, due to the French Legion of Honour Star being worn, the French service dress and the good likeness to contemporary pictures of him.

Miniatures were given to subjects as grateful gifts in recognition of services rendered.

Maybe an Army association with Napoleon 3rd sent William Trickett abroad in 1860, as stated in Sarah Curtis-Overton-Marshall's deathbed confession!

Napoleon 3rd with homes both in London and Paris, was certainly meddling in the political turmoil of Britain, Mexico and America at that time, also the Far East and William was in the right place and right profession – A possible answer to my hypothetical question. William could have given the miniature to Elizabeth as a farewell gift to her!

Perhaps one day the mystery will be solved, and I will find William Trickett Goad's future whereabouts, deeds and demise; hopefully giving us another story of family adventure.

More research for the future?

But maybe it is best that we leave this enigma at the heart of our family past, and just enjoy our stories of speculation.

Elizabeth's miniature painting

Story within a story: 'Elizabeth's Mementoes', fact and fiction

1907

The stooping old lady, wrapped in a shawl to keep out the chill wind, stumbled along the wide street. Clasping to her the precious bag, the contents of which she was delivering.

It wasn't heavy, but to her the most important thing she possessed. She looked up to see if she was in the right street, the sign said 'Windmill Road'. She had never been here before. Clutched tightly in her gloved hand was the paper her son James Stuart had given her of the address she needed.

In her pretty kitchen Maud sat polishing her treasured pieces of silver, she looked around her home and smiled at the thought of how Walter had fussed and seen they had all the comforts he could provide. After working in his father's grocery shop in Swavesey, Cambridgeshire, as a clerk, he went off to Brentford, London at the age of twenty one to earn enough money to be able to ask his sweetheart Maud to marry him.

It was 1900 when he had left home. Walter worked hard at the big store Kingham's, in the High Street, becoming head clerk and by 1906 had saved enough to buy this comfortable home for them in Windmill Road.

Maud had only been living here a short while – her first home as a bride, Walter James Hepher being her childhood sweetheart. He had always taken care of her, even as a child, although he was six years older, carrying her books to school and being around when needed. It seemed only natural that one day they would be man and wife. Maud's beautiful dark looks, inherited from James Stuart Goad's Indian heritage and her mother Mary Jane's Jewish family, both linked to make Maud a beauty.

She thought of her and Walter's years apart, how they had saved and worked hard. She had trained as a milliner in Cambridge. Leaving home at eighteen and lodging in the Petty Cury, in the centre of the city, in rooms over the shop. It was long hours and sometimes her fingers ached from the constant sewing and inevitable accidental needle pricks.

But she loved the coloured fabrics and wonderful feathers and decorations that adorned the hats she so skilfully created.

Then it was their wonderful summer wedding day with all their families around them at Swavesey – A day of love, lace and flowers. A happy day to remember.

Now she was a mother herself, little Marjorie lay in her cradle by the fire sound asleep, a tiny dark baby destined to be as beautiful as her mother.

Suddenly there was a knock on the door. Maud looked up surprised; she wasn't expecting anyone to visit that day. She took off her apron, smoothed her dress and hair and walked down the long hall to open the door. She stopped, for a moment puzzled and looked at the bent old lady standing there, shivering in the doorway. Suddenly she realised who it was,

"Grandma Elizabeth! Come in!" She took her by the arm and quickly guided her into the warm cosy kitchen and settled her into Walter's big chair by the blazing fire.

Elizabeth was faint and breathless; she had had a long and difficult journey. She sat for a while recovering her thoughts, the warmth of the fire and hot tea Maud had given her was making her drowsy.

Maud sat by and watched her aged grandmother. She could see she was exhausted and let her doze on. Elizabeth's mind kept slipping to the past, more real to her than the present lately. Dreaming of William, of dancing, of laughter and love and of fond embraces.

Maud thought of how she had always been a favourite of Grandmother Elizabeth, being her first grandchild and living only a short distance from each other in the village of Swavesey when Maud was a child. She had been just a skip through a footpath and she could be in her grandmother's farmhouse kitchen, with all the delicious baking smells and sparkling china and silver Maud loved. Grandma Elizabeth was housekeeper to the biggest farmer in the village, Mr. William Carter – a friend of her father's, James Stuart Goad, who also had a large dairy farm. Maud was surprised to see her Grandmother today; she hadn't seen her since her wedding day, at Swavesey a few years before. At the time when her Aunt Phoebe, Grandmother's sister, had so tragically died, she had suddenly decided to move away and left the Swavesey farm to live and work in Newmarket and so had not been such a big part of their lives from then on. She was always a quiet solitary lady, a bit apart from everyone. Like she was carrying a dream as well as living a life.

Elizabeth stirred, realised where she was, and reached out and took Maud's hand. "Thank you dear", she said, "I have come to see you before it's too late".

Maud saw the tears come to her eyes and gently squeezed her Grandmother's work gnarled old hand. "I've brought you my keepsakes of your Grandfather William. I want you to have them to keep as safely as I have all these years."

She showed Maud the photograph of William Trickett Goad, so handsome, with a flower in his buttonhole. "Taken on our wedding day", Elizabeth softly said with a smile. There was also a miniature of a special friend of William's, for whom he had done valued services and the newspaper telling of William's enlistment in the Army. "Oh! What a dashing man in his Ensign's uniform. He had a terrible time in India, it really coloured his life". Elizabeth then proceeded to tell Maud the story of her and William, of their meeting, courtship and love in the 1850s in London.

As she spoke Maud saw her Grandmother smile, even sparkle when speaking, and she saw glimpses of the dark beautiful lady she had once been. Maud listened, entranced and ultimately with sadness, put her arms around Grandmother Elizabeth and held her tight. For Elizabeth it was a release to know that Maud would carry her secret on, Maud whom she loved best. Maud who also knew what love was too, a love that her Grandmother could see she had with Walter.

"My life was always his", she smiled, "This life I've had has only been for James Stuart. I am not needed now he has the dear love of Mary Jane and family."

Maud promised to keep Elizabeth's mementoes and secret safe and one day tell baby Marjorie to do the same.

"One day perhaps someone will understand why and how this all happened and how special my William was and how we were parted", she said sadly. "But now I must go". She looked up and could see the winter dusk closing in through the window.

Elizabeth gathered all her strength, stood tall, wrapped her cloak and shawl tightly around her again. "Thank you, Maud". She wouldn't let Maud detain her, she had things to do. Sweet Maud! "No I can't stay, give my love to Walter".

She pressed the necklace she had been wearing into Maud's hand. "For you dear", she smiled.

She kissed baby Marjorie, tucked a special brooch into her tiny hand, and gave Maud one last hug and left her home, forever. Her task completed at last.

Outside Elizabeth clutched her shawl around her, the cold wind momentarily taking her breath away after the hours sitting by Maud's warm fire. The time talking of William had exhilarated her; it was like he was beside her now.

She caught a bus to where she had planned, stepped off, trying to ignore the nagging pain in her side, slowly walked to a place where she knew there was a seat and sat down.

She watched the people dashing around in the cold. It was getting towards the end of the day and the workers were going home in their droves, their coats tightly buttoned against the chill wind, not taking any notice of an old woman talking to herself on a seat by the river.

She knew the time by the big clock tower on the river bank, as it chimed away the hours. By late evening Elizabeth was still sitting, sleepily watching the gaslights, glittering on the surface of the dark water, as it rippled in the chill autumn wind. She, steadily getting colder and colder, but her head was too full of reveries of the past to notice. Talking to Maud had made it all so real again. Her thoughts were constantly of William and their time together.

Reality came to her in a wave of pain. With a deep breath she calmly stood and looked around. A small bent old woman, standing on the riverbank, the long wind-blown branches of the willows above casting their flickering shadows in the lamplight.

Dreamlike she gazed at the dark rippling water creating an illusory reflection of William in her mind. She sighed, and smilingly closed her eyes.

Later a black shawl could be seen floating on the glittering black water!

Author's note

No trace of Elizabeth Goad's death has been found yet!

In the 19th century, a socially difficult time for women on their own, the Times newspaper had a daily column titled 'Found Drowned'. It published lists of women found drowned in the River Thames.

The catalyst and inspiration for this story.

Inevitability

Nature revolves in its timeless seasons.
Death – Rebirth.
Creation – Evolution.
Our lives intermingled,
Our memories live on.
Whatever we've had can never be gone!
Just as Day follows Night.
After Winter comes the Spring.
So your hand will always be in mine.

Lesley Goad

This is dedicated to the life and love of William and Elizabeth Goad. It is one of the many poems I have written over the years. It speaks of the enduring spirit of love which lived on for them in James Stuart and Mary Jane; its legacy with us as a family today.

Our first Goad love story.

Chapter Five

William Trickett Reilly Goad 1836 – Unknown

'Our Indian Army Heritage'

Charles Elliott Goad
1812 - 1887
b. India

Harriett Darling Reilly
Reilly
1811 - 1870
b. India

William Trickett Reilly Goad
1836 - Unkn.
b. Calcutta, India

m.
1858?

Elizabeth Overton
1827 - Unkn.
b. Norwich

James Stuart Goad
1859 - 1928
b. Middlesex, London

Family Tree for William Trickett Reilly Goad 1836-unknown

William Trickett Goad

Map: India, 18ᵗʰ – 19ᵗʰ Century Goad World

18th-19th Century India Goad World

Himalayas

Simla

Delhi

Agra

Lucknow

Utter Pradesh

Arabian Sea

Calcutta

India

Bengal

Bombay

Bay of Bengal

Madras

Ceylon

Indian Ocean

William Trickett Reilly Goad, 1836 – unknown

Our Indian Army Heritage

Not a name to forget! So distinctive that I knew when it popped up on my laptop screen I knew there was no doubt he was the great great grandfather I had been seeking for several weeks. Elusive to past family attempts to find him. I was so thrilled to have tracked him down at last; even I had begun to feel that he didn't actually exist as most stories and family lore believed. But here he was. Now to find everything about him I could.

We find the Goad family of William Trickett in the 1700s living in Middlesex, London, England. His great grandfather (also William) 1731 – 1798 was married to Darling Thomas 1751 – 1811. They had a son Samuel Thomas born in London 1779, William Trickett's grandfather, who as a young man went to India to join the East India Company, as so many young men of his time did, to seek his fortune in one of Britain's outlying colonies.

In 1803 in Calcutta, Samuel Thomas met and married Maria Jane Boileau 1783 – 1823.

Born in India she came from an old colonial family of Huguenot French and Spanish descent. Samuel Thomas did well in India, eventually to become a Major in the Bengal Native Infantry.

So it seemed natural for their three sons, after having been sent back to London, England for their education, to join him in an Indian Army life: Samuel Alexander Boileau Goad, Howard Boileau Goad and Charles Elliot Boileau Goad (William Trickett's father) – born in Madras in 1812.

All were given their mother's maiden name as it was fashionable to do at this time. We follow the life of Charles Elliot our direct X3 Great Grandfather.

Charles Elliot became an Ensign in 67th Bengal Native Infantry, the natives being known as Sepoys, all the officers being British men.

In June 1834 he married Harriet Darling Cecellia Reilly, a distant cousin by looking at her name, as Darling was Charles' grandmother's name too.

Harriet too had been born in Calcutta, so they were probably both of the ruling East India Company families. This was a time in Empire where India was ruled with the consent of the British Government by the East India Company, founded in 1600. A truly remarkable organisation not shared by any other nation and unusually they were also allowed to raise their own Army, in which many generations of Goad men served and prospered, but also died.

Charles Elliot and Harriett's first two sons were born in Calcutta: Charles Boileau Reilly 1835 and 'Our X2 great grandfather' William Trickett Reilly, 1836.

William was born August 31st and christened in the Church of St. James, Calcutta, the following October; William, after his great grandfather, and Reilly his mother's maiden name.

Despite much research, I have been unable to find the connection for his unusual name of Trickett. Near family names are usually given to children for inheritance purposes, by linking them to a wealthy relative or childless friend.

Six more children were to follow, Charlotte, George, Fredrick, Joseph, Clara and Harriett.

Life at that time in India could be very precarious, prey to every passing disease, living always with the fear of a child suffering from sickness or death, coping with the heat, humidity, insects, monsoons and the clouds of dust. Also, their army fathers were often away fighting in Indian skirmishes on the borders. A tough life for army colonial families.

In the heat of the summer on the plains, wives and children escaped to the cooler climate of the Simla Hill stations, where Charles Elliot's elder brother Samuel Alexander lived and owned a large number of properties.

As Charles Elliot and Harriett had been born and bred in India they had adapted to its lifestyle and built up the obvious immunities, hence having eight of their children reaching adulthood.

The British colonials had created a way of life nostalgic of their lives 'back home'. They lived in large one storied homes called Bungalows (an old Bengali word), with large verandas all around, for cool shady outside living. They employed numerous Indian servants, attending to their every whim. The children were put into the care of an Indian 'Ayah' nurse maid who was the caring mother role to them.

Here we find William Trickett, his brother Charles Boileau and siblings having all the freedom, sights and sounds of India to enjoy. There were animals, ponies, servants to amuse them, and games to be played, as one big happy family.

But 1851 in the London census we find Charles, sixteen and William, fourteen, living in a boarding school in Tooting Graveney, Surrey; they had been sent back to England for schooling. What a shock England must have been for them, a long voyage, then to arrive in the chill of a northern climate, no parents or servants, then on to a rigid Victorian school life.

Colonial children were usually sent to England for their education when they were around seven years old to one of the numerous boarding schools opened for the purpose of Empire children. This arrangement often scarred the emotional development of the children and also their future relationships with their fathers and mothers who, in their separation, became virtual strangers.

Thank goodness Charles Boileau and William Trickett had each other for company and hopefully a few aunts and uncles in London.

In 1852 his brother Charles Boileau at the age of eighteen went back to Umballah, India to become an Ensign in the 56th Bengal Infantry, following in his father's footsteps. At that time local uprisings were occurring all over the colony, which had to be suppressed.

But by 1854 Charles Boileau is now with a regiment in the Crimea at Balaclava. A war fought by Britain, France and Turkey against Russia to keep the Mediterranean free of Russian influence.

On October 25th 1854, he fought and miraculously survived, in the "Charge of the Light Brigade" – one of the most dreadful massacres in British military history. One which changed the treatment and the way of life of the ordinary infantryman soldier in the future, with the care and compassionate help of people like Florence Nightingale their lives would improve.

Charles Boileau won a medal for bravery on that fateful day, but sadly on the 19th January 1855 his death is recorded in the Crimea, possibly from wounds or sickness. He was just twenty years old. How it must have affected William Trickett, to lose his older brother and childhood playmate; the person he was closest to. It could be now that his liaison with Elizabeth began. William Trickett had stayed in London; he hadn't rushed to join the army after school as expected of him. Elizabeth was now living in London, at St. George's, Hanover Square, Mayfair. We know there is a family of Goads living in this street at that time too. One can only surmise how they met, but meet they must have.

It was at this time too he could have met Napoleon 3rd as a young 'blade' about town.

In 1856 William's father Charles Elliott retired from the Indian Army after reaching the rank of Lieutenant Colonel, and eventually returning to England to reside in Kensington, London, accompanied by his wife Harriett.

How difficult it must have been for William Trickett, his parents estranged from him owing to the circumstances of their lives and upbringing, his younger brothers and sisters now also grown up and scattered.

Maybe this is why in 1858 William Trickett enrolled as an Ensign in the 32nd Foot Regiment Duke of Cornwall Infantry. Pressure from his father maybe?

With Elizabeth's mementoes, left with Maud Goad-Hepher was the original copy of The Times newspaper containing the announcement, declaring William Trickett Goad's enlistment:

The Times, Saturday, February 13th 1858.

Appointment of 'William Trickett Goad, gent, to be Ensign without purchase'.

The Times newspaper cutting

Ensigns are the youngest officers in a regiment. To be one you applied to the Commander-in-Chief and were then recommended by someone in whose responsibility the Commander-in-Chief feels confident (His father?). If the outcome of investigations into character is satisfactory and he can pass the exam, his name is entered on a register for a future commission when available. The Commander-in-Chief decides whether or not the commission has to be purchased. In 1858 to be an Ensign with the 32nd Foot Infantry Duke of Cornwall, cost £400 to buy, a considerable sum at that time. As the regiment was due to be sent to India to help quell the mutiny raging there, I expect William Trickett was fast tracked, free of purchase, because by March 2nd he was engaged in operations against Indian rebels at the Siege of Lucknow, India, led by Sir Henry Havelock. William Trickett, now found himself again in India, but this time at the heart of the Indian mutiny.

As an Ensign he would have been placed in command of a squad (8 men) to gain experience. Their primary role was to carry regimental colours into battle, which, whilst fighting, made them targets, resulting in a high mortality rate for Ensigns.

The conditions he would have experienced would have been atrocious: Living under canvas, with filth, insects, heat, dust and dubious rations. Sunstroke and heat apoplexy killed many men and there always loomed the fear of Cholera. So few treatments were available, the dubious use of arsenic, mercury mixed with chalk, the poison antimony in a glass of red wine for a purgative, and in the last resort rum and hot water.

Kill or cure!

Lucknow had been besieged by the Indian rebels for months, inhabitants were desolate and starving, with the city crumbling around them in the constant bombardment of cannon fire. The mutiny had been brought to a head by the Indian Sepoys, who had heard that bullet cases were to be coated in pig and beef fat and as when firing their guns, they had to bite off the bullet cap before loading, they rebelled.

Sepoys being either Hindu or Muslim, eating pig or cow was against both their religions. Slaughter on either side on a large scale followed, truly a shameful historical episode on both parts.

When William Trickett arrived in Lucknow, in 1858, with the 32nd Foot, they found a city of sick and half mad inhabitants. The hospital was overflowing with injured, army doctors doing their best, with no way of relieving the pain. Amputated limbs lay in piles all around and it was recorded at the time that no amputees had survived. The air was full of the stench from the cemetery, where they had to bury the dead after attacks, which inevitably added to the sickness.

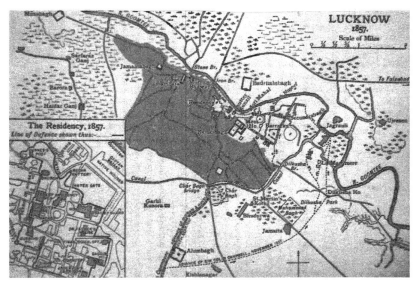

A map of Lucknow 1857

The 32nd were billeted in the Governor's Residency building. After bombardment one night, the roof caved in burying six men alive, only two could be dug out and saved.

They had to deal with prolific insects, flies smothering food, heat, dust everywhere and coping with snake and scorpion bites and then the prolific local guinea-worm, often several feet long, which burrowed into their and their horses legs and feet, this parasite affecting half the officers and men.

Truly a nightmare. All this and fighting the rebels too!

But by March 16th they had fought and secured the relief of Lucknow.

For his part in all this William Trickett was awarded the Indian Mutiny Medal, with the Lucknow Defence Clasp. A very rare medal today, sought after by collectors. Also the Governor General gave an additional year's service pension to each soldier for 'services rendered', after such a gruelling campaign.

One of the tragedies of the mutiny was that the British Native Infantry Officers had a deep affection for their native soldiers and sincerely believed that whatsoever happened in other regiments their men would remain loyal.

William Trickett must have been relieved to return to England with his regiment in late 1858. I would like to believe he then married Elizabeth. Their son James Stuart was born in late 1859 – sadly no trace of their marriage has been found yet, or James Stuart's birth certificate, but I shall keep searching.

What happened to William Trickett? Recent searches have found this:

The London Gazette, 18th May 1860.

"Ensign William Trickett Goad has been superseded being absent without leave."

(This is a Military term 'absent without leave', 'AWOL' ie. 'Absent from one's post or duty without official permission but not intending to desert.').

What of the consequences? This was a very serious offence. In peace time, it meant prison; in wartime, death.

Whatever happened one can only guess, he was just twenty four years old.

What could have caused this disappearance? Was it an undercover association with Napoleon 3rd? Did he go abroad as mentioned in Berry Wayman Tibbitt's letters?

Was he dead? If so, why didn't his family know? On other Goad family tree sites I also find William Trickett's death down as unknown.

Did the old military family 'close ranks' at the time on an event they didn't approve of?

Maybe Elizabeth believed he would come back to her one day! All I know is that, all her life Elizabeth cherished his memory, never remarrying as was quite usual for young widows at that time.

William Trickett came from two previous generations of military men. Who can say how his upbringing and life experiences affected him. Maybe his family didn't approve of his union with Elizabeth, a servant and country woman.

He bravely did his duty for Queen and Country in India. Surly he was a 'man of his time' and to be judged thus. All I know is that he is a part of our Goad story today and I am so glad that some family memories enabled me to bring him back to our family and reunite him with Elizabeth and James Stuart again, as part of our family heritage.

Appendix I: The Soldier

William Trickett Goad - Duke of Cornwall's 32nd Regiment of Foot

The 32nd Regiment of Foot of the British Army was first raised in 1702 as a regiment of marines to fight in the War of Spanish Succession.

It won its first battle honour in 1705 for the siege and capture of Gibraltar.

The 32nd landed in Portugal in 1808, and under the soon to be Duke of Wellington, fought in the battles of Rolica and Vimiero. They fought under Moore in the retreat to Corunna, and on returning to England they were part of the Walcheren expedition in the Netherlands where many were struck down with malaria. After being reinforced they returned to Spain, leading the assault on Salamanca and taking part in all the major conflicts right into France. For the final chapter in Napoleon's history, the 32nd fought at the battle of Quatre Bras, arriving about 2pm just in time to help halt the French advance.

The Cornish regiment were renowned for their blood curdling Death Howl before attacking. Two days later at Waterloo the 32nd were stationed opposite the French main attacks, stoically standing their ground before attacking Napoleon's assaulting troops. There were 647 men of all ranks at the start of 16th June 1815, and at the end of the two days there were only 131 men left standing: they suffered the greatest loss of any regiment on that day.

The regiment famously defended Lucknow from July to November 1857; Victoria crosses being awarded to William Dowling, Henry George Gore-Brown, Samuel Hill Laurence, and William Oxenham. The regiment's commanding officer, Col John E. W. Inglis, served as Brigadier in overall command of the Lucknow Residency during the siege. He was promoted to General and knighted for his services. The regiment was retitled and equipped as a Light Infantry regiment as a result of its contribution to the defence of the Residency, for which it also won a battle honour.

In 1881 it was merged into The Duke of Cornwall's Light Infantry. The colours of the 32nd Foot hanging in Monmouth Church are said to have inspired Sir Edward Hamley to pen these words:

> "A moth-eaten rag on a worm-eaten pole,
> It does not look likely to stir a man's soul,
> 'Tis the deeds that were done 'neath the moth-eaten rag,
> When the pole was a staff, and the rag was a flag"

William Trickett Goad and the Duke of Cornwall's 32nd Light Foot Regiment

Record Details for William Trickett Goad- 32nd Foot Cornwall Light

First Name	William Trickett
Initial	W
Surname	Goad
Rank	Ensign
Service	Army
Regiment	32nd Foot, Cornwall Light Infantry
Nationality	British
Campaign Medals	Indian Mutiny Medal
Clasp Awarded	Defence of Lucknow

The Indian Mutiny Medal

Instituted 18th August 1858 for award to British and Indian troops deployed against the Mutineers. The last of the Honourable East Indian Company's medal's issued on behalf of the British Government.

Description: Silver 36mm diameter with a swivelling cusped suspension. Obverse: the Diademed head of Queen Victoria and the words ' VICTORIA REGINA'. Reverse depicts a standing Britannia with a shield, presenting a wreath. Behind is a standing British lion; above is the word 'INDIA' and the date 1857-1858.

Bars; Five fishtailed bars were issued; DELHI-DEFENCE OF LUCKNOW-RELIEF OF LUCKNOW- LUCKNOW-CENTRAL INDIA.

Naming: Impressed in Roman capitals. Official replacements turn up thicker and naming in taller letters and showing the recipients service number (service numbers are not impressed on the original issue)

Ribbon: White with two red stripes.

Indian Mutiny Medal

Swavesey, Cambridgeshire, England

Profile of the Village of Great Grandfather James Stuart Goad

Swavesey was a settlement in Roman times, situated beside the old Roman road between Cambridge and Huntingdon. Evidence of an ancient castle remains and is believed to have been built during the campaign against Ely in 1071-72 by William the Conqueror. Ely was defended by the local Saxon hero, Hereward the Wake.

After many years of defeated battles with Hereward, William's soldiers were led across the high causeway from Swavesey, Aldreth, Haddenham and through old fen droves via Stretham by the Monks of Ely Cathedral, to hold on to their power and to avoid it eventually being ransacked by him.

Later Swavesey became a large mediaeval river port, with two docks. A drain channel ran north-west to join the River Ouse. The north, west and east boundaries are bordered by Fens – Mare Fen being the host to Skating Championships from 1880 until 1933.

Water-borne trade maintained Swavesey's prosperity and in the 1850s the population was 1300 strong with lots of agricultural and domestic trades. Water-borne trade discontinued at the end of the 19th century when a railway in 1847 was constructed between Cambridge and St. Ives. It replaced the docks for exporting from the local villages, who were sending farm and market-garden produce to London by boat. Railways also then aided the import of heavy goods and sand, coal, metal and fertilizers back for all the farms.

In 1845 more than two thirds of the cultivated land was arable. In 1886 several leading farmers formed The General Farming and Dairy Company Ltd, apparently a co-operative. It included 640 acres of arable and 360 acres of pasture, which gave an increase of rotation grassland. However, by 1895 more than 95% of the grassland had become permanent. Dairy farming considerably expanded between 1875 and 1895 – the time of James Stuart Goad, our Great Grandfather and dairy farmer. He farmed firstly at The Dairy Farm in the High Street, and latterly until 1923 at Ryders Farm, Swavesey.

Dairy Farm, Swavesey in 2014

St Andrew's Church, Swavesey

Chapter Six

James Stuart Goad 1859 – 1928

Mary Jane Jacobs – Goad 1863 – 1928

Our First Goad Farmers

Elizabeth
Overton   m.
1827 - Unkn. 1858?
b. Norwich

William
Trickett Goad
1836 - Unkn.
b. Calcutta, India

m.
Thomas   1860   Sarah Anne
Jacobs   Fitch
1832   1838 - 1873
1905   b. Lt Downham

James Stuart Goad   m.   Mary Jane
1859 - 1928   1882   Jacobs
b. Middlesex, London   1863 - 1928

Family Tree of James Stuart and Mary Jane Goad

Mary Jane and James Stuart Goad

James Stuart Goad – Mary Jane Jacobs

Our First Goad Farmers

James Stuart slipped his arms into the blue silk waistcoat his Aunt Phoebe had made as a gift for his recent 21st birthday, pleased with the reflection he saw in his mirror, as he had taken great care over his appearance to-day.

Two days earlier he had been in London visiting the wholesale markets of Shoreditch, selling the cheeses and produce of his uncle and aunt, Edward and Emma Hepher. He lived with them and his cousins at their large market garden in Duck Lane, Haddenham. Aunt Emma, like her Marshall sisters, was an expert cheese maker.

When returning to Cambridge on the train he found himself sitting in the same carriage as a beautiful dark haired young lady, who in conversation told him she lived in the village of Stretham, nearby to Haddenham.

Her name was Mary Jane, the eldest daughter of a local farmer Thomas Jacobs. Before parting, she invited him to join her and her family at the future Stretham Feast celebrations.

The Stretham Feast was a two day annual holiday held in the month of May, to raise funds for Addenbrookes Hospital in Cambridge, which was dependant on voluntary contributions from the local community it served. All neighbouring villages in their turn held similar fund raising days. Local Friendly Societies carried their brightly coloured banners and paraded the streets, being led by a loudly playing marching brass band.

Collecting boxes were willingly filled by villagers donating, all regarding it as insurance for their future. Everyone in the village attended wearing their Sunday best, if possible new dresses and hats, decorated with flowers and ribbons, the men sporting a new brightly coloured cravat or a just new cap and flowers in their buttonholes. It was an occasion for everyone to dress-up and to enjoy.

Set up in the village square overlooked by St. James' church, would be the swing boats and roundabouts, with their brightly painted horses, driven by a hand operated wheel. Stalls are set up on Front Street selling home-made rock and toys; also a photograph booth and shooting galleries. It was all the fun of the fair. A cricket tournament was played by village teams and there were races for the children, two days of fun and games for everyone.

On the final Tuesday evening a dance was held in the big upstairs room of The Red Lion, its windows looking out over the medieval cross in the square, viewing the fair and stalls lit up by flares at dusk.

A time of music and laughter and finding a new sweetheart.

It was Tuesday. James Stuart had arranged to meet Mary Jane by the church lychgate.

From across the street he saw her, looking beautiful in a new blue sprigged muslin dress, her dark hair in ringlets tied up with white ribbons, she smiling at him as he approached her, James Stuart could not take his eyes off her.

They spent the day walking, meeting the family and her neighbours, viewing the stalls, talking and enjoying each other's company.

He was introduced to her younger sisters, Sarah Anne, Elizabeth and Lydia, three more bright dark Jacobs beauties and, at the evening festivities, he then danced with them all in turn.

When that evening finally holding Mary Jane in his arms, and them spinning and dancing to the rhythm of the music played on piano and fiddle, by their laughter and words James Stuart knew they were destined to be together forever.

A day never to be forgotten.

They were married six months later, October 10th 1882, in All Saint's Church, Jesus Lane, Cambridge. Mary wearing her blue sprigged muslin, her newly married younger brother Jonathan and her sister Sarah Anne stood as witnesses for them on the day and to their future happiness together. A big family party was held at Mary Jane's widowed aunt Rebecca Harvey's home in Jesus Lane; her father's sister, who had been as a mother to all his children when Thomas's wife Sarah had died so young.

It was Michaelmas, the time for farm changeovers and rents to be paid, James Stuart had taken the tenancy of The Dairy Farm, by the old Swan Pond in the High Street of Swavesey, the village where he had been brought up as a boy. There living with his grandparent's William and Sarah Marshall, learning the skills of cheese making and the dairy trade from them both as he grew up. He had been planning and saving for a farm of his own for a long time. Now as a couple together they were destined to make dairy farming their future for forty happy years.

Dairy Farm in the early 1900s. James Stuart on the left and son Tom Goad on the right. Con, Mabel and Lilian are also in the picture. Photograph sent from Canada by Berry Wayman Tibbitt.

In Mary Jane, James Stuart had the ideal wife. She had been born and brought up on the Jacobs farm in Stretham, knowing all the ways of a farmer's wife; as a girl helping her mother and grandmother in the skills of the dairy, being part of a big farming family. She had been well educated at a school in Cambridge, and was quick, bright and pretty. She was just twenty and James Stuart twenty three years old, both young, strong and full of hopes for their future together.

By June 1883, James Stuart and Mary Jane's first daughter Maud was born.

Quickly the days went by. They were both working hard to make the dairy farm a success. James Stuart working to achieve a quality herd of milking cows, Mary Jane to running an efficient dairy, producing the butter, cream and cheeses. At this time people drank the skimmed milk, so the much needed by-products of butter and cheeses could be made with the cream. James Stuart selling to the markets he knew, as he had been taught by his grandfather William Marshall.

James Stuart joined The General Farming and Dairy Company Ltd, the Swavesey village co-operative. Its object was to share grazing, working together, to create a rising standard of living, helping each other to obtain prosperity for all.

The dairy aspect of the Fens was of great importance in the community and considerably enhanced the standing of a farmer locally. The farmer with a milk, butter and cheese making dairy, enjoyed enviable status within the community. His wealth was measured in the weight of cheeses and butter waiting to be sold in his dairy store. It was as good as or even better than money in the bank for them.

The breeding of cattle and the fertile Fen grazing grounds played a major role in the contribution of feeding the nation. In the 18th/19th century, the British Navy was classed as being victualled out of King's Lynn on Fen produce.

In 1884 James Stuart's dear grandmother Sarah dies, his new baby daughter born that year he calls Sarah Anne, but always calling her by her own special name of Nance. The farm flourished. James Stuart and Mary Jane soon had a large 'brood' to care for: son Thomas, 1886; James William, 1890; Stuart, 1891; George York, 1893; Constance May, 1894; Mabel, 1896; and lastly Lilian, 1899. Their family complete at the dawn of the new century, just two babies didn't survive, but that was a usual occurrence in these years of no antibiotics and many childhood epidemics. However, it was still very sad for them.

Such busy years for them all but so happy and so full of love, days of children and laughter. They, as a family, on Sundays attended the local Bethel Baptist Church, a member of The Free Churches Society. The Baptist faith, that both he and Mary Jane had been raised with. It gave great solace in the sad times which came to their life, when losing two of their babies at birth, and especially when helping cousins Berry Wayman and Ella through the sad tragedy of the death of their mother, James Stuart's dear aunt Phoebe – a shocking event which was so unexpected. Their cousins emigrated to Canada a year later for a new life, Mary Jane being a good letter writer, corresponded regularly with Berry until her death in 1928.

James Stuart was well respected in his Swavesey community. He played a full part in village life; always public spirited, he was voted onto the newly formed Parish Council when in 1898 they were set up by the National Government. He was elected by his village contemporaries as a member and continued as Vice-Chairman until he retired in 1921. He was trustee of many local charities and his advice was sought over many village problems. A well liked, conscientious and caring man to all.

As a family they had an anxious time when young Thomas caught the Polio virus and spent many months of treatment in the local isolation hospital. He eventually recovered but remained weak in one hip and leg, leaving him with a permanent limp, but he was still determined to be a farmer like his father.

James Stuart and Mary Jane delighted in their family. Bright and clever, all went to the village National School. Later, Maud went to train as a milliner in Cambridge, Nance went to The Royal London Hospital to train as a nurse. Tom is always by his father's side on the farm, also renting his own land to farm at Boxworth End. Stuart lodged at the nearby village of Sutton, training as a butcher, then in 1912 emigrating to America to join James Stuart's cousin Berry in Chicago. James William was an apprenticed carpenter and George York became a baker/ confectioner in the local Swavesey bakery. All good, useful trades.

After Maud's marriage to a Swavesey man Walter Hepher in 1906, they moved to Brentford, London. Sister Constance lodged with them and worked there in a drapery store as an assistant. Mabel, after finishing school, also trained as a milliner in Cambridge, but as a young girl, Lilian stayed at home to help her mother.

It is now the 20th century. Life is changing. Queen Victoria who reigned for 62 years has died and her son Edward VII is King.

James Stuart and Mary Jane now have the joy of being grandparents to Maud and Walter's daughter Marjorie, born 1907.

Thomas has married his sweetheart Ida Clark, from Histon Road, Cambridge and given them two new grandsons, John Stuart, 1914, and James Owen, 1916.

At this time James Stuart and Mary Jane moved to Ryders Farm, Swavesey, not far from their previous farm. It was the oldest house in the village, built in mediaeval times. James Stuart was now an experienced and respected farmer.

They loved living at Ryders, having big parties and picnics when the family were all home for weekends. Mary Jane was now able to enjoy creating a new garden, with the help of her trusty old gardener Mr Britchford, the house and garden watched over by a tall Wellingtonia tree, which is still there today. These were the halcyon days of the family before the clouds of war were to alter their lives for good.

Playing in the garden at Ryders Farm

Mary Jane Jacobs Goad in the garden at Ryders Farm

Mr Britchford the gardener

Mary Jane Jacobs Goad, with her five daughters: Maud, Nance, Constance, Mabel and Lilian. Under the Wellingtonia Tree at Ryders Farm, Swavesey

The Great War of 1914 shook the world, never to be the same again. James William and George York both joined the Army. Nance was nursing the wounded at The Aldershot Isolation Hospital. The people of Swavesey village did all they could for their country, sending their young men to fight, raising monies and knitting gloves, socks and scarves for the troops. They set up a Cottage Hospital in a private house, James Stuart, Mary Jane and girls all involved, raising monies and helping where they could.

George York was wounded in 1916. He was shot in the chest, the bullet going straight through his lungs, but still surviving to fight on a year later. They also received news that, in battle, he had endured a distressing German gas attack.

James William survived until 1918, but sadly died of dysentery and is buried far away from home in the country of Italy. So distressing for all the family.

James Stuart and Mary Jane were now sixty, both not in good health, forty years of farming life has taken its toll physically.

In 1922 Thomas, Ida and children, Jack, Jim, Betty and William (Billy), moved to Stretham Fen, Chittering. Tom was now managing his Uncle Tommy Jacobs' 400 acre farm, he who was Mary Jane's youngest brother.

George York was considering moving to Chittering too, to set up as a chicken farmer at Orchard Farm.

James Stuart and Mary Jane decided to retire and with daughter Lilian moved with George York to Chittering. When in the next year he married Maude, they rented Grove House, in the village of Stretham. The next years were happy here, although it had been a difficult decision to leave Swavesey, but Mary Jane was back where she grew up as a girl, her two brothers Reuben and Tommy, their wives and daughters now nearby. Their youngest daughter Lilian married Bert Peacock, her Wimblington farmer at the village church of St. James's in 1925. After the ceremony her Uncle Tommy Jacobs held a grand family party and dance at his home, Oakley House, a day for both families to cherish.

Grandchildren called in Grove House each day on their way home from school. Most of their family were living nearby and

James Stuart and Mary Jane were enjoying a well-earned retirement.

Mary Jane was due to go into hospital to have an operation for complications of her diabetes, Nance had returned home from her work in Malta to care for them at this time.

But before she has gone into hospital, James Stuart collapsed one evening and later that day he died of a cerebral haemorrhage. He was sixty nine years old.

But they were not to be parted for long.

Three weeks later Mary Jane also died in The Evelyn Hospital, Cambridge as a consequence of the operation, owing to the complication of getting gangrene in the thigh after an amputation.

The knowledge of antibiotics is in its infancy for coping with the control of infections and diabetes.

Twice in three weeks, seven of the achieving children of James Stuart and Mary Jane gathered to say goodbye to their parents. (Just Stuart in America and James William in a grave in Italy were not present).

They both had a Baptist service at Grove House before being interred in a double grave at Wood Lane Cemetery.

Nance's photograph sees it covered in an abundance of beautiful flowers.

Wood Lane Cemetary 1928

It was the end of an era for them all: Our 20th century great grandparents.

James Stuart and Mary Jane Goad – another Goad love story.

From the Cambridge Evening News

Funeral 2nd November 1928 Mr. J. S. Goad.

The funeral of Mr. James Stuart Goad, who passed away early Tuesday morning, took place at Stretham yesterday (Thursday) afternoon. Shortly after 2 o'clock the cortege left the house for the cemetery, the widow and family being conveyed in cars.

The service was conducted by Rev; G. J. Chamberlin of Ely, in the presence of a large assembly of Friends.

Mr Goad, who was sixty nine years old, had been in failing health for a considerable time. On Saturday night when retiring to rest, he had a sudden seizure and soon became unconscious, in which state he remained till the end.

The greater part of his life was spent at Swavesey, where for some years he was an active member of the Parish Council. Parish Council Rep; on the Board of Galons Charity and the Fire Relief Fund Charity (Frere Cottages) and a keen worker in connection with the village War Memorial Fund. He also served on numerous Committees and was Overseer of the Poor. He left Swavesey about four years ago. Including his widow he leaves three sons and five daughters.

Mourners included: Mrs. J. S. Goad, widow; Messers T and G Goad, sons.

Mrs J.W. Hepher, Miss. N. Goad, Miss, C. Goad, daughters; Mr and Mrs H. R. Ashby.

Mr and Mrs. B. Peacock, daughters and sons-in-law; Masters J. and O. Goad, grandsons.

Mr and Mrs T. Jacobs, Mr and Mrs R Jacobs, brothers and sisters -in-law. Mrs Bennett, Mrs G. Wright, sisters- in-law. Mr and Mrs J.W. Taberham, nephew and niece and Miss L. Jacobs, niece.

1859 – 1928

The Dairy Farm by Swan Pond, High Street, Swavesey,
Cambridgeshire (2014)

Ryders Farm, Swavesey 2012

Story within a story: 'James Stuart, the Meeting' – fact and fiction

Coningham Road, Shepherds Bush, London. 1887

James Stuart was sitting deep in thought, gazing out of the carriage window of the London train as he watched the countryside and towns flash by. He was on one of his regular trips to sell his wares at the big food markets of the city, proud of the fine cheeses that he produced and sold, from his farm in Cambridgeshire.

But today he also had another destination to fulfil. Two days earlier he had received a letter from his aunt Clara, telling him his grandfather Charles Goad was very ill and not expected to live much longer.

It was a considerable time since he had seen his grandfather. As a boy he would often visit his grandparents in their Kensington home. But since acquiring the tenancy of the Dairy Farm in Swavesey, and his subsequent marriage to Mary Jane Jacobs, and the birth of his three children, his life had become busy and full. He was a young man of twenty eight with all the responsibilities of a home, husband and father.

He had never known his own father William, who had died when he was a baby. He had spent his childhood with his maternal grandparents Sarah and William Marshall, having a country childhood around cattle and dairy, with all his Marshall cousins for playmates.

His mother Elizabeth living nearby as housekeeper at the big farmhouse of Mr William Carter, the largest landowner in the village. She living the life of a widow, but always hoping that her husband William, believed dead, would one day return, after disappearing when away on a mission for the Army.

He had been to see her the previous day to tell her about Aunt Clara's letter.

Even though she was now sixty years old, he could still see the beauty she had once been, standing tall in her full black dress, her thick white hair piled high on her head in the fashion of the time. Her only concession to the severity of her dress as a widow was the small exotic broach she wore at her throat, of gold and coloured jewels.

She encouraged him to go and see his dying grandfather. William's father, the severe upright, retired Indian army officer, but a father-in-law who had been kind to her when William went missing, he also grieving then, at loosing another military son, but as a military man himself, he knew all about the duty to his country.

The jolting of the train ended James Stuart's reveries. He had arrived at Liverpool Street station, and firstly went to visit the big wholesale food market where he quickly did his important farming business transactions.

Now, to catch the underground line to Shepherds Bush. He had never ceased to marvel at this feat of engineering of twenty years; men burrowing below the land's surface like moles; trains travelling through dark tunnels, with holes to the surface to let the smoke out. Not a comfortable ride, but a way of taking the population of London quickly and safely to their daily destinations.

Soon he found himself outside the door of his grandfather's home in Conningham Road. He looked up and admired its fine proportions and putting his hand on the shiny brass knocker, noticing its unique shape of an Indian elephant's head, he knocked to let the family know of his arrival.

When inside, the house seemed so quiet, a world away from where James had come from. His Aunt Harriett smiled and greeted him and then quickly took him to his grandfather's room. He quietly approached the still figure lying in the darkened room, heavy drapes drawn across the large windows.

Lying in his bed, drifting in and out of consciousness, Charles heard the sound of someone close by. He turned and tried to raise his head from the pillow.

"William my boy! You came!" he gasped breathlessly, his pale eyes filling with tears.

His dry clawed hand reached out and held onto James Stuart's coat sleeve.   The old white-haired man looked up and whispered in a harsh distant voice, "We don't have much time, I'm so sorry my son; forgive me?"

But the effort and shock of the moment was too much for Charles. His eyes closed and he fell back onto the mound of soft pillows, breathing heavily, beads of sweat glistening on his hot fevered brow.

James Stuart gently released his arm from the fixed grasping hand and looked down at his dying Grandfather lying in the large bed, looking so small and pale, struggling for breath. Thoughts raced around his mind, quietly accepting the realisation he had been mistaken for his father, whom he had only seen in a photograph. "I certainly must look like him." he mused. He knew there had been harsh words between his father and grandfather, who didn't agree with his son's involvement with the Emperor Napoleon 3rd and his schemes for power. Obviously when nearing the end of his life he was trying to make amends with William.

James Stuart was now twenty eight years old. No longer the child he had been when here on his last visit. "Grandfather, we've had so many years apart," he thought, "So much pride and so many unspoken words! His father and mother certainly had a story to tell!"

His head was full of these thoughts and mixed emotions.

Charles opened his eyes and James Stuart took his hand and whispered ," Grandfather, I have come to say goodbye," Hearing his voice, the old man smiled in recognition of his grandson, and with a feeble voice said, "James you are so like your father, I'm so proud you have grown into such a fine young man". But with the effort of these words Charles's eyes closed again, his hand still holding onto James Stuart's with him so glad to hear his grandfather's words.

James Stuart had no fear of death; he had been brought up by his other grandfather, William Marshall, in the Bethel Baptist faith. He and Mary Jane attended the local Chapel in Swavesey each Sunday.

Charles, breathing heavily, had now sunk into a deep sleep. James Stuart sat for a while, still holding his grandfather's hand, thinking of the past and now knew how blessed he was with his wife and little family. He decided to himself to look to the future. He must talk to his mother Elizabeth and help her too.

He quietly whispered to his grandfather lying so still," Dear grandfather, we must let the disappointments and regrets of the past go, and be at peace," squeezing his hand when speaking, hoping he could hear, wherever his mind had taken him, but there was no more James Stuart could do.

His Aunt Clara had quietly come into the room and he intimated to her that it was time he should leave.

He bent and kissed his dying grandfather goodbye, and squeezed his hot dry hand now lying limp on the white counterpane. He gave one last backward farewell glance, as he reached the door, at the still sleeping figure in the bed and he quietly left.

He collected his hat and gloves, and politely giving his "commiserations and goodbyes" to his aunts Clara and Harriett, stepped out into the fresh sunlit air of the busy streets of London.

Now, home to dear Mary Jane, Maud, little Nance and baby son Tom. It was time now for his own dreams and future.

Chapter Seven

The Swavesey Children of Ryders Farm

The Swavesey Children

Maud	Sarah	Thomas	James	Stuart	George	Constance	Mabel	Lilian
1883	Anne	1886	William	1891	York	May	1896	1899
1965	1884	1961	1890	1935	1893	1894	1977	1937
	1940		1918		1979	1945		

Family Tree – The Swavesey Children of Ryders Farm

James Stuart, Mary Jane and family

The Swavesey Children of Ryders Farm

The nine Swavesey born children of James Stuart and Mary Jane Goad have come to our 21st century family mostly as memories. Our family branch being descended from Grandfather Thomas Goad. There are some childhood memories of a few Great Aunts and Uncles by many of the cousins today. Paddy has memories of Great Uncle George and tales told by his father Bill, of his young times with his Uncle and Aunts, when as child in Stretham.

Great Aunt Maud, after marrying Walter Hepher, moved to London. Her story is in the next chapter. Her grandson John has happy memories visiting Hill Farm as a child with his mother Marjorie, for Mollie Goad and Douglas Marchant's wedding day in 1949 Mollie being Tom and Ida's youngest child. Tom will have his own important story later.

Mabel and Lilian, Bethel Baptist Church

Mabel 2nd at back, Lilian seated far right

His other oldest sister Sarah Ann, always known as Nance, although she died in 1940, was always spoken of and greatly loved by all the family and whose interesting life is written separately. James William sadly died in 1918 in Italy – the shadow of the Great War touching the family. George, surviving the dark war days, loved by all, baker, soldier and poultry farmer, lived on to the grand of age of eighty four. Another chapter later of his and his brother James William's army life, and Stuart's family in America. Constance was a gifted actress and singer, performing at many local charity concerts, always leading the village singing of the National Anthem at the final curtain. She gave a memorable performance of 'The Duchess' in 'Alice in Wonderland', when it was produced magically at dusk on a warm summer's evening, in a lantern lit woodland garden in Swavesey. All in aid of raising funds for the Swavesey Memorial Hall in the early 1920s. On the day of its opening Constance gave to all attending, a wonderful rousing rendition of 'Land of Hope and Glory', much to the pride of her parents.

She then went to live in Stretham, as she married local corn-dealer Russell Routledge in 1932. He began his working life as a baker but by WW2 was trading in corn. Flour being the link I expect! His father was the village Mission Chapel Minister, sent from London at the turn of the 20th century; the Chapel being in a little black tin hut in Pond Lane.

Nance, Mabel, Con and Lilian

Con, Mabel and Nance

Russ' and Con's wedding, 1932

Mabel in the garden at Ryders Farm

Photograph sent from Canada by Berry Wayman Tibbitt

Aunt Con and Russ (as they were known) lived at the Bakery, in Cage Lane, Stretham, then in Short Road. She, as a girl had spent many holidays in Stretham with her cousin Irene Jacobs, Uncle Tommy's daughter at Oakley House, the big house on the High Street corner of Top Street. Irene consequently became her bridesmaid when she married Russell at St. James', Stretham in 1932. We have some wonderful happy photographs of the wedding day thanks to her sister Nance's photo album, handed down in the family to me by cousin John Howes. Constance was in Cambridge with her Uncle Tommy Jacobs on the day he died in The Lion Hotel, Petty Cury; she had always been close to her Jacobs family. Her name can be seen today on the Champions Board for the year 1944 at the Stretham Bowling Club. Sadly Aunt Con died in 1945 after an operation for gall-stones at Addenbrookes Hospital, Cambridge. Her bright personality so missed by Uncle Russ who lived on into the 1950s, and fondly remembered by all the present day cousins.

Aunt Mabel, was pretty and artistic, and had trained as a milliner, like her sister Maud. See the pretty hats in the Swavesey picnic photograph. In 1918 she married Horace Ashby, a local Ely man and civil servant, at St. Andrews Church, Swavesey .They too got very involved in the village fundraising for The Memorial Hall, Mabel playing the piano and Horace producing shows and also acting "Comic Turns." Once Horace dressed as a magician, calling himself "Watteau Billie", and gave a skilful display of magic; all the fun of the evening later reported in the local newspaper.

Later they came and made their home at Waterbeach, near Cambridge.

Horace died in 1956. Mabel lived on until 1977 at their home, The Homestead, Meldreth, near Royston, Hertfordshire, where they had finally settled. Mabel aged eighty one when she died. Two good and happy lives.

Lilian, the youngest and last sister came to live at Grove House, Stretham, in 1924 with her father and mother when they retired. In 1925 she met and married Arthur Bertram Peacock, (always known as Bert) a farmer from Wimblington, near St. Ives.

For her wedding at St. James's, Stretham she wore a white silk georgette dress trimmed with silver, with veil and wreath of real orange blossom from Kew Gardens (a gift from her niece Marjorie Hepher, who later married a Kew Garden Botanist, Frank Norman Howes). She had her wedding reception at Oakley House, the home of her Uncle Tommy Jacobs.

They were to live at Lattice Farm, Wimblington and subsequently had a daughter, Daphne, in 1927. Thanks again to Aunt Nance's photo album we have a photograph of Lilian and Daphne when she was about ten years old. Significant, as Lilian died in 1937 at the age of thirty seven. No more is known of the family or Daphne after this.

One conclusion, which can be seen from Aunt Nance's photograph album, is how loving and close the large family stayed through the years, even when they had all left home and scattered to live their own lives.

Another tribute to James Stuart and Mary Jane's family life and love.

Russ Routledge and Horace Ashby
(married to Con and Mabel)

Goad Swavesey Picnic
Left to Right: Horace Ashby, Mabel, Tom, Stuart, Nance, her beau?,
Walter Hepher, Maud?, Lilian, George, James, Con.

Maud Goad- Hepher 1883 – 1965

'Keeper of Memories'

At the Dairy Farm, Swavesey, Cambridgeshire, the summer after the marriage of James Stuart and Mary Jane Jacobs in 1882, a baby girl was born to them. They decided to call her Maud, a popular name of the time. She had the striking dark colouring of her mother and grew up into a very beautiful young woman.

The eldest of five sisters and four brothers, her life was never dull. Days at the Dairy Farm were full of family fun. She attended the National School in the village of Swavesey, Cambridgeshire and was very bright and did well. In 1901 when she was eighteen she went to train as a milliner in Cambridge, lodging over the shop in Petty Cury. She had been walking out with Walter Hepher for a while and they were intending to marry one day. Walter in 1901 left Swavesey went to board in New Brentford, Middlesex, London, he was twenty three years old and working as a grocers clerk. He was the son of Jesse and Harriett Hepher, who kept the grocers shop at 1 High Street, Middle -watch, Swavesey, where he had started work as a young man. His father was to become later the Registrar of Births and Deaths for the Swavesey District. Both Maud and Walter worked hard for their future together, they had known each other all their lives, their families closely knit through the years, as both living on the High Street.

By 1906 Walter and saved enough to buy 'Fernbank', a house on Windmill Road, Brentford and that year he and Maud were married and started their happy life together.

The wedding took place at St. Andrew's Church in Swavesey, uniting the local families of Goad and Hepher. Their wedding was a grand summer country affair. We have a photograph showing both families in all their finery and lace, Mary Jane and James Stuart proudly sitting beside their beautiful bridal daughter Maud. A true Edwardian scene.

Maud's brother James William later went to war with Walter's brother Wilfred. But that is another story. James Stuart's Aunt Emma Marshall had married an Edward Hepher, a Swavesey man, a generation before. He had been a market-gardener in the village. Later, James Stuart lived with them in Haddenham, as a young man. The Goad and Hepher families are intertwined through the years. James Stuart's Uncle William Overton had lived in Swavesey as a child with a Hepher family related to his Grandmother Sarah. Also, little Lucy Hepher was living with her and James Stuart in 1871. Lots of family ties.

It's 1911. Walter is thirty three, head of house and occupation is clerk. Still living in Fernbank, Windmill Road, Brentford. Maud is twenty eight and they have a daughter Marjorie, born June 1907.

Through the years we see photographs of this little family, proud Walter with his two dark beauties; Marjorie, so like her mother, Mary Jane and James's first grandchild, who had wonderful memories of staying with them at Ryders Farm, Swavesey as a girl. Also Maud's sister, Constance May, who, aged seventeen is boarding with them. She is working as an assistant at the local drapers store in Brentford. Maud and Walter's life was very happy; he was a very successful business man, working hard at Kingham Brothers food wholesalers, in High Street, Brentford, Middlesex.

Kingham's was a wonderfully old fashioned grocery firm, importers of bacon and Sanderson's self-raising flour. Bacon curers in the old style; they had their own wharf almost opposite Kew Gardens and many products were brought directly by barge from the London Docks. All tea produced in the world markets was brought to the London Auction houses to be sold. Kingham's packed and sold their own special tea called Kin-Gama. By the time Walter retired he was a director of this large company, a true credit to his character and hard work.

Maud and Walter were very proud to be able to send their daughter Marjorie to St. Paul's girl's school, Hammersmith, where her music master at the time (early 1920s) was the composer Gustav Holst – he who wrote the wonderful 'Planets Suite'.

In the late 1920s Marjorie met a young South African botanist, Frank Norman Howes, whilst playing tennis at the Kew Gardens Tennis Club and they married in 1931. In 1944 Maud and Walter became proud grandparents, when their grandson John was born.

Maud and Walter's wedding, 1906

Marjorie's wedding, 1931

Frank later became the head of the department of Economic Botany at the famous Kew Gardens. Life was good for them and their family.

After over fifty years of happy marriage, Walter dies at the grand old age of eighty two in 1962. Maud following three years later also aged eighty two.

Thank you Maud, for keeping safely the mementoes of your Grandmother Elizabeth. Her treasures were safe with you!

Another happy Goad Love Story.

Sarah Anne Goad 1884 – 1940

'Aunt Nance – Nurse and Nanny'

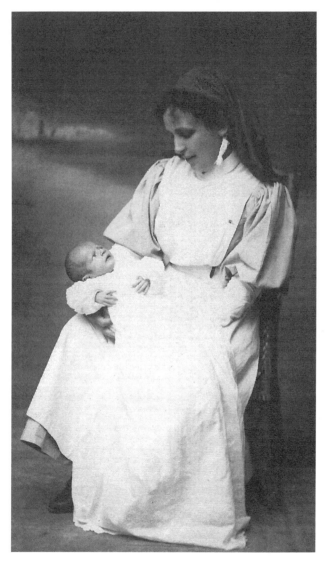

Sarah Anne Goad

Sarah Anne, second daughter of James Stuart and Mary Jane Goad, was given the name of her late grandmother and aunt, also her paternal great grandmother who had died that year. But all her life she was to be known as Nance, even on the 1911 census at the age of twenty seven, she chose to declare herself by this name of her own when working at the Royal London Hospital.

Born in 1884 her childhood on Dairy Farm, Swavesey was happy and lively, she was close to her elder sister Maud. Four brothers were born in quick succession after her: Thomas 1886, James William 1890, Stuart 1891 and George York 1893, to whom she played 'little mother'. Proving to be loving and practical, helping her mother Mary Jane and delighting in her three little sisters, Constance May 1895, Mabel 1897 and finally Lilian 1899.

As a child, her brother Thomas contracted Polio, a worrying time, as he would have been in the local Isolation Hospital until his recovery, and this would have been a big concern in all their lives.

We are not sure what year Nance joined the Royal London Hospital for her training, but we see on the 1911 census her living at the Nurses Home in the Parish of St. Boltoph, Whitechapel. The street address is The London Hospital. Her occupation is 'Hospital Nurse'.

The Royal London Hospital

To become a nurse Nance had to apply with two character references and to be interviewed by the renowned formidable Matron Eva Lückles.

After being accepted she would have been given a mauve check dress with removable sleeves, white bib apron and cap. She would do a six weeks trial, doing various menial tasks, such as sorting laundry, dusting beds, giving meals, bedpans and sewing shrouds. After acceptance and three months had passed, she would be asked to sign a contract to complete a two year course and if then qualifying, having to commit to working a year as a 'London' staff nurse.

A ward photograph – Nance is on the far left

A training nurse had to take regular examinations to receive certificates of achievement. Days were long and tiring; up at 6.15am, breakfast at 7.00am, then Ward Duty, a two hour midday break, finally finishing at 8.30pm after evening lectures. Lights out was at 10.30pm. This routine was six days a week with two weeks' holiday per year, all for the salary of approximately £20 per annum.

Thank goodness Maud, Walter and sister Con were living within easy reach in Brentford, and the train services were good between London and Swavesey for visits.

How proud James Stuart and Mary Jane must have been of her.

But now it was 1914, England was overshadowed by the terrible war with Germany. Nance is now a fully qualified nurse, and desperately needed by her country. The next we know we find her nursing at the Aldershot Isolation Hospital. It was the first British base to take the casualties from the Battle of Mons in the western front. We have several photographs of her then. In one she is pictured in a large group of Officers, Medical Nursing Staff, NCOs and men, dated 1915. Also, one taken in one of the wards with wounded soldiers dated 1918. I can find no trace of her having joined the Queen Alexandra's as an Army nurse. Research tells me 'The London' sent groups of nurses wherever they were needed at the time, even to private patients.

Nurse Edith Cavell, from a Norfolk family, was also a trainee at The Royal London in the early 1900s, the time Nance was there. She took up a post as Matron at a hospital in Brussels, Belgium. Caught up in wartime events, when Germany occupied Belgium, she nursed and helped numerous soldiers escape home. A devout Christian she nursed English, French and German alike. When discovered by the Germans in 1915, she was arrested and tried, even after international protests she was found guilty and quickly shot early the next morning, and branded as a traitor, much to the shock to the rest of the world.

In her home city of Norwich, Norfolk, by the Cathedral with its majestic spire, there stands in Tombland a statue in her honour.

What an auspicious time for Nance to take up her vocation and what sadness she must have experienced in her wartime hospitals. Ever conscious of the perils of war and being reminded of her dear brothers James William and George York away fighting in France. But by 1919 Nance was looking to her future, after her four arduous years of wartime nursing she decided to go for more training, this time specialising in women's and children's health.

She took a post at Queen Charlotte's Hospital, Hammersmith, London, the first maternity unit in Europe. The hospital was founded by King George 3rd's wife Charlotte in 1739, originally being called Queen Charlotte's Hospital for 'Lying In'. Even today it is still renowned for its women's and children's services.

Nance belonged to a generation of women who paved the way in many professions and proudly showed the worth of women's skills in this changing 20th century world – culminating with them all finally obtaining the vote in 1929.

Wartime nursing at Aldershot

Letter and last personal words to Aunt Nance

Dear Aunt Nance, Thank you so much for the album of lovely photographs; it has helped me see how you touched everyone's life. You were thirty years old and it was 1924 and with your new nursing skills you decided to leave hospital nursing and become a Nanny to the Rusby family. Naval Commander and Mrs Rusby engaged you to care for their new born son Cameron. You sailed to Malta, where you were all to live, travelling there in his command ship 'The Queen Elizabeth.' How proud you look holding Cameron at his baptism on board. Holy water was put in the ship's bell for the occasion.

There are also lots more photographs of happy times in Malta.

But 1928 brought you back to Stretham, to care for your mother and father at Grove House. Both now elderly and ill and you stayed with them till the last.

But your life was back to Malta again and your, now two, surrogate children.

Cameron was joined by baby Stuart, then in 1932 it was back to Weymouth for the Rusby family and a shore posting.

The 1930s appear full of Nanny friends and babies and children. All seem special to you. You always so professionally dressed in your starched Nanny uniform. Two pages of your album are of niece Marjorie's wedding to Frank Howes in 1931 and sister Con's to Russell Routledge in 1932, pictures of lovely happy family days. The last photographs of you are on a happy day out visiting Hinkley Woods, with a friend, niece Marjorie and her husband Frank. All in your Sunday best, pretty dresses and summer hats, it is 1937 but another time of war is looming on the horizon.

You came back to Stretham to live, your surrogate children now grown up. You called your home 'Ryders', a reminder of memories of past childhood happiness in Swavesey, a place so special to you all.

Sister Con and Russ now live in Short Road, Stretham. Sister Mabel and Horace live in nearby Waterbeach. Brother Tom, Ida and family are now living at Hill Farm, Stretham by the old windmill. Brother George and wife Maude are farming poultry at Orchard Farm, Chittering. All still so close.

But in 1940 you fell ill and sadly died at the young age of fifty six. You were such a caring sister to be missed by all your sisters and brothers.

On October 2nd you were laid to rest in Wood Lane cemetery, close by your dear mother and father, James Stuart and Mary Jane. Maud's husband Walter was your executor and dear Maud saved your photograph album, which has been so important to me.

Later, it was looked after by Marjorie, then John, helping me to picture family life and to write this labour of love today. Without this album I could not have painted such a clear picture of your life today.

Dear aunt Nance, You are a true Lady of the 20th century and an Aunt to be proud of.

Nance with Cameron on board HMS Queen Elizabeth, 1920s

Nance, Marjorie and Frank Howes

Aunt Nance

'The Dawn of Modern Nursing and the London Hospital'

In 1859 Florence Nightingale published her 'Notes on Nursing' after her experiences at the Crimean War. After meeting a lot of opposition, she eventually, in 1860, opened a nurse's training school at St. Thomas's Hospital, London, helped by the support of many enlightened people of the time. A conscious charity ethic in society and social changes at the end of the 19th century was enabling women to work outside the home. The past stigma that the nursing of the sick was only for women of low character had changed. The nursing care for the sick had become more important. With the new understanding of hygiene helping recovery, added to the use of the drugs, cocaine and morphine, the patient was cared for in a more professional way. Hospitals were benefiting from this awareness by the ready support of the great and good of society and as always by Royal Patronage. Although old beliefs, like scarlet bed covers to repel lice were difficult to change.

Nursing was an institutional life; every hour had to be accounted for, no privacy, except when sleeping and very little life outside the hospital. This had to be a true vocation for everyone following this path in life, all had to remain unmarried.

This is the dedicated life of service Aunt Nance Goad chose at this time in nursing history. James Stuart Goad's cousin, Sir Frederick Treves of Joseph Merrick (Elephant Man fame) was surgeon and teacher at The Royal London Hospital at this time. Is this why Nance chose to go there? We know so little, but it is possible.

The Royal London Hospital was built in 1753, with private funds as a charity hospital for the poor and sick of London. It was situated in the East End of London at Whitechapel, had seven hundred beds and depended on the great and good of society for its upkeep.

It had a Medical School. Private physicians from the West End, (Harley Street) visited twice a week to do ward rounds, to operate if necessary and lecture to student doctors and nurses in the evenings.

Adam and Eve in the Hospital 'Garden of Eden'

The treatment of the poor was free, but if the illness was incurable they were refused admittance, owing to overcrowding. The only other option for the patient then was the workhouse, to die a pauper's death.

The running of the hospital and the staff was done by the famous Matron Eva Luckless (featured in the 2005 BBC. television series 'Casualty 1900s'). She was a friend and disciple of Florence Nightingale and ruled The Royal London from 1879 until her death forty years later in 1919 – always in the manner of a Headmistress or Army Commander, a great disciplinarian, but always wanting the best for all.

She saw that her hard working nurses had a garden provided for their recreation. It had fountains and rose bushes, doves, ducks and deckchairs. There was even a penny-in-the-slot machine to dispense boiling water to make the all-important 'cup of tea'. Nurses called it The Garden of Eden.

We see a photograph in Nance's album of a statue there, of two children, sheltering under an umbrella, titled 'Adam and Eve'. Nance must have been so familiar and happy here, spending free hours enjoying the garden, created in the heart of London.

The Royal London Hospital is still a place of renown today, part of our great NHS.

James William Goad 1890 – 1918
George York 1893 – 1979

James William, second son of James Stuart and Mary Jane Goad. After leaving school at Swavesey, Cambridgeshire, he took an apprenticeship as a carpenter. George York, the last of four sons, when finishing his schooling, served as an apprentice baker and confectioner at the local bakery in the High Street, Swavesey, Cambridgeshire.

In the 1911 census, James William is living in Chalfont-St-Peter, Buckinghamshire, working for a building company as a carpenter. Also lodging with him is Wilfrid Hepher, also a carpenter, brother of his sister Maud's husband Walter. As schoolboy friends they had decided to keep each other company while working away from home.

But now it was the year 1914. War with Germany had been declared, so all three boys volunteered for the army. James William joined the Royal Army Service Corp. He was the first Swavesey soldier to qualify for the 1914 star medal, having enrolled August 1914 and been sent quickly to France. Wilfred joined the Royal Engineers. George York, the 9th Suffolk's. Sadly James William lost his friend in 1916 when Wilfred was killed at The Battle of the Somme. By then Wilfred had achieved the rank of Sargent, and had been awarded the DCM.

James's role in the Service Corp was to supply and transport. As a driver he saw, over his four years' service, many theatres of war; Arras, Ypres and The Somme – experiencing many futile battles.

In Flanders, in the summer of 1918 he was taken ill and died of dysentery, a big hazard of communal life and trench conditions, he had seen and suffered so much in four years. He was just twenty seven years old and they buried him in the war cemetery at Montecchio, Precalcino, Italy. James William and Wilfred's sacrifices are commemorated on two war memorials. One at Chalfont-St-Peter and in their home village on the memorial cross in the churchyard of St. Andrew, also on the Roll of Honour in Swavesey Village Memorial Hall.

War memorial, St Andrew's church, Swavesey

With so many sons of England being buried on foreign soil, the government decided that every grieving community would have a war memorial. The national Cenotaph was also erected in London and in honour of the fallen, decreed on the 11th day of the 11th month, that red poppies should then be worn, and that the nation, on the chime of the 11th hour, was to stand for two minutes in remembrance of their sacrifice. This was the beginning of The Royal British Legion and its constant work for war veterans and their families.

Such was the magnitude of the death of 15 million men in WWI and its impact of the losses affecting every family. With the now universal education it brought to everyone the realisation of the value of each human life.

Poplars, 1907 James William Goad back row 2nd right, Wilfrid Hepher back row far right

Opposite page: A photograph, taken in a studio, of James William and George York with their five sisters: Maud; Nance, in her nursing whites; Mabel; Constance and Lilian. Walter Hepher, their brother-in-law and niece Marjorie are there too. Both brothers are in their Army khaki.

It was lucky for them to all be home together at this time, and probably their last leave as a family. They all look serious and conscious of the times they are living in. Only Thomas and Stuart are not there.

Back row: James W, Maud, Walter, Con, George In Front: Lilian, Marjorie, Nance, Mabel

George York Goad

By 1916 George was a Sergeant. We have a copy of a letter sent to his parents in that September. It is from the Army Records Office to notify them that George has been admitted to the South African General Hospital, Abberville, France, suffering from gunshot wounds, also a copy of his letter written to his parents on arrival.

No./5319/PkCas

(If replying, please quote above No.)

Army Form B. 104--80.

————————————— Record Office,

————————————————— Station.

—————————— , 191 .

SIR,

I regret to have to inform you that a report has this day been received from the War Office to the effect that (No.) *15319*

(Rank) *Sergt.* (Name) *G. Y. Goad*

(Regiment) *9th Suffolk* ~~was admitted on 18 9/16~~ ~~is dangerously ill at~~

to 1st South African Gen: Hos. Abbeville suffering from *Gunshot Wounds Chest.*

I am at the same time to express the sympathy and regret of the Army Council.

Any further information received at this office as to his condition or progress will be at once notified to you.

I am,

SIR,

Your obedient Servant,

Mr James Goad   *C. Barrow 4H.*

for Officer in charge of Records.

(785.) W. 6939—2690. 500M. 7/15. N.P.A. Ltd.

Forms

B. 104-80

Z

Letter from the Army Record Office

1st South African General Hospital
Ward 13
B. E. France
19-09-16

Dear Mother,

Just a line to let you know I am getting on a bit and came here yesterday.

Came down here on a barge down one of the rivers of France, it was much better than coming on a train, you don't get jolted about. I can do without that I can tell you.

They are very kind to us in this Hospital. You couldn't be looked after better.

I think I am lucky in getting here. All of us came here that went down the line in the barge. I expect my letters will go astray now till you get this address.

So, write by return, won't you. But mother, you need not worry about me as I shall get on all right. I didn't think I was made to stop a German bullet. I haven't done so at the present, as this one went straight through me. How is Horace (Mabel's young man?) getting on? Hope he is all right, also old Billy (his brother, James William) He never wrote to me as you said sometime back he was going to. I think this is all this time.

Will write again in a day or two.

Hoping this will find you well with

> *Love to All From Your Loving*
>> *Son George*
>> *G. Goad Sgt.*

What a lovely optimistic letter, and it is good to know that his prediction of a German bullet was true. Although it was eleven months before he was sent back to France again, after a long convalesce in England, as the bullet had passed right through his lungs. But he survived all future battles he was in, and was eventually discharged in 1919.

James William, George York and nursing sister Nance all saw first-hand the terrible events of WWI. But it was a war which touched everyone's life, with most families having a father, brother or son in France.

All believing they were fighting 'The War to End All Wars'.

George York

George York's medals

George came back to the family in Swavesey, helping his father and joining in the drive to raise monies for the Memorial Hall. We see in newspaper announcements George being MC at the fund-raising local Whist Drives held in the National Schoolroom. In 1923 he took up poultry farming at Orchard Farm, Chittering, near Cambridge with his father and mother, who then retired from Swavesey. Now being a neighbour to his brother Thomas at Chear Farm. In 1926 he met and married Maude Elizabeth Willetts, from Sussex. His parent's, James Stuart and Mary Jane then moved to live at Grove House in the village of Stretham.

George and Maude married at her home Shoreham-by-the-Sea in the local Methodist Church. Their daughter, Mary Elizabeth was born in 1927 and always a good friend of her cousin Billy, her Uncle Tom's youngest son who loved to spend his holidays helping his Uncle George with the chickens, as only living across the fields on the next farm. When Mary grew up she trained as a school teacher, afterwards living and working at Isleworth, Middlesex.

Maude, George's wife, sadly died in April, 1947, only forty seven years old.

Luckily he had his brother and family nearby, but happily in 1949 he remarried to Winifred Lower, a local welfare nurse, and retired Methodist Missionary.

George and Winifred, 1949

They lived at Orchard Farm but later retired to 1, Oakham Cottages, Castle Grove Road, Chobham, Surrey. In 1965 Winifred died and we see from probate she left George £4,625 – a considerable sum then. George, now seventy two, moved to live with his and Maude's daughter, Mary, who had never married, still teaching in Isleworth and living at 55, Worten Way.

In July 1979 at the age of eighty six he died; a good long life.

Known and loved by this generation of Goad cousins.

The last link for them to James Stuart and Mary Jane Goad's 'brood' of Swavesey.

Cambridge News Obituary: Wheeler J.W. Goad.
9th August 1918

The sad news reached Swavesey this week that Wheeler James Goad, ASC has died from illness on 28th July, while serving in Italy. Wheeler Goad was universally loved and respected, and the tidings of his death were received with general regret. He was the first Swavesey man to volunteer for service at the outbreak of war, joining the ASC on the 18th August, 1914. On the 5th October 1914 he went to France, thus gaining the 1914 Star, and he was the first Swavesey man to appear in the village wearing the ribbon of that distinction when he came home on short leave last March. He served continuously in France until last November, when he proceeded with the British troops to Italy. William Goad was a fine example of a thorough Englishman and a true hearted soldier. His body lies resting in sunny Italy, and his friends will always remember that, "there's some corner of a foreign field that is forever England".

'Wheeler' An Army term for a Driver.

James William Goad, with research I have seen he was known as Will or Billy by all who knew him – the family using his second name so as not to confuse him with his father.

In Memory of
James William Goad
Driver
T2/016992
7th Div. Train, Army Service Corps
who died on
Sunday, 28th July 1918. Age 27

Royal Army Service Corps

Montecchio Precalcino Communal Cemetery Extension, Italy
Plot 2. Row A. Grave I.

Montecchio Precalcino is a town in the Province of Vicenza, 4
kilometres north of Dueville and 16.8 kilometres north of the
town of Vicenza. Take the autostrada A31, Vicenza Schio, and
leave it at Dueville. Follow the signs for Montecchio Precalcino.
On arriving in the village a CWGC sign will be seen. This
cemetery is always kept open.

From April 1918 to February 1919 those who died from wounds
or disease in the 24th and 39th Casualty Clearing Stations were
buried here or at Dueville, and in December 1918 and January
1919 some also of the dead from the 9th Casualty Clearing
Station. Certain graves were brought in after the Armistice from
the small Communal Cemetery Extensions of Trissino, Lugo
and Caltrano. There are now over 400 1914-18 war casualties
commemorated in this site.

Swavesey

Chalfont St Peter

James William Goad

In memory of James William Goad

Painting: Waiting for a New Dawn

Waiting for a New Dawn

In the sapphire shades of night,
She bathes the world in a silver light,
Looking down on the earth below,
Life wakens from sleep in her gentle glow.
Timeless motion in her silver beams,
Blue moon shadows enfold silver dreams.
And the eternal promise brought by a dove
Welcomes a new dawn.

Lesley Goad

The sentiment of the poem inspired by the painting, both created by me, is peace and new beginnings.

It is here for James William and George York, remembering their years of sacrifice in France.

Stuart Goad 1891 – 1935

'Son of the New World'

Stuart Goad
1891
1935

Mabel	James	Harold	Christine
1922	Francis Goad	Wesley Goad	1929
1964	1923	1925	1958
m. Roger	1950	1992	
Fredrikson			

In 1891 Mary Jane gave birth to a son, he was the third successive son of four, and named Stuart after his father James Stuart. He was their fifth child, their previous son, James William being born just the year before.

He grew up on Dairy Farm, Swavesey, Cambridgeshire. At the age of five he attended the village National school, joining his older brothers Thomas and James William and his sisters, Maud and Sarah Ann and a year later younger brother George York. The four brothers had a typical country childhood out on the farm, being so close in age they always had a playmate.

By 1899, his three younger sisters were born, Constance May, Mabel and Lilian, now the family was complete.

Too soon the happy days and times of childhood on the farm were over.

On the 1911 census we see Stuart aged nineteen, living in the nearby fen village of Sutton, whose church tower I can see on the skyline from my kitchen window, known locally as 'the pepper pot', by its unusual shape. Close by is the city of Ely, its Cathedral is known as the "Ship of the Fen", as it is seen silhouetted on the flat Fen horizon in all weathers.

He is living at Bow Cottage, as a lodger, and is working as a Journeyman Butcher, following in the skills of his Uncle Reuben Jacobs in Stretham, the next village, his mother Mary Jane's brother. The choice of butchering was very complimentary to farming.

Most villages at this time had more than one butcher's shop on their High Street.

Only his eldest brother Thomas followed their father James Stuart into farming.

James William chose to be a carpenter and George York a baker. All good valued skills.

But Stuart was a Goad with a sense of adventure and at the age of twenty one, in 1912, he sailed from Liverpool, England on the RMS Lusitania, bound for New York, America, for a new life in the 'New World'.

At this time the Lusitania was the prize liner of the Cunard Shipping Company.

Built to be the fastest ship in the world, with good weather the Atlantic Ocean crossing could be as short as six days. At the time Stuart travelled to America in the Lusitania, her newly built, "faster" sister ship was due to make her maiden voyage; the ill-fated Titanic. A voyage with dire consequences for all aboard her and a story known to all, from the great films made of this chilling iceberg disaster.

In 1912 Stuart's journey would have perhaps ended with different circumstances if he had chosen to travel on the Titanic in that fatal month of March.

The Lusitania was to have its own story. On May 1st 1915, in the midst of WW1, travelling from New York to Liverpool, she was torpedoed and sunk by a German U boat off the coast of Ireland. 1,196 people were drowned, just 764 survivors.

This sinking helped change the course of the war. Many American nationals who were travelling on board had died and with America being a neutral country at this time, this event helped bring them into the European theatre of war.

On the passenger lists for the Lusitania leaving Liverpool, on March 9th 1912, we see 'Stuart Goad, son of James Goad of Dairy Farm, Swavesey, Cambridgeshire'. He was bound for 'Chicago, Illinois', to work as a butcher.

He was to join Berry Wayman Tibbitt there, James Stuart's cousin who had emigrated there a decade before. Berry had mentioned this fact in a later letter to Mabel Goad - Ashby, Stuart's sister.

The next time we see Stuart is on the 1919/20 USA Federal Census. He is living in Genoa City, Wisconsin and married to Ella Porath, she having been born there, and they having a son John, born in 1917.

Next he is living in Pennsylvania, now married to Viva Lent, also having been born in that State. They have a daughter Mabel, born 1922 and a son, James Francis, born 1923. By 1925, the family are back in Genoa City and son Harold Wesley is born, followed by daughter Christine in 1929.

A twice married man, with a family of five children, he is experiencing all the highs and lows of life. Is he still butchering? I cannot say. There is so little information on the census. He is obviously thriving with his family around him.

Sadly his death is reported in 1934, at the young age of forty three, leaving his young wife Viva to bring up their young family alone. We know his descendants are still living in Genoa City today.

James Stuart Goad

2013 Appendix

Great Uncle Stuart's 'Immortality' - Our American Adventurer

CAMBRIDGE WEEKLY NEWS

6th June 1919

SWAVESEY MAN IN U.S.A.

"Our Swavesey representative had this week received a letter from Mr. Stuart Goad, youngest? son of Mr. J. S. Goad, Ryders Farm, Swavesey, from Genoa Jet, Wisconsin. Mr. S. Goad says that he joined the USA. Army on 15th June, 1918, and was attached to the US. Machine Gun Training School Camp at Augusta, Georgia, as an instructor. On July 19th he was promoted sergeant, and on the 15th January last (1919 he was discharged. A number of officers attending the Training School were British Officers. Genoa Jet is only a little town with a population of about 800, yet it contributed 198 "boys" to the US Army."

After having an interesting afternoon visiting the local Swavesey historian Mr. John Shepperson and buying from him his book of newspaper extracts, titled, "A Village during the Great War." When reading it I was thrilled to find the above snippet on one of its pages.

I had little information of Great Uncle Stuart, as you will have seen from my previous writings. It led me to thinking of the copy of a letter I had been lent by cousin Gillian Goad-Johnson, written by Stuart's older daughter, Mabel Goad-Fredrickson, which she had sent to her Aunt Mabel Goad-Ashby, then living in Waterbeach, Cambridgeshire. and dated January 20th 1959.

In this letter she writes news of all her family, concluding that she has just one married brother Harold Goad, still surviving of her four siblings. This is news of 50 years ago.

Stuart's daughter Mabel's 1959 News

Stuart had 5 children: John by his 1st wife Ella Porath and 4 more by his 2nd wife Viva Lent. A sad story to come.

(1) John died in1948 in surgery, aged 31, leaving 1 son.
His name is now on the Genoa High School 'Honor Roll'.

(3) James Francis in 1950 was killed in a car accident aged 27, leaving 2 daughters.

(5) Christine in 1958 died of a brain haemorrhage aged 29, leaving 1 son.

(2) Mabel and (4) Harold are living near each other on the same street, also mother Viva next door at Christine's home, looking after her husband and son.

It was a long shot, but I felt I must try to see if there is a chance of contact with Stuart's two remaining children's 21st century family, to help complete my 21st century picture of 'Our Swavesey Children's descendants.

I put together an explaining letter, a copy of my book introduction, photographs and copy of Mabel's original letter of 1959.

I did two complete copies, addressed one to 'The Goad Family' and one to 'The Fredrickson Family' sending them both to Mabel's address of 50 years ago. Knowing that her brother Harold Goad and family also lived nearby, I included my e-mail address and sent it all by air-mail. I waited in hope.

Three days later I had an e-mail reply from Debbie Goad, wife of Barry Goad, Harold's third son and Stuart's Grandson.

Paddy and I couldn't believe our eyes, a reply so soon! So a new adventure begins for us.

She said she was thrilled and promised to have a family meeting and then come back to me with news. Signing off as 'American Cousin-in-Law'. So now another wait!

Viva Lent, Stuart's second wife, mother of Mabel, James Francis, Harold Wesley and Christine, was sadly left a widow in 1934 when our Great Uncle Stuart died. The youngest, Christine was only 5 years old.

We see her on May 1ˢᵗ 1935, as a founder member of 'The Genoa American Legion Auxiliary,' to become a First Officer of Unit 183 and presiding as their Chaplain.

Preamble to the Constitution of the American Legion Auxiliary

"FOR GOD AND COUNTRY, we associate ourselves together for the following purposes: To uphold and defend the Constitution of the United States of America;

to maintain law and order; to foster and perpetuate a one hundred per cent Americanism; to preserve the memories and incidents of our association during the great wars; to inculcate a sense of individual obligation to the community, state and nation; to combat the autocracy of both classes and the masses; to make right the master of might; to promote peace and goodwill on earth; to safeguard and transmit to posterity the principles of justice, freedom and democracy; to participate in and to contribute to the accomplishment of the aims and purposes of The American Legion; to consecrate and sanctify our association by our devotion to mutual helpfulness."

We can see how by being involved in this organisation Viva and her family became part of the wider community in their lives and the friendship, help and support it would have brought them.

Viva never remarries; she has much family sadness to bear over the years as we see below, and cares for, in their turn, her bereaved grandchildren; her Faith hopefully giving her the strength and comfort to carry on.

Mabel Goad-Fredrickson, born 1922, died in 1964, aged 42, just four years after writing her letter to her English family.

She left a husband and 4 children, the youngest being only 7 years old.

Another sad event for all. I have had no response from her Fredrickson family yet.

James Francis Goad, born 1923, died 1950 aged 27.

James Francis Goad

James entered Service on March 13 1943, Company 1, 378th Infantry, 95th Division.

He trained at Camp Joseph T Robinson, Arkansas; Camp Shelby, Mississippi; Fort Riley, Kansas; Shreveport, Louisiana; and Fort Sam Houston, Texas.

He was sent overseas for operations on June 6th 1944 (*An auspicious date for Britain),* returning to America on June 29th 1945; One of the soldiers known in Britain as GIs.

He fought in the European theatres of war unknowingly beside his Goad cousins; His Uncle Thomas's sons Jim (James Owen) and Bill (William). All were simultaneously in action in the theatres of war in Northern France, Central Europe and

Rhineland. James being wounded in action, qualified for the award of The Purple Heart.

He served for 2years 7 months 39 days; and was discharged on November 21st 1945 at Fort Custer, Michigan. His decorations show the extent of Service:

American Theatre Ribbon; 3 bronze campaign stars; Combat Infantry Badge;

Purple Heart Medal; Good Conduct Medal; European -African – Middle Eastern Theatre Ribbon; World War II Victory Medal.

James in his civilian trade was a carpenter.

Thank you from us all here in England James. Your Grandparents James Stuart and Mary Jane would have been proud of you.

Harold Wesley Goad, born 1925, died 1992 aged 67.

Harold Wesley Goad

He attended Genoa City High School like his older brothers and sister.

On June 29th 1943 he entered Service joining the Air Corps. He trained at Camp Grant, Illinois; Gulfport Field, Mississippi. He was discharged on November 4th 1943 at Gulfport Field, Mississippi, after serving just four months as the rank of Private.

It didn't say why on his record, but one must surmise it was a health reason owing to him being awarded a Good Conduct Medal on leaving.

He joined his mother Viva in the American Legion Auxiliary, Genoa City, Wisconsin Branch – Playing in the Legion Soft Ball Team of 1947, finishing 4th in the league.

Harold's trade was also as a carpenter.

Harold was twice married and like his father has 5 children: Bonnie and Benjamin by first wife Carol.

Bonnie married Douglas Noyce and has 3 daughters and 1 granddaughter.

Benjamin married Mary Anne Loucks and has 1 daughter.

Harold's second family:

He married Jean Rae Katzenberg and had 3 children: Larry Rae, Mary Christine and Barry Scot.

His 2 eldest children have no family but Barry is married to our correspondent, cousin-in law Debbie and he is step father to her 2 sons, Jacob and Justin and grandfather to Jackson.

It is so lovely to have the American Goad photographs and delight in their likenesses.

Thank you Debbie for your family Goad voice from across 'The Pond'

How lovely it is to hear of Stuart's descendants, all cousins to our family here today.

Last word about Stuart: On his American WWI Army record he gives his name as James Stuart. I searched his birth certificate and early census and he is down as just Stuart! But like his cousin Berry Tibbitt, after leaving England his family is always in his thoughts; he called his 1st daughter Mabel after his sister, son James with the name of his brother and father. So adding James to his own name seems a natural thing to do when so far away from home. A loving link to his father James Stuart.

We know Stuart died in 1935, aged 43, but so exciting to know his and our Goad family are still living in Genoa City, Wisconsin today, and that our James Stuart and Mary Jane's family genes are thriving in the United States of America.

Bonnie (Noyce), Larry Goad, Deb (Tuckner), Barry and Mary Goad

Barry and Debbie Goad

Stretham, Cambridgeshire, England

The Village of the Jacobs and Goad Family

Painting of Ely as seen from Stretham/Little Thetford area

The Doomsday Book records, 'Stradham' as having the Abbots of Ely Fisheries.

Stretham is a small fenland village situated four miles from Ely on the A10 artery road between King's Lynn and London.

It is 53 feet above sea level, Ely being 85 feet above.

Cambridgeshire is one of the driest counties of the British Isles, Stretham's average rainfall being 24 inches per year. The River Cam flows on its North East border. The River Great Ouse to the south west joining the Cam near Stretham Ferry Bridge.

It has one of the largest beam engines in the fen, which is open to the public, operating by electricity today for demonstrations of its past historical use.

The old windmill is beside the A10 and is now a house, but in 1936/1945 it was used by the Royal Observers Corp. In 1962/1968 it was a Cold War Observer Post.

Outside the Red Lion Inn is the 15th century cross, the most perfect example surviving in the country.

The church is dedicated to St. James, in the diocese of Ely; its Patron, the Bishop of Ely. The church contains a black marble memorial for Anne Brunswell, 1667, the wife of a Rector and sister of Sir Christopher Wren, the architect of St. Paul's Cathedral, London.

St James' Church, Stretham

In 1850 the population was approximately 1200, with 7,000 acres. It had a Post Office and a railway station, opened in 1866; the Ely to St. Ives GER. line. Closing to passengers in 1931, but continuing on for the local fruit and vegetable trade to send to markets until 1964. In 2001, the population was 1,700, owing to 20th century building.

The Victorian Infant School is now used by the Stretham Play Group, a new school being built in 1978. In the times when all children were educated until the age of fourteen in the village, they went to what was known as The Middle School, by the Red Lion, which is now for industrial use. The children now go by bus to either Witchford or Soham Village College.

The old Methodist Chapel in Chapel Street is now a house, but there is still a Post Office and a village store. The Strict Baptist Chapel, attended by our Jacobs ancestors in Read Street, is now empty and derelict.

All the small farms have gone from the village, all land mostly being farmed by large contractors. If someone were visiting from the 19th century they would not recognise parts of the village by its changes. Many of which have occurred within living memory.

But community and village life is still just as important.

I have to thank the Stretham Parish Council for the accurate information and figures of Stretham, obtained from the book produced for the village in 2000, 'The Stretham Millennium History', produced by The Cambridge Heritage Associates.

A Tribute to Beatrice Stevens BEM

As I sat to write my notes of Paddy's local Stretham grandfathers and uncles of the Jacobs family, I realised most of what I knew I had 'gleaned' from the writings of Beatrice Stevens, our late local historian and schoolteacher.

I had the pleasure of meeting her several times and being entertained in her home. Her memories and affection of our late father Bill Goad was endearing.

She had taught him at the village infant school in the 1920s, in her early days of teaching there – and when speaking of him, always calling him by his childhood name of Billy.

I also had the pleasure of her giving me the gift of two of her books, which she personally wrote in for me.

How she would have been interested in my project today; how I would love to 'pick her brains'. But thankfully I have her memories at least. I do hope she wouldn't feel I was plagiarizing her work; I am just using her reminiscences as the 'icing on the cake' of my basic text – Popping in her 'little gems' to enliven my script.

Hopefully she would give me her blessings, especially as we both share the same name, Beatrice and the same birthday!

I hope she will accept my thanks and tribute to her.

Sketch showing the 15th Century cross

Chapter Eight

The Present Day Goad Jacobs Ancestors

'From Meshach to Mary Jane'

The Story of Shadrach, Meshach and Abednego
from The Old Testament of The Bible

During his rule, King Nebuchadnezzar of Babylon built a gigantic gold statue and insisted that all his subjects worship it, threatening that anyone who disobeyed would be thrown into a fiery furnace.

While most of the populace promptly obeyed, three young men-- Friends of the prophet Daniel-- named Shadrach, Meshach and Abednego refused, because they worshipped only one God.

Nebuchadnezzar was furious and summoning the three men offered them a last chance to bow down before his statue or be hurled into the furnace. "Then what god will be able to rescue you from my hand?" he mocked.

Shadrach, Meshach and Abednego replied to the King, *"O Nebuchadnezzar, we do not need to defend ourselves before you in this matter. If we are thrown into the blazing furnace, the God we serve is able to save us from it, and he will rescue us from your hand, O King. But even if he does not, we want you to know, O King, that we will not serve your gods or worship the image of gold you have set up"*.

Daniel 3:16-18

This only made the King angrier and he ordered the furnace to be made seven times hotter. So fierce were the flames that the soldiers who threw the three men into the fire were burnt immediately. The King expected to see the three burnt to a cinder but to his amazement, not only did he see the three men standing unruffled, he saw a fourth man there too. Awed, he asked the men to come out.

Shadrach, Meshach and Abednego walked out. Their bodies and clothes had not been burnt at all. They didn't even smell of smoke.

Then Nebuchadnezzar said," Praise be the God of Shadrach, Meshach and Abednego, who has sent his angel to rescue his servants! They trusted in him and defied the Kings command and were willing to give up their lives rather than serve or worship any god except their own God. Therefore I decree that the people of any nation of language who say anything against the God of Shadrach, Meshach and Abednego be cut into pieces and their houses be turned into piles of rubble, for no other god can save in this way.

And the King promoted them to higher jobs in the Kingdom.

Daniel 3: 28-29

Shadrach, Meshach and Abednego

Our Jacobs Ancestors

William
1605 - 1657
b. Brinkley

Mary Day
1605 - 1638

John
1623 - 1707
b. Brinkley

Anne Robinson
1610 - 1705

Richard
1665 - 1723
b. Brinkley

Etheldreda Clark
1667 - Unkn.
b. Soham

Joseph
1711 - 1756
b. Brinkley

Anne Pheabody
1719 - 1771

1.Mary Stickwood
1778 - Unkn.

Jonathan
1756 - 1828
b. Cambridge

2.Phebe Bright
1787 - 1862

3.Susannah
Cornwall

Jonathan
Mary
Joseph

Ellen
Isaacc
Shadrach
Abednego
Meshach
1793-1884
b. Cambridge

William
Jane

The family tree of our Jacobs Ancestors

'From Meshach to Mary Jane'

Shadrach, Meshach and Abednego, three brothers from the Old Testament and also three brothers from our Jacobs ancestors.

Meshach is our X3 Great Grandfather who was born in 1795 in the village of Chesterton, now a suburb of the City of Cambridge.

The three brothers in the Bible endured a trial by fire for their faith.

Let's hope Meshach's only trial by fire, was his love for Sarah Sheldrick, a Stretham woman, whose father owned Gravel Farm, whom he married in St. James' Church, Stretham in 1818. So bringing his branch of the Jacobs Family to Stretham to live.

Meshach was a man of the land like his forefathers. He and Sarah settled into a cottage on what used to be called Gravel Road, the old unmade track, now upgraded and known as the Newmarket Road, leading to the village of Wicken. Ferries were used to cross the two rivers, the Little Ouse and The Cam, before the bridges were built. Stretham being part of the old Isle of Ely.

The first census we find Meshach on is 1841. He is forty five and Sarah forty four. With son Thomas aged ten, Mary Sheldrick, aged nine and Rebecca, aged seven. Meshach is declared as a Labourer. By 1851 the family of Meshach were living at Green End, him still an agricultural labourer, as is his son Thomas, now twenty. Just three of them living at home. By 1861 Meshach has reached the age of sixty seven, still labouring on the land, and Thomas is now classed as a 'Pig Jobber.'(dealer).

I researched and found Meshach and Sarah had had seven babies born alive.

James	Jonathan	John	Thomas	Mary	Rebecca	James
1818	1820	Sheldrick	1832	Sheldrick	1834	1837
1819	1838	1824	1905	1833	Unkn.	Unkn.
		1905		1898		

Only two living children being given their mother's maiden name!

Infant mortality was a part of all families' lives at this time, there was very little to combat the diseases and epidemics that came periodically. You needed a strong constitution to survive to adulthood. Four of their babies reached adulthood. Jonathan reached just eighteen. Rebecca married William Harvey and lived in Cambridge, she and her spinster sister Mary Sheldrick helped brother Thomas so much with his family later, when he was left a widower. Loving aunts to all his children.

In 1861 son Thomas, our X2 great grandfather married Sarah Ann Fitch, a woman from nearby Little Downham, and brought her to live at Green End, Stretham.

Babies soon followed. Mary Jane 1863, Jonathan 1864, and Sarah Ann 1866, (in memory of her grandmother) as sadly in 1866 Meshach's wife Sarah died. They had been married for forty eight years. Her gravestone can be seen today in St. James' churchyard, Stretham. On it written:

In Loving Memory
of Sarah
Wife of Meshach Jacobs
Aged 69 years
Also of
Mary Sheldrick Jacobs
Her Daughter who died
August 5th 1898
Aged 66 years

The latter inscription obviously added later by her brother Thomas.

By 1871 Meshach is still classed as a Labourer, living now at Pump Lane, Stretham with his son Thomas, daughter-in-law Sarah and children.

By 1881, at the age of eighty seven, he is on the census as a general labourer, still with Thomas and family. What a long hard working life he has had on the land, ultimately owning his own patch of land in Stretham, acquired by his tenacity and hard work. When Meshach died at the grand old age of 90 years and 11 months, he had laid the foundations and example for the future success of his son Thomas and grandsons Jonathan, Reuben and our 'uncle Tommy Jacobs'.

Meshach's gravestone is in St. James's churchyard, Stretham, still there today. On it written:

In Remembrance of Meshach Jacobs
Who Died December 30th 1884
Aged 90 years 11 months
"Let Me Die The Death Of The Righteous
And Let My End Be Like His"

Jewish origins but he appears a Christian of his time.

I found his probate too:

"Jacobs Meshach. Personal Estate £132.10.

27th January 1885. The Will of Meshach Jacobs, Late of Stretham in the Isle of Ely, in the County of Cambridge. Yeoman, who died 30th December 1884 at Stretham, was proved at Peterborough, by Thomas Jacobs of Stretham, Farmer and Dealer, the son and sole Executor.

How well he had lived his life – the old historic title of Yeoman given him by the County Clerk. Looking up the correct meaning it says:

> *"Man holding and cultivating small landed estate of landed value 40 shillings.*
>
> *To serve on juries, to vote for a knight of the shire.*
>
> *Historically a servant in royal or noble household"*

A trusted and true man able to vote! A hard working man of the soil! A life well lived, Meshach an ancestor to be proud off and respected.

How glad I am to have found him for you all.

His son Thomas, by the time Meshach had died, was farming 20 acres and employing 2 men. Sadly his wife Sarah had died in 1879, leaving Thomas with a young family to raise. She had only been forty one years old. Her health had obviously suffered after giving birth to seven surviving babies in fourteen years.

Another woman of her time! Her headstone can be found in St. James's church yard today. On it is written:

Affectionate Remembrance of Sarah Anne
Wife of Thomas Jacobs
Who died March 3rd 1879 Aged 41 years
"Many Are The Afflictions Of The Righteous
But The Lord Delivereth Them Out Of Them All"
Psalm XXIV. 19

He and Sarah Anne had seven surviving children:

The first child was daughter Mary Jane born 1863 (destined to be the wife of James Stuart Goad and our great grandparents), Jonathan born 1864, Sarah Anne born 1866, Lydia born 1868, Elizabeth born 1871, Reuben born 1873 and finally Thomas, born 1876, known as 'Tommy' Jacobs, the most successful farmer and cattle dealer of them all.

Thomas, by 1891, had acquired more land and was becoming very successful as a cattle dealer. He never remarried, but with the help of his sisters Mary and Rebecca. In their turn each of his family lived with her and went to school in Cambridge, she now widowed and living at 34, Jesus Lane, later in 35, Bridge Street.

Sarah Anne and Elizabeth married, Lydia returned to Stretham to be with their father. In 1882 Mary Jane married our James Stuart Goad.

Son Jonathan became a dealer and farmer in Stretham. Reuben and Tommy were to figure greatly in the life of Stretham at the turn of the 20th century. More of them later.

The last we find of Thomas Jacobs is on the 1901 census. He is now seventy two, a dealer and employer. Lydia is at home looking after him. She is a spinster, aged thirty one. Young Tommy is there, aged twenty three and an employer too. They are now living at 1, Read Street, Stretham, in a large farmhouse called Laburnum House, with yards, barns and land behind, also having a living in servant to help Lydia run the home.

The family are reaping the rewards of their years of hard work.

In 1905 Thomas dies at the age of seventy five. He is buried in Wood Lane Cemetery, Stretham, where his headstone can be seen today.

On it, it says:

In Loving Memory Of Thomas Jacobs
Who Died December 1st 1905 Aged 75 years
"Asleep in Jesus"
Also Of Lydia
Daughter Of The Above Who Died March 3rd 1903
Aged 34 years
"Peace Perfect Peace"

Oh! Lydia gone too!

Thomas and family worshipped at the Strict Baptist Chapel, just next door to their home in Read Street.

In 1906 Thomas's probate was granted:

Jacobs Thomas, the elder, of Stretham, Cambridgeshire, died 1st December 1905. Probate London, 12th March to Godwyn Ladington Archer* Esq, Jonathan Jacobs cattle dealer and Thomas Jacobs farmer. Effects £123-5s-0d"

A good life and success story to hand onto his sons, two of them already established farmers and dealers like him.

*Goad Solicitors today, Archer and Archer, Ely.

John Sheldrick Jacobs

I must now write a few lines about Thomas's elder brother John Sheldrick Jacobs; Meshach and Sarah's third born son of five. At the time of writing this, I have just found him online in another family tree – also, this wonderful photograph of him taken 1898 aged seventy four, which I have printed here.

Is there a likeness of family today? I would like to think so!
Certainly lots of Jacobs genes in the Goads.

John Sheldrick Jacobs

John Sheldrick (his mother's maiden name) was born in 1824 and died in 1905, the same year as his younger brother Thomas. He was living at 2, Chapel Walk, Stretham in his latter years. He was a labourer all his life, just like his father, leaving Stretham for a few years to live in Ousden, Suffolk, near Bury-St-Edmunds, to work as a pipe laying labourer. Before leaving Stretham he had married a village woman Mary Richardson, at St. James's church in 1851. They had four surviving children. Mary must have died, as in 1860 he married Rebecca Money, also a Stretham woman, at St. James's too.

We next see them on the census of 1881 and 1891, by then returned to their home village of Stretham. They have nine surviving children; three born at Bury St Edmunds.

While researching I find the name Jacobs to be very common in the anglicized Jewish community, which makes accurate research lengthy and difficult. Not many sons born in this generation either .Maybe his daughters married into local families! Lots of Jacobs genes in our near neighbours perhaps? All too distant to research, but I do find with research, John Sheldrick also owned his cottage and small piece of land in Stretham, also a Yeoman and hard-working just like his father Meshach.

It is lovely to have Paddy's X2 great grand Uncle John Sheldrick Jacobs' photograph. A family face from the past.

Now we have reached the 20th century.

Life in Stretham was thriving for many small farmers, although it was a hard-working occupation. But many men aspired to working a small plot of land for extra income, to keep a pig and grow food for their family. Doing other work as well, all the small trades were in Stretham, including shops containing everything for hearth and home; cobblers, barbers, dressmakers, butchers and bakers to name a few.

Also a multitude of ale houses to slake your thirst at on the way home from work.

Where were Meshach's three grandsons in these changing times?

Jonathan, Reuben and Tommy

The eldest, Jonathan, born 1864, grew up working the land beside his grandfather Meshach and father Thomas. He was a farming man through and through.

On the census of 1881, at the age of seventeen his profession is already given as farmer, when researching I found this original document:

"Declaration to the England Marriage Bond and Allegations"

The Parish of St. Dunstan's in the West, in the City of London

Jonathan Jacobs just eighteen, declaring he is twenty-one and Mary Elizabeth Hazel, also of age and declaring they had been resident in the Parish for fifteen days.

16th January 1882. Both from the county of Cambridgeshire, I guess they had eloped! It's not often the bridegroom is the younger!

I looked at their marriage in the church register and found their witnesses were an F. Charles and Annie Martin. A previous wedding three days before had also been witnessed by Annie Martin too! I guess they had professional witnesses!

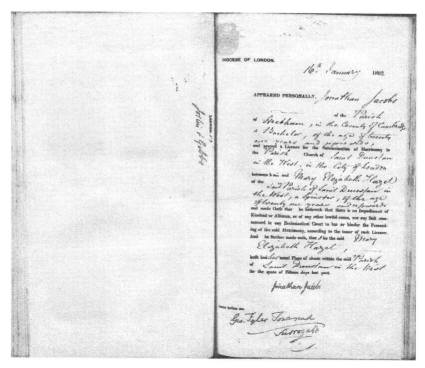

Jonathan Jacobs marriage to Mary Elizabeth Hazel

Mary Elizabeth was twenty four, the daughter of Hannah Hazel, widow, a farmer of 140 acres, employing 5 men and two boys.

Farming at Hazel's Farm, Bedwell Hay Lane, Little Thetford.

The previous ten years had been difficult for the Hazel family.

Hannah's husband Henry died, leaving her to run the farm. She had the added grief of burying four of her children. Just Hannah and her two oldest children now surviving, Mary Elizabeth and son Frederick, aged twenty, so perhaps Hannah had been reluctant to see Mary leave home!

But all seems to have turned out well with Mary and Jonathan, as twenty years later we find them living at 21, Long Lane, Stretham, him aged thirty seven, Mary, forty four. Jonathan was now a very successful farmer and dealer. They have had four daughters, two dying in infancy; Lillie Mary and Annie Eliza surviving to adulthood. I find the Jacobs genes do not seem to produce many sons.

As a Master farmer, Jonathan was of considerable importance in Stretham. On weekdays, when he could be seen dealing cattle in the local markets, he always wore respectable black.

In appearance he was not unlike England's King Edward VII, 'portly and regal 'some would have said.' Sporting the same full beard too!

His Sunday 'black' was a full frock coat, a glossy top hat and a silver-topped ebony cane. He truly looked 'King of Stretham'.

Mary Elizabeth, whom he affectionately called Lizzie, always wore black too. Her Sunday black was a full dress of shiny black satin. Only the lavishness of the trimmings added variations. She was a busy bustling lady, who always accompanied Jonathan every week to Chapel. They attended the strict Baptist Chapel in Reads Street, next door to his father Thomas's home at Laburnum House.

They would often attend the other Chapel in the village as a courtesy, owing to Jonathan's friendship with another successful local farmer Charlie Wright.

When attending chapel it would be like royalty arriving. His seat was prepared with cushions and carpet on the floor and hassocks, not for kneeling, but to put his feet upon. Whether it be strict Baptist or Methodist Chapel, there was a pew in each of them, which no-one else dared to venture in.

Ultimately they lived in Cambridge House on the Wilburton Road, Stretham, where Jonathan could lean on his gate and watch his younger brother Tommy's cattle pass by, to and from Cambridge market, to his holding yards at Oakley House, Top Street.

Jonathan died aged fifty three, 9th April 1917.

Jonathan's probate:

"Jacobs Jonathan of Cambridge House, Wilburton Road, Stretham, Cambridgeshire. Cattle dealer, died 9th April 1917. Administration Peterborough, 7th May to Mary Elizabeth Jacobs, widow. Effects £201."

Mary Elizabeth died in 1924 aged sixty seven, still living in Stretham with her daughter Lillie Mary.

Jonathan was a very successful Jacobs grandson of Meshach, third generation of farming Jacobs in Stretham. His larger than life presence and personality would surely have been missed by the village folk.

His Jacobs mantel will be taken up by his younger brother Reuben, born 1873.

Sent as a teenager to be a butcher's apprentice, he lived in Bridge Street, Cambridge with Aunt Rebecca Harvey, his father's sister – and butchery being a complimentary skill to the pig and cattle farming industry.

In 1897 Reuben returned to Stretham to live. He had courted and married Alice Langford, nee Wright, landlady of The Chequers public house. She was a widow with two children; Percy, twelve and Laura, six. Alice was thirty five to Reuben's twenty four.

The Chequers was situated in the centre of the village on Front Street by St. James's church, opposite the Red Lion Inn, the old cross and the Post Office.

Reuben set up a butcher's shop behind the Inn, and kept pigs in the yard too.

In the daytime he was a busy smallholder and butcher and in the evenings he was serving the beer as "mine host".

Another generation with the Jacobs work ethos.

In 1898 Alice and Reuben had a daughter Victoria and a year later a son Archie was born. They kept house at The Chequers for twenty five years, Archie joining his father in the butchery trade. He only left Stretham when his father died in 1930.

He set up in trade in Willesdon, London, where he married an Edith Cutts, in 1931.

His last butcher's shop was at 143, Long Lane, East Finchley, London, until his death in 1961. I couldn't find out if Archie had any children, especially sons, as at the moment there is no trace of any next generation Jacobs boys, as Jonathan and Tommy only had daughters.

It is interesting Archie left Stretham after his father died, he obviously needed new beginnings in his life and also in 1930 the country was in the middle of a great economic depression, a time when men made to their Capital City for employment.

After thirty years of being at the hub of village life, Reuben died in the Evelyn Nursing Home, Cambridge on 24th January 1930, aged fifty six.

1930 Probate:

"Jacobs, Reuben of Glenfield, Stretham. Died 24th January 1930, at the Evelyn Nursing Home, Cambridge. Administration Peterborough, 10th February to Alice Susan Sarah Jacobs, widow. Effects £119-1-2d".

Alice was a widow again at sixty seven. They had retired from the busy life of trade to live in the village at Glenfield (the whereabouts of this house is unknown to-day). Reuben was a successful butcher and publican for over thirty years. Alice lived on into her eighties and ended her life living with son Archie in London.

The last of the three sons of Thomas Jacobs, and youngest grandson of Meshach, is another Thomas (always known as Tommy), as I will also call him. He was financially the most successful of all.

He was quick of speech, quick of wit and quick in his actions and medium of build and full of energy. A well respected dealer in the world of farming and cattle at all local markets, when as a young man, he rode everywhere on horseback.

He dressed as all wealthy farmers of his time, in a good tweed jacket and waistcoat, with a watch chain across his chest. Breeches, brown boots and leggings of the finest leather, polished to a resplendent shine. To complete the picture was a silver topped cane, which he twirled as he talked, striking it on his leggings to emphasize a point he was making.

His young life was spent with his father Thomas and grandfather Meshach. His mother died when he was only three years old, so he could hardly remember her.

His Aunt Mary Sheldrick and Aunt Rebecca Jacobs-Harvey in Cambridge cared for him and he had lots of older brothers and sisters for company.

He was always called Tommy to distinguish him from his father. By the time he was twenty three he was a dealer and employer. His father Thomas was now seventy two, so Tommy was mostly running the farm at Laburnum House, Reads Street. Sister Lydia died in 1903 and two years later his father followed in1905.

In1904 Tommy courted and married Rachael Crisp, a woman he had met while visiting sister Mary Jane and James Stuart at their farm in Swavesey. Rachael being born in Swavesey. He was twenty eight and she twenty six. They were married in St. Andrew's Church Swavesey, Cambridgeshire and started married life at Laburnum House Farm; their baby daughter Constance Ethel arrived soon after in 1904.

The third generation of Jacobs brothers were now big employers in the village, helping raise prosperity for all. Daughter Irene May was born in 1906. Both his daughters loved to visit Swavesey cousins at Ryders Farm, all becoming great friends. Of course we see no male issue again, this fact eventually influencing the outcome of all the lives of the present day Goad family.

Then in 1912 came the terrible fire at Laburnum House Farm, which destroyed Tommy's holding yards and barns. He had been visiting the Saturday Cambridge cattle market and, on returning home, he was devastated at the sight he saw. Burnt barns and yards full of tethered stock, a horrific scene that was to be talked about and remembered for a long time in the village.

Soon afterwards, Tommy bought the big seven room Oakley House Farm, on the corner of Top Street. It was time for a new beginning after the horror of the fire.

Oakley House had large bay windows at the front, giving him a good view of his brother Reuben's Inn, The Chequers in Front Street, and he could watch his cattle in the street when being driven home from the Cambridge market.

His big yards, behind his house, had overnight holding bays big enough for all local cattle travelling to and from the big central market in Cambridge. Using his smaller barns and yards for his farm, once a year the yard and big barn was scrubbed and decorated with greenery and used for the Chapel Anniversary tea and dancing celebrations.

As Tommy got older he bought himself a Ford car to travel about in; a sign of his growing prosperity and of the changing times.

The local barber, George Spicer, became his chauffeur.

Paddy's dad, Bill, told him the story of Uncle Tommy needing to go on an urgent journey. George had removed the plugs from the engine to dry out.

"Can't go yet", said George, explaining about the plugs.

"Never mind the plugs," said Tommy, "Put them in when we get back!"

Tommy's knowledge of cattle and horses was better than of cars!

Tommy, having no sons, and now owning a considerable amount of land and farms locally, spoke to his nephew Tom Goad, his sister Mary Jane's eldest son, and gave him the opportunity to come to Stretham and manage them for him.

Tom had been a tenant farmer at Boxworth End, Swavesey for twenty years, and was married to Ida Clark, they had three children with another on the way.

It seemed a good move to make, to go and manage Uncle Tommy's 400 acres.

So a new life began at Chear Farm, Chittering – the next village to Stretham on the Cambridge Road.

It was 1922. A big wrench to leave Swavesey where he had been born and had always lived, but farming was changing. Life was different after the Great War of 1914-18.

His father James Stuart was close to retiring too, so he decided to give up Ryders Farm, the place they had all loved so well. He and Mary Jane came firstly to Orchard Farm, Chittering with son George, who was starting a poultry farm. Then, when George married, went to live in Grove House, on the corner of Green End and Newmarket Road, Stretham (previously the home of the owner of the Grove Foundry Works, the Wesley family).

This was the end of an era at Swavesey for them all, but Mary Jane was back in the village of her birth. And the history of the lives of the present Goad family in Stretham began.

Tommy loved the buzz of Cambridge market on Saturdays. He met old friends and planned good deals, enjoying the talk and laughter of it all.

On February 15th 1936, at the Red Lion Hotel, Petty Cury, Cambridge he collapsed and died of a heart attack, aged sixty. His death certificate says it all:

"Cause of Death: *1a Cardiac Failure*
                               b Myocardial Degeneration
                               c Cirrhosis of Liver
                               d Optic Atrophy
Informant and in Attendance: C.M. Routledge, Niece of Stretham".

Constance May, sister Mary Jane's daughter was there with him at his end! He was buried at Wood Lane Cemetery, Stretham. His headstone is there today, inscribed thus:

IN LOVING MEMORY OF THOMAS JACOBS
WHO DIED FEB 5th 1936
ALSO HIS WIFE RACHAEL ELIZABETH
WHO DIED OCTOBER 30th 1961
AGED 74 YEARS

Tommy's 1936 Probate:

"Jacobs, Thomas of Stretham, Isle of Ely. Died 15th February 1936, at the Lion Hotel, Petty Cury, Cambridge.
Probate London, 16th March to Rachael Elizabeth Jacobs, widow.
Effects £9,157-17-2d. Re sworn £10,221-6-9d.

His elder daughter Constance Ethel had emigrated to Malaya in the 1930s. Marrying in Singapore, the reception was held at the famous Raffles Hotel. Her husband, Eric Dimock, elder son of Mr and Mrs John Dimock of Plantation Farm, Stretham, had gone to manage a tea plantation for the company Ampar Tenang.

In 1942 and before the Japanese invaded, she managed to escape with her two daughters, Joan and Jill, returning to England via Australia. Eric was captured and sent to Changi camp and worked on the notorious Railway of Death. He survived but returned home to England in 1945, far from well. They ended their working life farming in Cambridgeshire, Constance dying in1966 and Eric 1991.

Daughter Irene May married Norman Westren and lived in Cambridge.

Tommy's wife, Rachael, went to live in Cambridge and died in 1961.

In Rachael's Probate, her effects left to Irene were: £ 22,707-11-1d.

Tommy Jacobs was another true family success story, not just because of his wealth, but a tribute to his tenacity and hard work.

A life lived to the full right to the end .The last Jacobs in Stretham.

But Thomas Goad and his descendants will carry the Jacobs genes on – Thomas, the first farming Goad in Stretham and the great grandson of Meshach Jacobs, the first farming Jacobs in Stretham.

Miniature painting of Napoleon III

Picture showing uniform worn at the time of the Indian mutiny

Uncle Edward Hepher's sign

'Autumn Leaves'

 II

'She bathes the world'

'Dawn over Stretham Fen'

REMEMBER
THEIR LIVES ARE
IN YOUR HANDS

CREW OF A BRITISH DESTROYER GOING ON WELL EARNED LEAVE

SAFELY HOME

because
nobody talked!

World War II propaganda poster

Certificate awarded to Bill after crossing the equator in January 1946

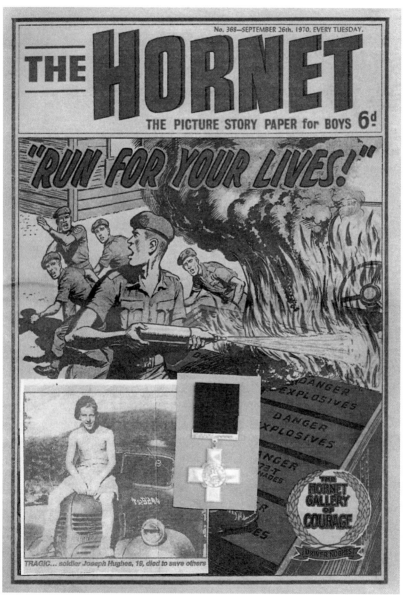

Joe's story on the front cover of The Hornet (reproduced with
the kind permission of RCDC Thomson & Co. Ltd. 2014)

Bill's medals

Painting of Hill Farm House

Paddy's Oak tree

Chapter Nine

Thomas Goad 1886 – 1961

'Stretham's First Farming Goad'

James Stuart Goad
1859 - 1928
b. Middlesex, London

m.
1882

**Mary Jane
Jacobs-Goad**
1863 - 1928

**Thomas
Goad**
1886
1961

m.
1914

**Ida Clark
Goad**
1887
1971

Thomas Goad family tree

A. Hendrey   *Godmanchester
St. Ives and Ramsey*

Thomas, Stretham's first farming Goad

Ida Goad, 1914

Thomas Goad, 1886 - 1961

'Fen Farmer' and 'Life on Hill Farm'

I am conscious, as I write of Paddy's grandfather Tom Goad, that many reading this will have their own childhood memories of him and stories handed down to them by their own parents. They are Tom and Ida's children; Jack, Jim, Bill and Mollie.

Hopefully these memories will be enhanced by their own perspective, when reading the words I write today. I, as a writer, see only by listening and by research through the 'Tunnel of Time.'

Thomas was the first son of four; the third child of James Stuart Goad and Mary Jane Jacobs-Goad of The Dairy Farm, Swavesey, Cambridgeshire. He was born in 1886 and named after his grandfather and uncle on his Jacobs family side, both Stretham farmers. How auspicious for his future, as to where and how Thomas would eventually choose to live his life.

Tom grew up happily in his big family of nine children, loving to be out on the farm with his father, especially around the stock dairy herd or playing in the fields with his three younger brothers; James William, Stuart and George York, all the games every generation of boys dream up.

One day when playing Tom felt very ill; he kept losing his balance and falling over when he walked. It had been a hot summer and the polio virus was diagnosed.

This meant many weeks in the local isolation hospital, having careful nursing and treating his wasting leg muscles with hydro-therapy and massage in the hope of containing the virus damage to his nervous system.

The illness we now know as the virus poliomyelitis had been known for thousands of years, with isolated cases all over the world. However, with the knowledge and education of hygiene in the late 19th century, the natural resistance to this virus, which had been inbuilt into mankind for generations declined.

In the 1880s the first major epidemics began to occur in Europe, usually affecting children between 6 months and four years.

We are not sure how old Tom was, but we know he was left with weakened muscles on the one side of his body, hip and leg, giving him a permanent limp – A victim of the world's first polio epidemic.

Luckily, Tom was a strong boy and as he grew up, his natural strength compensated for his disability. He was determined to be a farmer like his father, and after finishing his education at the Swavesey National school, he began helping his father full time.

We see this on the 1901 census. Tom is fourteen and is working on the Dairy Farm.

By 1911, aged twenty four, he has taken the tenancy of his own farmland at Boxworth End, Swavesey, but still living at home with his mother and father. The census tells us he is already an employer. He is a young man with a determination of life and the will to succeed.

By 1912 his younger brothers have all left home. James William has gone with his village friend Wilfrid Hepher (sister Maud's brother-in-law), to Chalfont-St-Peter, Buckinghamshire, to work as a carpenter.

Stuart, after training as a butcher in the nearby village of Sutton, has emigrated to America to seek his fortune.

George York is an apprentice baker and confectioner at the village bakery, in the High Street, Swavesey.

Sister Maud has married Walter Hepher and has a daughter, Marjorie, born in 1907, and living in Brentford, London.

Sister Nance has gone to London too, to train as a nurse at the renowned Royal London Hospital.

Constance was a draper's assistant in a store in Brentford, and lodging with her sister Maud and Walter.

Only Mabel, training as a milliner and Lilian, still at school, were at home with him and their parents.

By 1914 Tom has courted and married a woman from Histon Road, Cambridge, called Ida Clark, and they set up home in a cottage at Boxworth End, Swavesey, near to the land where Tom farmed.

Soon their son John Stuart was born, always to be known as Jack. We have a wonderful photograph of Jack, under two years old, sitting on his Grandfather James Stuart's shoulder at Ryders Farm.

Now the Great War had begun, Tom saw two of his younger brothers enlist in the Army. James William joined the Army Service Corp as a driver. George York joined the 9th Suffolk's. Tom had been registered unfit for Army service, but had been left on the Army reserve lists for the future.

But of course farming was a very important occupation, providing food for an island nation being blockaded by German U boats around its shores.

In 1916 a baby brother for Jack was born, they called him James Owen. When young he was always known as Owen, but in later life to be called Jim. In 1918 a daughter Betty arrived.

In 1918 Tom, still on the wartime reserve lists, was called to go before the National Service Medical Board in Cambridge on June 26th for a new assessment, as Britain was conscripting all able bodied men for a last big push to defeat Germany.

He was declared to be: *'Permanently and totally unfit for any form of Military Service and discharged from any liability to be called for future service"*

He was thirty one years old, 5ft 71/2" tall, weighed 140lbs, and even to the detail of him having a mole under his right eye was noted. But there was no reference to his past illness of Polio. To fail this strict medical, meant he was very disabled and shows what tenacity of life Tom had, to be able to successfully follow his chosen occupation he loved.

Meanwhile, in the village of Stretham, Uncle Tommy, Mary Jane's youngest brother was dealing in cattle and farming. Buying up local land and growing ever prosperous. He decided he needed a farm manager for his land on Stretham Fen in the next village of Chittering. He approached his young nephew Tom and asked if he would like to take it on.

M.N.S. Form R 2079.

(WARNING.—If you lose this Certificate a duplicate cannot be issued.)

CERTIFICATE TO BE ISSUED TO A MAN IN THE ARMY RESERVE WHO HAS BEEN FOUND BY A NATIONAL SERVICE
MEDICAL BOARD TO BE PERMANENTLY AND TOTALLY UNFIT FOR MILITARY SERVICE.

Region No. *198699*

Full Christian Name and Surname *GOAD Thomas*

of *Swavesey, Cambs.*

(Registered Address as on Registration Card.)

A member of the Army Reserve was on the *21st* day of *June*, 19*18*,
found by the National Service Medical Board at *Cambridge*
to be permanently and totally unfit for any form of Military Service and it is hereby
certified that he is discharged from liability to be called up for Military Service.

Dated this *26th* day of *June* 19*18*

(Signed) *Russell*

Assistant Director of Recruiting.
For Minister of National Service.

Stamp of Area Recruiting Office.

*Description of the above-named man on the *21st* day of *June 1918*

Age *31 8/12*

Height *5 ft 7½ in*   Weight *140*

Marks or Scars ....

Signature of above-named man *T. Goad*

* Should agree with particulars on the Medical History Sheet A.F.B. 178.

(1787) Wt.11702/427. 2500 Bks.—900 21-12-17. J.R.&C.

N.B.—Any person finding this Certificate is requested to forward it in an unstamped envelope to the Secretary (R.1.), Ministry of National Service, London, S.W.

National Service Medical Form

It seemed like a good move for the little family as they were fast outgrowing the cottage at Boxworth End and farming life was changing after the four years of war. Tom would be overseeing 400 acres and dealing with all that entailed.

It was a big step forward, and so, excitingly, they made a new beginning at Chear Farm, Chittering. It was the dawn of the Goad family at Stretham.

It was now 1922.

The previous few years had been difficult; WWI had brought many changes, including the sad death of his younger brother James William, to be buried in a graveyard in Italy so far away. This loss had affected them all, being such a close family.

So life began anew for all at Stretham and Chittering.

Brother George was now raising poultry at Orchard Farm, Chittering with his retired parents, James Stuart and Mary Jane and daughters Con and Lilian. Then later they took the tenancy of Grove House, on the corner of Green End Lane, Stretham, when George married Maude in 1924.

Tom, Ida, Jack, eight, Jim, six, Betty, four and baby William, always as a child called Billy, were brought to live at Chear Farm, Chittering. Two years later the family was complete when daughter Mollie was born.

Jack, Jim and Betty were now all pupils at Stretham Infant School in the High Street.

Tom and Ida were now at a busy time of life; lots of hard work, but a real feeling of achievement for them too.

Sadly in 1928 James Stuart, Tom's father suddenly died, and three weeks later mother Mary Jane followed after a fatal operation in hospital.

All the Swavesey children gathered in Stretham at Wood Lane Cemetery: Maud with husband Walter and daughter Marjorie, now twenty one, living in London; Nance, who had returned from her work as a nanny in Malta, to care for them; Constance, who was now courting Russ Routledge, the Stretham baker in Cage Lane; Mabel now living in Waterbeach, near Cambridge, with her husband Horace Ashby; Lilian, married to her Wimblington farmer, Arthur Peacock (Bert), now with a three year old daughter Daphne; and George York, home from the Army, raising poultry at Orchard Farm, Chittering, with his wife Maude and baby daughter Mary Elizabeth.

On the farm next door to George, Tom, Ida and family, all busy on Chear Farm.

Only Stuart is missing, far away in America and James William lying in a grave in Italy.

It was a sad day for them all as they stood together by the abundantly flowered grave. All with so many happy memories of Swavesey, their childhood and latterly Ryders Farm, where they had gathered to picnic and party in their halcyon young days before 1914, until the clouds of war and separation came to change their lives. The end of an era for them all.

Tom and Ida's family were growing up fast. It was now the 1930s, the time of the Wall Street crash and the Worldwide Depression, with massive unemployment and poverty.

Tom worked hard, times were uncertain, but he was a good farmer. He had always had an ambition to have his own farm again. Jack was now over twenty years old and working by his father's side. Jim was training as a baker under the wing of his uncle Russ Routledge, now married to his Aunt Con. Living with them at Cage Lane, as bakers kept early hours.

Betty had gone to London to train as a nurse in the footsteps of her Aunt Nance.

Bill spent a lot of his teenage years helping his uncle George with his chickens at Orchard Farm; he and his cousin Mary being great childhood friends.

Mollie was now a scholar at Stretham School, being taught by the late Beatrice Stevens, a 'born and bred' village girl, and later to be local historian, B.E.M. and author.

In 1936 uncle Tommy Jacobs died. Changes were happening, bringing uncertainty over the farms. After Probate they were sold to Mr. B. Chambers and Tom continued to manage them for him; still living at Chear Farm.

But Tom had been looking and saving for a farm of his own. He was interested in Hill Farm, situated by the old Windmill, Stretham. The tenant, Mr. Driver was ready to retire, so with much advice from his farmer friends and three good references, sent to the Ely Cathedral Church Commissioners, who owned the land, he applied to become the next tenant.

After fulfilling all the criteria they demanded of him, they granted Tom the tenancy, for him to begin farming, there at Michaelmas, 11th October 1937.

Since the Middle Ages, 'Michaelmas' was the traditional day to pay rents and bills, and the day recognised as the last day of Harvest.

The feast of St. Michael is celebrated on September 29th, but with the reform from the Julian to the Gregorian calendar of 1752, there was loss of 11 days in the calendar year. Michaelmas tithes and rents were moved on 11 days.

Tom Goad's tenancy rents were from October 11th as the Ely Cathedral Commissioners were using the date of 'Old Michaelmas Day'.

Excitedly, Tom and Ida duly moved into Hill Farm House. Their son Jack, twenty four, and thirteen year old Mollie moved with them. But son Bill, fifteen, had other ideas than being a farmer. A lively, clever boy, he was fired with the imagination of seeing the world.

He had listened to the tales of an old village sailor, and that November he left the home of his Uncle George where he was living, to be a boy sailor on HMS Ganges, a training ship at Shotley, in Suffolk. His story will be told in the next chapter.

Hill Farm had 100 acres, one rood or goad*, 18 perch. The farm's yearly rent was £150, a considerable sum to find in 1937. Rents were paid bi-annually, April and October (Lady Day and Michaelmas).

*See 'What's In A Name Chapter'.

Paddy on horseback with Uncle Jack

Tom, Ida and family at Hill Farm
Back row: Sally, Bill, Bess, Betty, Jim, Joan /Kate, Jack, Mollie, Doug
Middle row: Richard, Tom, Gillian, Ida, Paddy.
Front row: Christopher, Robert.

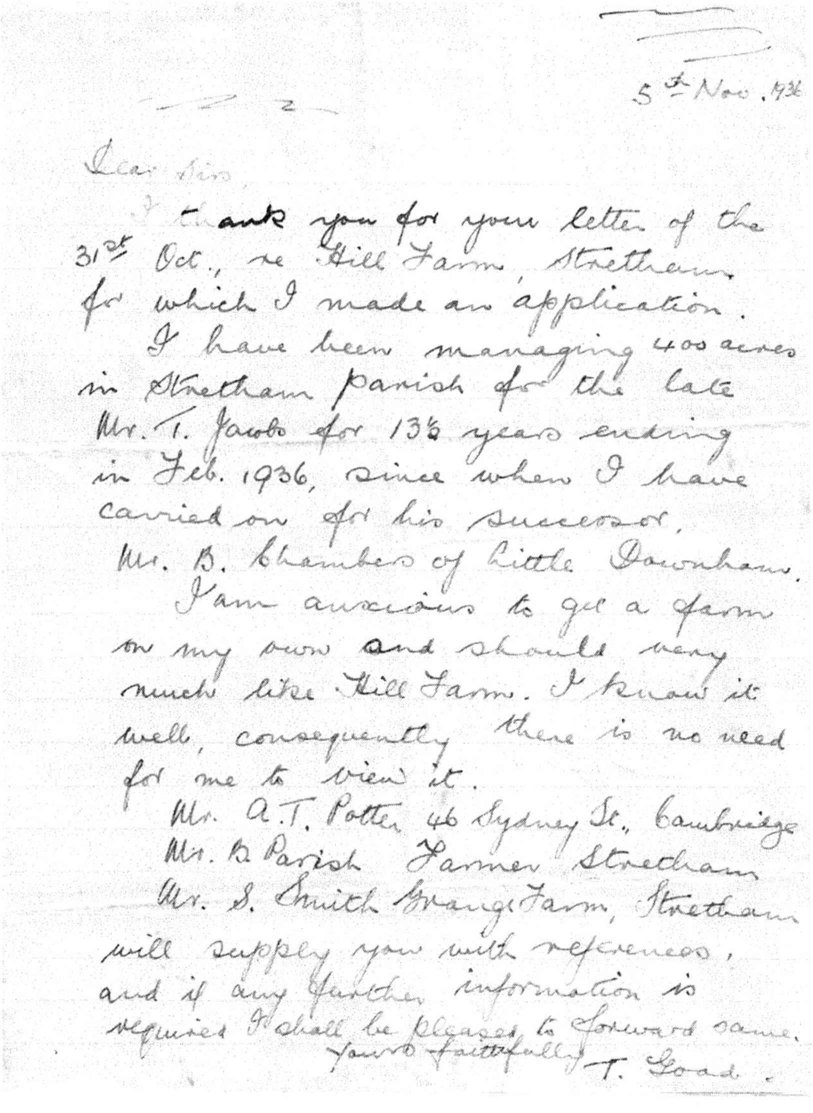

5ᵗʰ Nov. 1936

Dear Sir,

I thank you for your letter of the 31ˢᵗ Oct., re Hill Farm, Stretham, for which I made an application.

I have been managing 400 acres in Stretham parish for the late Mr. T. Jacob for 13½ years ending in Feb. 1936, since when I have carried on for his successor, Mr. B. Chambers of Little Downham.

I am anxious to get a farm on my own and should very much like Hill Farm. I know it well, consequently there is no need for me to view it.

Mr. A. T. Potter 46 Sydney St., Cambridge
Mr. B Parish Farmer Stretham
Mr. S. Smith Grange Farm, Stretham

will supply you with references, and if any further information is required I shall be pleased to forward same.

Yours faithfully,
T. Goad.

Tom's letter to the Cathedral Commissioners, 1936

Hill Farm now became the hub of the family of Tom and Ida Goad. Tom now felt the pride of his own land, even though it was tenanted, but it was such an achievement for them both.

But all too soon there came another war to contend with in their lives. In September 1939, Adolf Hitler declared war on Poland by invading their boarders with the German Army. This politically involved the whole of Europe, and eventually the whole of the civilised world. History repeating itself in Tom and Ida's lifetime.

Son Jack, aged twenty five, wasn't eligible to fight, as farming was declared a reserved occupation. But he became a part of the all-important Home Guard of Local Defence, endearingly known as Dad's Army today.

Stretham Home Guard. Jack is seated 4th from the right

Again, as an island nation, food production was all important. The import shipping from America, Australia and New Zealand was being targeted in the Atlantic Ocean, causing acute rationing in Britain. Farming production to feed the nation was paramount. The slogan 'Dig for Britain' was for everyone to do, on every spare patch of land. So Tom and Jack set to, to 'do their bit'.

Hill Farm flourished; it was mixed arable, pigs, cattle and chickens, working horses and orchards of fruits. Tom had a large vegetable garden and a house cow to make them self-sufficient. Ida made butter and cream cheese in the dairy. Just as Tom's ancestors, his great grandmother Sarah Marshall and great Aunt Phoebe Tibbitt and mother, Mary Jane had done a century before; family life skills for more than four generations. Son Jim went to war to do 'his bit' too. He was conscripted to join the Royal Army Catering Corp, having trained as a Master baker with his Uncle Russ Routledge.

At Stretham Tennis Club, he had previously met Bess King, from Lakenheath, Suffolk. They married in September 1939, setting up home in Brooke Lane, Stretham, and son Robert was born in 1941, Tom and Ida's first Grandson. Jim's Army wartime took him to the Middle East theatre of war, with a long spell in Egypt, then on to Jhansi in India. They do say 'an army marches on its stomach'. Jim saw to it they were all well fed and fighting fit.

In 1946 he was discharged and safely home to his family, and to the birth of his second son Richard.

In the 1930s Betty Goad had been in London training and working as a nurse. When war was declared she came back to live at Hill Farm in Stretham and joined the Ely Division of The Red Cross. Her nursing skills were needed in these uncertain times. She also served voluntarily at the Royal Air Force Hospital in Ely.

Ely hospital had opened in 1940, to care for the wounded airmen returning from bombing raids over Europe. They were stationed at the airfield in Witchford, the next village.

The sound of their Lancaster Bombers taking off and flying overhead filled the Stretham night sky during the Battle of Britain years.

The village of Stretham 'adopted' a ward at the hospital. Taking parcels to cheer their lives, and writing letters for men with injuries and burns, and reading to the sick.

It was a very emotional time for all, visiting the young men, some disfigured and wounded – sometimes seeing them only once, not knowing if they were discharged or had died.

'Goodies' were collected from villagers to make Christmas stockings for all.

When the war years were over Betty, like her Aunt Nance before her, became a Nanny.

Betty Goad and the Stretham nurses

Ultimately she joined the household of Major William Spowers, retired Household Cavalry. He was now a book and ancient manuscript expert at Christies Auction House in London. Born in Australia and educated at the famous Geelong Grammar School, which was also attended by our own Charles, Prince of Wales, for a time.

Betty Goad took care of William and Antonia Spowers' three sons: Hugo; Adam; and Rory, born between 1960 and 1967. Paddy remembers Aunt Betty bringing Hugo to stay at Hill Farm House when a baby and watching him being bathed in a bowl on the kitchen table. William Spowers bought Betty her own car, the revolutionary new 1960s little 'Mini', with the number plate WS 52, which she proudly drove.

One day he came to Stretham to visit. He drove and parked his large pale blue Rolls Royce in front of Mollie and Doug Marchant's home in Berry Close. A car of its like never before or since seen on that small village council estate.

He was proudly entertained to a delicious tea by the family.

In the late 1960s, Paddy was driving his great uncle George York back to his home in Chobham, Surrey, after he had been visiting his nephew Bill Goad at Millway, Stretham. They called to have tea on the way home with George's niece Betty Goad at the home of the Spowers family at Wintlesham, Surrey. During the afternoon William Spowers invited Paddy to join him in a swim in the family pool; he even lent Paddy a pair of trunks to wear! As wealthy as he was, he acted as a true gentleman to all. When William Spowers retired he created The Wintlesham Arboretum. It is today regarded as a masterpiece in the grand tradition of landscape, the best in Britain. It is situated between the villages of Lightwater and Wintlesham, Surrey and consists of 65 hectares. It is now administered as 'The Spowers Charitable Trust' for the advanced education in the study of trees and birds. Betty Goad lived and worked for the family, very much loved, until her death in 1985.

In 1939 Bill Goad met Sally Hughes whilst his ship was docked at Greenock, near Glasgow, Scotland for refuelling. This was an intense and dangerous time for him, sailing in a destroyer on Arctic Convoys. A few hours of shore leave was so welcome after the rigours of wartime sea battles.

In July 1943, mother Ida went with Bill and Sally to Buckingham Palace* to see King George VI pin the Albert Medal on her son's chest, a tribute to her son's bravery at sea and a proud day for Ida, Tom and the family. * See Bill Goad's Story.

One month earlier in June, at St. James's Church, Stretham, Bill and Sally were married, a happy wartime interlude for all the family and a chance to have one of their family 'gatherings'.

In April 1944, son Christopher Thomas was born, another welcome grandson for Tom and Ida. Bill's war is written in the next chapter.

Mollie Goad enlisted in the ATS on the 21st July 1941. She told her son David that she had walked the four miles to Ely to enlist, so as to avoid the arduous task of the strawberry picking season which everyone was expected to partake in.

Private Mollie Goad was stationed at the Central Ordinance Depot, Weedon, Buckinghamshire. Being only seventeen when she volunteered (her father must have forgiven her defiance) she was employed doing clerical duties concerned with the issue of small arms, rifles and machine guns, including the Bren and Lewis guns. She was proudly chosen to be part of The Guard of Honour, when HRH Princess Elizabeth, The Princess Royal, (now our present Queen Elizabeth II) visited Weedon on November 5th 1943.

Mollie spent her war in Buckinghamshire, a world so different from Hill Farm. Five years later she was safely discharged on January 3rd 1946, her life's experiences now having made her an independent woman.

It is 1944. Tom and Ida have two grandsons, Robert and Christopher. Their family is scattered by war, a difficult time emotionally for all. Whenever they could everyone gravitated to Hill Farm; there was always a welcome for them – and their friends – from Tom and Ida. Her wonderful fry-ups of farm produce in the old kitchen and family gatherings, helped to ease the worries of the times.

How everyone celebrated on the 8th May 1945, when Hitler was defeated. It had been a long and difficult six years of war, especially as everyone believed at the beginning that it would be over by the first Christmas.

Life was still hard, rationing still continued, Tom and Jack were still busy, employing men to help in everyday work. Tom was now almost sixty. Jim and Bill were still fighting in the Far East and Korea.

Betty, on one of her visits home, brought her nursing friend Mary Fisher to stay, who then became a regular visitor to the farm. On one occasion Mary bought her sister Joan with her, from their home in Wolverhampton, West Midlands.

Jack was smitten! He had found the girl for him, duly married her and set up home just across the road from Hill Farm at Berry Green.

Jim came back from 'his war' to continue working with his Uncle Russ; Aunt Con had sadly died in 1945. Jim and Bess's second son, Richard, was born in 1946.

Bill and Sally's second son Patrick John (Paddy) came along in 1947.

Jack and Joan's first daughter Gillian was born in 1948.

In 1949, Mollie married Douglas Marchant whom she met during wartime; Doug had been serving in the Royal Navy. It was a big family party, held at the farm, after a ceremony at St, James's Church in Stretham. Nephews Robert and Christopher were pageboys. Mollie and Doug then also made their home in one of the houses at Berry Close.

Private Mollie Goad

Tom and Ida on Mollie's wedding day in 1949

Tom with Mollie on her wedding day in 1949

The years of work showing in Tom's hands, his stooping walk, the result of his body being weakened by childhood Polio

Tom, Ida and the wider family
Back row:Douglas, Christopher, Jack, Bill, Jim, Robert, Richard
Centre row: Gillian, Joan, Mollie, Tom, Ida Betty, Bess, Sally.
Front row: Cathryn, John, David, Timothy, Martin, Paddy.

In 1953 Tom and Ida became the proud owners of Hill Farm, Stretham, son Jack and now Bill by his side.

Jack, Jim, Bill, Mollie, their spouses and families were all living either at Berry Green or Berry Close for the next few years.

New babies were born to Jack and Joan; Cathryn in1950 and John in 1952.

Also Mollie and Doug had David, 1953 and Timothy, 1956.

Bill and Sally's third son Martin was born in 1955.

Wartime austerity was easing off. They were all one big happy family together.

Tom and Ida were happily surrounded by their adult children and grandchildren. At seventy Tom was still working out on the farm every day with his sons, Jack and Bill.

There were gatherings in the old kitchen for Ida's fried breakfasts, afternoon teas and cake after the day's work. Grandchildren called in after school, before going home, doing chores on the farm on Saturday mornings for their 2/- (10p) pocket monies from Granddad. Jobs like cleaning the mangold wurzels ready to go in the chopping machine to make cattle and pig food; straightening bent nails with a hammer and many more. Gillian and Kate kept busy washing the numerous chicken eggs.

They enjoyed the long harvest holidays, when Fisher cousins from Wolverhampton came to stay. Nieces Ina and Anne Free, niece Jean Clark and families, Carter cousins, Betty's friends, Madge, Eric and family all visited. There were so many happy days of laughter, family and friends – All gathering in the old kitchen for meals and Paddy accidentally swallowing the Christmas pudding silver sixpence one year!

They used to meet in each other's homes for a party. Sally's piano being carried to wherever it was for a big family sing-song.

One year Bill and Sally took Chris, Paddy and Martin to Yarmouth for a caravan holiday. Jim, Bess and family brought Tom and Ida to visit for a day out. Grandfather Tom just sat and enjoyed the sea air, not getting out of the car or even taking off his coat. Quite out of his comfort zone!

We have a lovely photograph taken in the old orchard around 1958; all the family together in their Sunday best, Tom and Ida proudly sitting in the centre with all their progeny around them. It's a picture to cherish.

Berry Green, Stretham, 1960s

Paddy remembers his Grandfather reciting a poem to him.

"On yonder hill- There stands a mill.

If it's not gone- It stands there ..

He would hesitate for Paddy to say *"still!"*

Tom would always add the word *"yet"*. It became a laughing game between them.

Kate (Cathryn), Jack's youngest daughter, also had a similar poem with him.

She recalls he teased her with:

Kate, Kate as sure as Fate,
You'll have to marry me.
Or else I'll have a notion
Of diving in the Ocean
And splashing all the Mermaids
At the bottom of the sea!

(Adapted from the chorus of a Victorian Music Hall song by Harry Dacre d.1922)

Tom obviously had many old rhymes and much practice in the past, having been the elder of six siblings, the youngest three being girls and two older sisters.

Today's era of grandchildren will all have their own special memories of grandfather Tom, a fun gentle man, who was never heard to speak a swear word.

Many mention the hot spoon placed gently on the back of your hand, with a twinkle in his eye, when at the tea table.

Also of Tom's farm dog called Ceasar, loved by all, and named after the dog he had as a boy on Dairy Farm, Swavesey.

By being married to Paddy, his grandson, I have his special memory of when, in 1956, he was admitted to Brookland's Isolation Hospital, Cambridge with suspected Polio, after having shown all its symptoms. After then being diagnosed with encephalitis and having a difficult operation on his spine, a few weeks later when he was well enough to go home, he was taken first to see his grandparents at Hill Farm. His grandfather Tom was sent for off the farm; he came into the kitchen and immediately kissed Paddy. The smell of working granddad and tobacco impressed the moment forever in his memory, his only remembered time of being kissed by him.

Tom was obviously remembering his own experiences of Polio as a child and thinking of the ultimate consequences for Paddy at nine years old. Paddy never forgot this act of love from his grandfather Tom.

Tom's health was failing. He began to use crutches to help him get around the farm. Before, when he was more mobile, he rode an old bicycle to inspect his crops. Later he was pushed around in a wheelchair by his grandsons to view the farm, his hip and leg finally letting him down. The years of hard physical work had taken their toll.

Paddy remembers when about ten years old, Tom asking him to drive the tractor and take him out on the farm to look at the fields and crops. Feeling so grown up and pleased to be asked, as he knew how to start and drive the tractor. But when far out on the farm it stopped, unfortunately Paddy had never mastered the technique of how to restart it. But he was saved by Jim Russell luckily working in the next field.

Grandfather Tom also not being mechanical and having never driven a tractor had no idea either what to do!

Memories of his uncle Tommy Jacobs and his car plugs! All 'men of their time'.

Latterly when Tom was completely incapacitated and having to lie indoors he enjoyed listening on the radio to the 15 minute daily fictional serial of the farming family at Brookfield Farm, Ambridge. Titled 'The Archers', subtitled, 'an everyday story of country folk'. A popular serial still broadcast.

Also a line was rigged up out of the kitchen window passing through a hole in the frame, attached to tin cans outside. This was so Tom could tug the line to keep the birds off the chicken's feed corn situated outside in the orchard by his window. He had to feel useful to the end!

It was October 13th 1961 and things were never to be the same. Tom died at Hill Farm. His heart just gave out. He was 18 days short of his 75th birthday. A week later, after a short Baptist service at Hill Farm, he was laid to rest with his parents, James Stuart and Mary Jane Goad and all his Jacobs family in Wood Lane cemetery.

A very much missed granddad, husband and father.

A new era was to begin on Hill Farm.

Ida lived on until 1971, continuing to live in her home at Hill Farm.

Jack and Bill were now farming together.

Ida was cared for by all, never to be alone for long. Breakfasts and teas were still in the old kitchen.

Ida had led a sheltered life. For her, her home came first with Tom and family. She never went out and worked on the farm, but made cream and butter in the dairy.

She was a good cook and dressmaker, and always changed her dress for afternoon tea. She proudly said she had never had her hair cut; when she brushed it out, it came to her waist. She then wore it twisted into a bun at the nape of her neck.

For many years Mrs Doll Fletcher helped her in the house and did the washing for her.

She loved to entertain her sisters, Edith, Hilda and Mabel to tea on their visits to her, arriving on the bus from Histon Road, Cambridge, where they all lived. All identical in appearance to his grandmother Ida in Paddy's memory!

Grandchildren called in to see her every day after school, and took it in turns to sleep in her home each night for company, she was never alone. A truly loved Nana.

Tom and Ida shared forty seven years of love, family and farming. He had been brought up in the Bethel Baptist tradition – as all his siblings were. Tom never drank alcohol or swore and on his few outings he loved to go to market. He became a respected local farmer, always working hard and bravely overcoming his childhood physical adversity.

A loved father and grandfather to be proud of.

We look back and praise his and Ida's achievements.

Another Goad Love Story.

Tom and Ida with Mollie, Bill, Betty, Jack and Jim

Mollie, Bill, Betty, Jack and Jim in 1980s

"Dawn Over Stretham Fen"

Painting "Dawn over Stretham Fen"

I created this painting after first visiting Ely, and seeing Ely Cathedral dominating the skyline. This is here for Thomas and Ida Goad who brought their family from Swavesey to settle and farm here in Chittering/Stretham in 1923.

Life is all about new beginnings, full of hopes and promises, and a tribute to their success in ultimately buying Hill Farm, Stretham.

I chose the following poem for Thomas. The sentiment speaks for itself.

> God gave all men all earth to love,
> But since our hearts are small.
> Ordained for each
> One spot should prove
> Beloved over all.

> Rudyard Kipling

In Loving Memory

of my dear husband

Thomas Goad

Who passed peacefully away, 20th October, 1961

Aged 74 years

Service private at Hill Farm, Stretham
on Tuesday, 24th October, at 12 noon
followed by interment in Stretham Cemetery.

Hill Farm,
Stretham, Cambs.

In loving memory

Painting of Hill Farm

Chapter Ten

William (Bill) Goad A.M. G.C. 1922 – 1994

The Ganges Boy who 'Joined the Navy to see the World'

Thomas Goad
1886
1961

m.
1914

Ida Clark-Goad
1887
1971

William (Bill) Goad
1922 - 1994

m.
1943

Sarah (Sally) Hughes Goad
1922 - 1988

William (Bill) Goad family tree

Bill In Whites; Worn when in the Far East. The uniform changed from blue to white when at Gibraltar

William (Bill) Goad A.M. G.C. 1922—1994

'The Ganges Boy who 'Joined the Navy to see the World'

May 10th, 1922: William was Tom and Ida's last child to be born at Boxworth End, Swavesey. He was called William after Tom's younger brother who had died in WWI in 1918. Billy as a child but always known as Bill to the later generations.

Before he was a year old he was brought with his brothers, Jack and Jim, and sister Betty, to the farmhouse at Chittering to live. His father Tom was now manager of Chear Farm, Stretham Fen, overseeing 400 acres for his uncle Tommy Jacobs.

In 1924, two years later his sister Mollie was born to complete the little family of Tom and Ida.

Bill grew up on the farm on Stretham Fen. He was a strong and healthy boy, clever and full of life. He spent many happy hours in the summer months swimming and fishing on the banks of the River Cam and Little Ouse (known locally as 'the old west'), that flowed their way through the farmland.

He went to school at Stretham Village School. In the infant class he was taught by Beatrice Acred (later Stevens) who was later to be awarded the BEM for services to the village of Stretham, as school teacher, governor, local historian and author.

She still called him Billy, when speaking of him to Paddy and I.

His eldest brother Jack, when he finished schooling, went to work on the farm with his father Tom; Jim trained as a baker at the Routledge Bakery in Cage Lane, Stretham.

Betty always had the dream to be a nurse like her Aunt Nance, father Tom's elder sister, and eventually went to a London hospital to train.

Bill (as we knew him) liked to spend his time with his Uncle George, a poultry farmer at nearby Orchard Farm, Chittering. Helping him with his chickens, ultimately as a teenager moving in to live with him, Aunt Maude and cousin Mary Elizabeth.

In 1936 his great uncle Tommy Jacobs died. So his father Tom had decided to look for his own land to farm.

In 1937, at Michaelmas, the decision was made to begin a new life as tenant farmer at Hill Farm, Stretham, situated by the old windmill on the Ely Road.

Bill had grown tall and strong, and now aged fifteen he was helping Uncle George full time. He enjoyed working with chickens, but he felt his future life was not in farming. He had a great curiosity of life and the world. He had listened to an old sailor in the village telling tales of life at sea. These tales cast a spell on a youthful imagination, telling of the romantic life of a sailor and seeing the world for free. For centuries boys with a thirst for adventure had 'run away to sea'.

So, in the long tradition, Bill too decided to go and 'see the world' for himself.

He volunteered to be a boy sailor. In 1937 he joined the training ship, HMS Ganges, at Shotley in Suffolk, the next county to Cambridgeshire.

Naval training had been based on board ship since 1866, but by 1906 a shore base had been built at Shotley on the bank side of the River Stour, opposite the port of Harwich, Essex – A traditional shipbuilding area for more than 200 years.

HMS Ganges' aim was ''*to turn out disciplined and self-sufficient young men possessing confidence, courage, endurance and a sense of Service, professionally trained to take their place in the fleet''*.

The Royal Navy Training Establishment was to equip the 20th century sailors with the skills for the new breed of ships and warfare of the future. The old days of sail have truly gone.

In the early days, the old style sailing ship trained sailors accused the 'Ganges Boys' of being trained in a 'Stone Frigate'. But its tough training still stood a boy in good stead for life at sea, where the 'Ganges Boys' were soon to be held in great respect.

One of its objects was physical fitness and a lot of hours were spent in the gymnasium, so that a boy was healthy, robust and competent to care for himself when at sea. Their biggest problem was teaching boys to swim, an essential skill for a sailor.

Bill, after his boyhood years of diving and swimming in the river pools by the Royal Oak (now the Lazy Otter) at Stretham, soon obtained his proficiency and lifesaving certificates.

It was a hard tough life; early rising, cold showers and acute discipline. As with any boys living in close proximity grudges arose. They were made to fight it out in the boxing ring. "Best to be settled in public"!

Speaking of this time, Bill remembers the cold showers to be endured and of always feeling hungry. A favourite supper of his was cooked dried peas and a large wedge of cheddar (obviously very plain food), and of competing for and eating the discarded cheese rind off others' plates. Food was eaten in silence. Occasionally one plate of food was removed by an instructor before they entered the mess, so they had to jostle and fight to stand behind a plate, the weakest often had to go hungry as a punishment. It was called 'character building'.

Bill's natural strength and abilities carried him through, adapting to this strict regime. He had joined as a 'Boy Second Class'. His weekly pocket money was 1/- (5p) rising to 1/6d (71/2p) when he became 1st Class.

The first seven months he spent in preliminary seamanship classes, school work and physical training, including all sports and athletics.

In this one year training Bill was able to take two weeks leave at Christmas, two at Easter and three weeks in the summer. Otherwise he was confined to barracks. A few outings to the village of Shotley were sometimes allowed to spend pocket monies. The most difficult thing was that smoking was banned, which lots of boys found hard to cope with, as then we were a nation of cigarette smokers.

It was at this time Bill got his naval nickname as 'Lofty', having now grown into a young man of over six foot. A name to stay with him throughout his service.

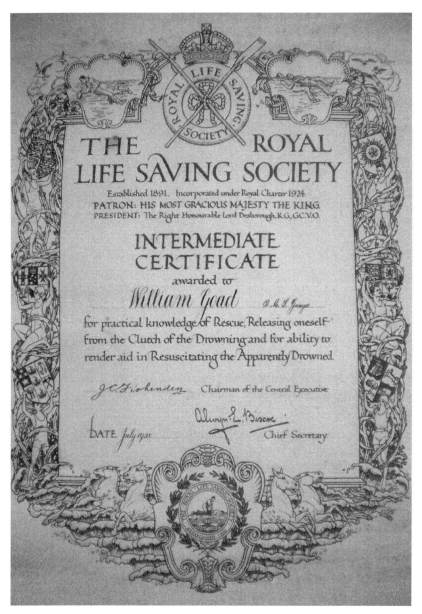

Lifesaving Swimming Certificate

After Bill's seven months were up he passed to 'rating' First Class. He then went onto a five week course on mechanical training, followed by gunnery instruction. After completing all this successfully, Bill was sent to sea in HMS Pembroke to implement the practical use of all he had learnt in the classroom.

He then returned to HMS Ganges to be 'kitted out'. He was then ready for sea.

His first ship was HMS Dragon, where it was recorded that he had injured his left hand when *"a ship's hatch slammed down trapping his middle finger"*, needing him to see the ship's surgeon. Not a good beginning!

While training with the Grand Fleet in the summer of 1939, Bill now on HMS Mashona, escorted to Liverpool the Liner 'Empress of Australia', with King George VI and Queen Elizabeth on board.

In September 1939, Germany, led by Adolf Hitler, declared war on Poland, which ultimately included Great Britain. As a young and inexperienced sailor, Bill was to be in the thick of it all, to see and experience so many terrible events of history.

Sailing on HMS Mashona, a destroyer of the Tribal Class, Bill was to be part of the guarding convoys in the Atlantic Ocean and Arctic Ocean.

Merchant ships bringing food and supplies to Europe from America, Australia and New Zealand were being sunk by the skilful German U-boat commanders.

The most effective way of dealing with this German threat was the convoy system which had been devised and previously worked well in the same situation of WWI.

The organisation of groups of merchant ships under escort of small warships, with defensive tactics, and the invention of devices for detecting submarines underwater, helped turn the tide against the U-boats; tactics thankfully which resulted in eventually winning the battle of the Atlantic in 1943.

Bills first taste of war came on 25th/26th September 1939, when HMS Mashona went to the assistance of HMS Spearfish, a submarine, which had been severely damaged by German action off the coast of Ireland. They rescued the crew and safely escorted her back to England without incident.

He is now at his base at Scapa Flow, the historic natural harbour in the Orkney Islands, ready for the long trips out on the Atlantic and Arctic convoys.

Sailing down either the west coast of Scotland to Greenock, the only large dock on the Clyde, or Rosyth in the east, on the Firth of Forth, where they docked for refuelling (Naval term, oiling) or repairs.

One day, while out on shore leave in Glasgow, he met 'the love of his life', Sarah (Sally) Hughes, a Scottish girl from Pollockshaw Road, Glasgow. Part of the famous 'Gorbels' district. Her father was a Railway Inspector. Sally was the eldest of four, she being only seventeen, like Bill. Her brothers, James, Joseph and Francis, were still not old enough to enlist.

Sally was very musical and had a lovely singing voice. Every leave from then on, when he was docked in Greenock or Rosyth, Bill spent in Glasgow with her and her family, welcomed by her parents in their home like a son.

Sally

On May 10th 1940 Bill had become eighteen. He is now classed as Ordinary Seaman and was a ship's gunner, searching the Arctic seas around Scapa Flow and Norway, guarding merchantmen and hunting for U-boats.

Bill, as a young naval rating, was featured on a Government propaganda poster, titled, *"Crew of a British Destroyer going home on a well-earned leave".*

The message is: *"Remember Their Lives Are In Your Hands, Safely Home Because Nobody Talked"!*

You see Bill first off his ship, after action at sea. All the crew are going home on leave.

In wartime spies were thought to be everywhere and you had to be conscious of careless talk. The most famous posters were *"Careless Talk Costs Lives"* and *"Dig For Britain"* urging the importance of growing food for all. Today we see *"Keep Calm and Carry On"* printed on numerous artefacts as nostalgia.

In 1940 Bill kept a small diary of his days at sea, although it had to be written and kept carefully in case he was captured as a prisoner of war and his writings gave away any information to the enemy. I have deciphered and transcribed it, and it is separately printed later as an appendix. It gives his perspective of one year of being a young naval rating on a destroyer in the Arctic convoys. His first ship was F59, HMS Mashona of the Tribal class. They were built to match those of Germany.

Young Gunner William Goad

Wartime propaganda poster

She was built in Scotland and commissioned in 1938.

There was the idea that each ship of the class would sail to the country where the tribes lived. In the event, only HMS Ashanti (Bill's next ship) was to fulfil this.

She visited the Gold Coast (Ghana) in 1939. Here she was feted by the local Ashanti tribe, whose witchdoctors cast lucky spells over her and gave her gifts of a silver bell and a gold shield, but importantly also 'the Juju' doll, which they mounted on the pompom gun deck, which by tradition was always to be respected by the crew.

On the reverse of the photograph we have of it, Bill has written *"Old Hairy Legs"*! Obviously an endearment!

Bill's story of events on Ashanti is told later; such a 'lucky' ship for him.

With his diary he is truly 'Putting us in the picture' of life in the early days of WWII and all its dangers.

Ashanti JuJu

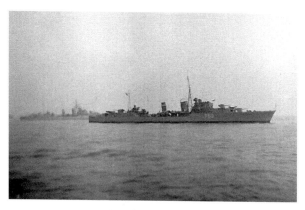

HMS Mashona

On the 24th May 1941 HMS Mashona was part of the operations in the sinking of the German Battleship Bismark. On the 27th she was cruising off the north eastern coast of Ireland, and having been out for four days she was getting low on oil, when they were attacked by a wave of Luftwaffe aircraft. Mashona was struck on the Port side penetrating No 1 Boiler Room, which exploded and blew a big hole in the side of the ship.

She listed to Port, the guns were then hand trained to Starboard, to fire at any target overhead. (Bill was a gunner). Any unnecessary gear was thrown overboard to no avail; she was listing further with each roll. Orders were given to abandon ship. Luckily there was an hour's lull in the bombing and HMS Tarter was able to pick up survivors and take them to Greenock. Forty six men were lost in action.

Now on her side HMS Mashona was scuttled with torpedoes by HMS Sherwood and HMS St. Clair and sunk to a watery grave, east of the Irish Aran Islands.

It was stated in The Ely Standard, June 6th 1941, *"News has been received that Billy* Goad is in hospital, wounded following the sinking of HMS Mashona, after taking part in the hunt for the German Warship Bismark".*

*His old schoolteacher Beatrice Stevens was the local Ely Standard correspondent, hence the "Billy".

Bill had been wounded in the chest when she sank. After three months in hospital and resting at home, by September 1941 he is back at sea on his new ship. All the surviving company of the Mashona have been transferred to HMS Ashanti, which had just had a refit. The experienced Mashona crew gave the Ashanti a flying start as they were such a unified crew with full knowledge of how a Tribal worked and they stayed together as a successful team until late 1943.

In the summer of 1942 Ashanti was sent as the part of Convoy Pedestal to relieve the Mediterranean island of Malta; its people were starving and living in caves underground. Germany and Italy were trying to blockade and bomb this British base to surrender. It was of such a strategic importance to the North African Campaign for all. For the people's endurance and bravery at this time the whole Island was awarded the George Cross.

The battles and losses on this campaign made it a very difficult time for Bill.

It is now 20th September 1942. Bill is back on Arctic convoys, twenty one years old and still a gunner on HMS Ashanti. Three years of cold, icy rough seas, hunting German U-boats and Warships, and being attacked by German Bombers.

He is now 'Leading Seaman' and given the Royal Navy nickname of a 'Killick'* because of the anchor on his badge (*Killick: 16th century name for a ship's anchor, a heavy stone in a wire cage).

Now experienced in all aspects of his job on board ship, this is the time he was tested; a moment showing what his years of training had been leading to.

Firstly, I will generally put you in the picture!

HMS Ashanti was providing cover for convoy QP-14; a German submarine was detected. Depth charging did not produce any results and contact was lost. Ashanti, running low on fuel, interchanged positions with HMS Somali on the inner screen and awaited a favourable opportunity to refuel. Somali took up Ashanti's position and was immediately hit amidships by a torpedo from the German sub', U703. The damage was very extensive. Only the upper deck was holding the ship together. Most of the crew were transferred to other ships except for 80 who remained aboard for damage control. It was decided by the Captain, Colin Maud, to try and salvage her so the Somali was taken in tow by Ashanti. After towing the crippled ship for 420 miles in flat and calm seas, the weather conditions began to change. Becoming what is known as katabatic conditions, that being, very cold air sweeping down off Iceland meeting the warmer temperature of the sea causing the reaction of violent and unpredictable winds and snowstorms, dreaded by all.

In these terrible Arctic conditions Somali's remaining plates buckled and she folded in half and sank on the 24th September. Forty men were lost but amazingly HMS Middleton managed to save over thirty men from the raging seas.

Now I quote eye witness accounts and citations so you see a clear picture of events.

Eye witness Peter Belchamber RN sets the scene:

On the 20th September, HMS Somali was torpedoed by U703. This came soon after being "straffed" by German aircraft which had caused the damage, though confined above the water-line. She, together with HMS Ashanti, warships and destroyers, was escorting Convoy QP 14 back from Murmansk to Scapa Flow. The torpedo hit the Engine Room and all on watch were killed. Rum was quickly handed out in the event of the crew ending up in the North Sea. Life rafts were lowered over the side without anyone remembering to secure them to the ship and they floated away.

Around 80 personnel were left on board to try and get the ship to Iceland, the rest of the crew having been taken aboard the sister ships.

The Captain, Lt: Commander Colin Maud, disagreed with the Chief Engineer and decided to try and save the ship.

Before long the diesel generator failed and Ashanti came to their aid and fixed a tow line. All went well for about 400 miles, until the fourth night when a Force 10 gale and blizzard caused the tow line to break and HMS Somali broke in two.

First the stern sank and the bow end rose steeply and the order was given, "abandon ship". Those who jumped off the Starboard did so to their death. The rest went down the guard rails Port side. There was only one life raft left, but as the air temperature was lower than that of the water, the only crew to survive were those who ironically did not manage to get onto the raft from the water.

Meanwhile on the Ashanti Lt. Lewin and Leading Seaman William Goad climbed down a scrambling net, Goad grabbing hold of Captain Maud, who, tradition has it, was holding a bottle of Whisky."

The next eye witness account is from a Times newspaper interview with Lt. Lewin in 1989.

The Late Lord Lewin, Former First Sea Lord, Chief of the Defence Staff, Falklands War. Life Peer, Knight of the Garter and Chairman of the Trustees of the National Maritime Museum.

He speaks of an experience at sea in the Arctic that still remains in sharp focus.

"We were with a Convoy 800 miles north of Jan Mayan Island when our sister ship Somali was torpedoed by a U-boat. We took off all but 70 of her people and took to tow for three days and four nights. It was my job to get a power line shackled to three or four hundred yards of towing cable so that her pumps could be started.

This worked but on the last night it blew a Force 10 gale and a blizzard. There was a blue flash and we knew the tow and power lines had parted, so we switched on our search lights and saw that the ship had broken in two and was sinking. A tremendous sea was running and we tried to save as many as possible.

Leading Seaman Goad and I went down our side on a scrambling net to reach survivors in the water. He went out on a line and brought in their Captain. I grabbed their First Lt: but the ship was rolling, he was very heavy and covered in oil and I lost him."

The horror of that night stayed with him; the loss of comrades' lives and the combat they fought with the raging seas as well as the enemy.

Bill wrote about this event to his mother Ida Goad, of his thoughts and feelings in a letter of 24th February 1943. It was written in reply to her letter to him, telling him of his Albert Medal Award. The contents are printed later as an appendix to his story.

The Citation of 4th February 1943

Issue Admiralty Fleet Orders

"The King has been graciously pleased to give orders for the following appointment:

For Great Bravery in Saving Life at Sea,
'The Albert Medal'
Acting Leading Seaman William Goad.
CJX 156149

"Leading Seaman Goad went over his ship's side, on a line, in water well below freezing point, and rescued an unconscious man. It was blowing a full gale and there was a very great risk that he would either be washed away by the breaking seas, or swept under the bilge keel of his ship which was rolling heavily."

Bill was very modest about this honour and always maintained he was just doing his job just like many others.

The Albert Medal was created in 1866 for 'Saving Life at Sea'. It is an extremely rare medal and was not lightly bestowed. It is rarer than the Victoria Cross. It is bronze, with a royal blue enamel background and a blue and white ribbon. The reverse is inscribed with the name of the recipient and the description of the deed – unique to this decoration.

The criterion for the award of this medal is:

"Daring and heroic actions performed by mariners and others in danger of perishing, by reason of wrecks and other perils of the sea."

Captain Colin Maud, whose life Bill saved, presented Bill with a clock engraved on the base with the words:

"Thanks Chum" Colin Maud 24-9-42.

The clock still sits on our hall table today, but after seventy years it now doesn't tick!

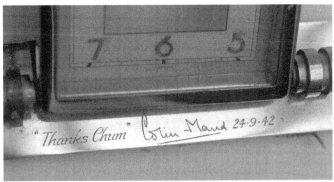

Clock and inscription "Thanks Chum"

Colin Maud, sporting a fine black beard, full of fun and a charismatic officer, went on to be a Commander RN. His exploits in the Normandy invasion of 1944, as Beach Master, were featured in a film made in 1950, called, 'The Longest Day'.

The famous British actor of the time, Kenneth Moore played the role of Maud.

Colin Maud, while on duty, always carried a distinctive stick*. He even lent the actor Kenneth Moore his original stick to carry when filming.

A story which could not have been told if Bill Goad had not rescued him from the Arctic Seas in 1942.

Serendipity!

How our lives are shaped by the people who touch them!

*See chapter 'What's In A Name?'

On the 19th of June 1943, Bill and Sally were married at Stretham in St. James' Church, The White Ensign being flown at the entrance of the church.

Her family all came down from Glasgow. His shipmate and friend, Leading Seaman Dan Maloney, AKA 'Ginge' was his 'best man', who wrote and read the following poem at their reception on Hill Farm.

St James' Church, Stretham

Bill and Sally's Wedding

Left to Right: Tom and Ida Goad (Bill's parents), Den Mallony (a Naval friend), Mollie Goad (Sister), Sarah and John Hughes (Sally's parents)

Bill's crossed the mighty ocean and braved the rolling seas

And I know to-day he will not mind a little bit of tease,

In the King's Royal Navy he's loved by all his mates,

And to-day he takes to himself the mate of all mates

****

We love to sing his praises, to tell of what he's done,

The rescue of his Captain and his fight against the Hun,

To his friends he's known as "Lofty" and he justifies that name

Not alone in stature but in his countries fame.

****

He's not in the ship's nest to-day but on England's strand,

And we welcome Bill and Sally with all our hearts and hands.

They're launching out on life's road with Stretham's every blessing,

And I'll not detain you longer for time is really pressing.

****

Now medals may come your way Bill,

But the greatest treasure on earth

Is a wife that suits your comfort

And a new "Lofty" to give birth.

I found this safely saved in Sally's special box of cards and photographs.

As Bill only had a few days' leave, they honeymooned at his Aunt Mabel and Uncle Horace's home in Waterbeach. They always remember being awoken on their first morning as husband and wife by Aunt Mabel playing on her piano, 'Jesu, Joy Of Man's Desiring' – forever after, Sally and Bill's favourite tune. A tribute to Mabel and Horace's continuing sense of theatrical fun.

But Bill was soon back on board ship and back at sea.

Buckingham Palace, July 1943, Albert Medal Presentation Day, with other Ashanti Crew, Mother Ida Goad, far right, Sally 4th right and Bill behind.

In July 1943, with thirteen other members of the crew of HMS Ashanti, Bill proudly took his mother Ida and Sally to Buckingham Palace for King George VI to pin the Albert Medal on his chest. After the investiture there was a group photograph taken by the Queen Victoria Memorial statue outside the front of the Palace.

A day for them to remember always.

The Ashanti, Bill's lucky boat, was one of 4 of the Tribal Class of the 28 commissioned, to survive wartime conflict. The old witchdoctor's spell was stronger than the hazards of the sea and the aggression of the enemy.

The three others were the Eskimo, Nubian and Tarter.

But The Ashanti was now due for another refit, so in early 1944, Bill was transferred to HMS Nith, now having been promoted to Petty Officer.

Petty Officer William (Bill) Goad

Then it was June 6th, the time of the Normandy Invasion; HMS Nith was sent to be the D-Day Headquarters of the British Landings, firstly landing 231 Infantry Brigade on 'Jig' Green Beach. They then commenced duties in routine control of convoys to the assault force zones, acting as a radio ship co-ordinating the action. In order to be readily recognised while performing her duties, her stack and bridgeworks were painted bright red for the occasion.

Bill once said to me, "The action was chaotic and he felt like he was in a position of 'come and get me'." On June 24th she was attacked by German JU 88 modified to be a 'Mistel', an experimental weapon. Simply a plane filled with a shape charge and guided by a mother aircraft. There were 10 casualties and 26 wounded and they were then safely towed to the Isle of Wight for interim repairs, then on to a dry dock on the Clyde in Scotland for modification.

Thankfully Bill, even in the thick of battle, survived all that came his way.

Also in April that year, their son Christopher Thomas was born (The 1st of 3 'Loftys').

It is now 1945. There were celebrations at the defeat of Hitler, when on the 8th May the German surrender was signed.

But it wasn't over for Bill. He was then sent to Arakan, India via Gibraltar and the Suez Canal, to take part in operation Dracula (the retaking of Rangoon).

Once completed, HMS Nith was chosen to be the Headquarters of The Senior Officer in Charge, and to participate in operation Bibber to retake Thailand. But Japan surrendered in August 1945, after America exploded the first nuclear bombs at Hiroshima and Nagasaki. In March 1946 Bill and HMS Nith departed India for home and came back to become part of the Reserve Fleet at Harwich, England.

Sadly Sally had news in 1946 that her youngest brother Joseph had been killed. He had only been in the Royal Army Service Corps for less than two years.

He was serving in Hong Kong, helping the post war clean-up of surplus ammunition, moving it to a safer place. He was posthumously awarded the George Cross for his bravery on the occasion of his death.

The Citation reads as follows:

"He attempted single handed to extinguish a fire which had broken out in the back of a three ton munitions truck he was driving. Hughes's brave efforts and his shouted warnings, to everyone else in the vicinity, to get clear of the blazing vehicle undoubtedly prevented severe loss of life when the explosives blew up, fatally wounding him."

He was just nineteen at the time, how proud Sally was of him; a husband and a brother being awarded the highest honours for bravery.

In 1970, 'The Hornet', the picture paper comic for boys, featured Joe and his war time bravery on the front page, a photograph of this is included.

In 2006 Paddy and I, with his daughter Helen, attended an unveiling of a commemorative plaque in Glasgow. Joseph was being honoured by his family's local community. In St. Joseph Church, in the City of Glasgow, now a community centre, there is a glass case containing his citation, photograph and a facsimile of his George Cross. His original is held at the HQ of his Regiment at Aldershot.

Paddy, Helen and Lesley at Joe Hughes' memorial

Front Cover of Hornet Comic Telling Joe's Story

The Hornet RCDC Thomson & Co. Ltd. 2014. Used by kind permission.

Bill was then to be involved in the Korean theatre of war, away from his growing family again, fighting in a conflict still not resolved today.

But not before their second son, Patrick John (Paddy) was born on November 5th 1947. When first seeing Paddy when he was 'newly born', a big baby with black hair, lying with clenched fists in the air, Bill declared he looked just like an 'Irish boxer' and that they would call him Paddy. Sally compromised and agreed to call him Patrick, but to this day he is called Paddy. He was taken to Bill's ship HMS Tyne, moored at Harwich, to be christened in the ships bell, fulfilling an old naval tradition.

Sally settled and made a home at Mill House, Ely Road, Stretham, for their two boys.

By 1953 and having sixteen years of knowing nothing else except the discipline of Navy life, Bill decided to turn his back on 'life at sea', and come home to Stretham and be a farmer. He had been away from his Sally and boys far too long.

He is quoted as saying he was "tired of being shot at." Most of his naval career was spent in different theatres of war. He had achieved the rank of Chief Petty Officer, he had never been disciplined, in his conduct record he is noted as being 'superior'.

He was the epitome of a true sailor and 'Ganges' had done their job well.

Paddy recalls the day Bill came home for good, he was six years old and had only seen his father intermittently since he had been born. He was playing in the street, a taxi stopped and a man called out to him. He saw his elder brother Chris shouting and running down the street. Paddy suddenly realised it was his Dad whom he knew was due to be coming home. He jumped in the taxi, sat on his father's lap and Bill put his Navy cap on his head which Paddy proudly wore all day. He had his father home, they were a complete family at last.

Bill joined his father Tom on Hill Farm, working alongside his older brother Jack, learning a new trade and settling into a new life's routines. Not always easy for a person who had roamed the world for years.

All the brothers and families lived either in Berry Green or Berry Close, opposite the farm. Also sister Mollie, husband Doug and family too.

The happy years of the 1950s passed by. In 1955, Sally and Bill had their third son, Martin. For Bill, this time he had the novelty of being a true, hands on father.

Bill was settling in on Hill Farm, he was enjoying growing vegetables and flowers in his large garden at Berry Green, a contented family man at last.

In 1956 Bill received a letter from Admiralty House, Chatham, to say that they were building new homes for sailors at the shore base. The roads were being named after men in Nore Command, who had been decorated with honours.

So Goad Avenue is there today.

Goad Avenue, named after William Goad

In 1964 he and Sally had 'Millway' bungalow built, on the corner of Mill Drove, opposite the old windmill. A new era had begun as proud home owners, Bill making the garden beautiful with an obsession for roses filling it with glorious colours and scents.

In 1971 Bill was offered by the Government the opportunity to exchange his Albert Medal for its equivalent, the George Cross.

No more Albert Medals were to be awarded; the grading of medals was being reassessed.

After great thought, Bill declined. He decided that, "The King had placed his medal on his chest and that was good enough for him." He kept his Albert Medal, even though he could legally put GC after his name.

He became a member of the VC/GC Association. He and Sally and two guests (other family members), attended and enjoyed various 'dos' in 'high places' in London with the 'great' and the 'good'. It was bi-annually and Bill enjoyed meeting contemporary wartime compatriots and looked forward to visits to Buckingham Palace for 'tea' with the Queen. All this done with proud Sally by his side.

After his father Tom's death in 1961, Bill continued farming with his brother Jack. As well as the pigs, chickens and arable, they added a successful beef unit. These were happy years for the brothers bringing up their families on Hill Farm, creating a good farming partnership for twenty five years.

Sadly in 1988 Sally caught Meningitis, after years of learning to live with Parkinson's. It was serious. Six months earlier, Bill and his brother Jack had sold Hill Farm to Jim's sons Robert and Richard.

Retired, Bill and Sally were hoping they would enjoy more of the foreign holidays they had begun to take. After five months in a coma, Bill by her side every day, Sally sadly died. She was only 65.

She was his true sweetheart, he said later he so missed her 'Wisdom of Life'.

Everything he did, he did for her.

To combat his grief and loneliness Bill decided to become a Voluntary Hospital driver. A new career, he enjoyed the routine and meeting new people, and made lots of new friends. He had a new kitchen installed and learnt to cook, and grew flowers in his garden for charity. He visited all his extended family, becoming its networking link and keeping busy, with his little terrier Ella for company, named after his favourite singer Ella Fitzgerald.

HOME OFFICE
Kingsgate House 66 Victoria Street London SW1E 6SS

Telephone 01-828 4366 ext 1521

W Goad Esq GC
"Millway"
Ely Road
Stretham Ely
Cambs

Your reference

Our reference
HON/64 101/4/59
Date
2 December 1971

Dear Mr Goad

ANNOUNCEMENT MADE BY THE PRIME MINISTER ON 21 OCTOBER 1971

'The Albert and Edward Medals were instituted in 1866 and 1907, respectively, as awards for outstanding gallantry in saving or endeavouring to save life. Since 1949, however, no Albert or Edward Medals have been awarded – except posthumously – and the general public are no longer as conscious as they were of their significance and status.

It has been represented that the effect of this is to deprive surviving holders of those medals of the recognition which is their undoubted due. I am glad to be able to announce, with the approval of Her Majesty The Queen, that all surviving holders of the Albert and Edward Medals will be required forthwith to exchange their awards for the George Cross. My right hon. Friend the Home Secretary will now issue advice to those concerned. Pending completion of the exchange they will be entitled as from today to add the initials G.C. – instead of A.M. or E.M. – after their names.'

You may already be aware of the Prime Minister's announcement on 21 October 1971 that holders of the Albert Medal are required to exchange their award for the George Cross. A copy of the announcement is enclosed for your information.

As you will see, you are now entitled to add the initials G.C. after your name instead of A.M.

You will from now on be regarded for all official purposes as being a holder of the George Cross. This includes the award of the gratuity as a holder of the George Cross instead of the Albert Medal, and you will therefore find in due course that your monthly payments (which will be for the same amount) will be paid by another Department instead of the Home Office.

The transfer is automatic and there is nothing you need do, except that if you wish to exchange your medal for a George Cross medal you should send it to this Department (Room 444). If you would like us to send you special registered envelope for this purpose would you please write and let me know.

Yours sincerely

(MISS) R M GAYNES

Letter from the Home Office offering an exchange of medal

231

In 1994 Bill became ill and after a short while in hospital, he died on Christmas Day, saying wryly to Paddy on Christmas Eve, "I think I've got my timing wrong."

Stalwart to the last!

He had asked for a Humanist Funeral and the music chosen by the family says it all: 'Jesu, Joy of Man's Desiring'. Of course! Memories of Bill and Sally's wedding.

Ella Fitzgerald, 'Every Time You Say Goodbye'.

'What A Wonderful World' Louis Armstrong.

The poem 'If' by Rudyard Kipling was chosen to be read as a tribute.

His obituaries appeared in The Times and The Daily Telegraph – much to the pride of his three sons, Christopher, Paddy and Martin.

A dearly loved father by us all.

Bill and Sally were another true Goad Love Story.

Bill and Sally's Honeymoon Picture, 1943 – Bill's favourite

Words by 'Billy Goad' for his childhood teacher Beatrice Stevens.

Written in 1994.

"Early in 1944 I was appointed to HMS Nith, one of a type named after rivers and when D-Day came in June of the same year, we took part in the landings, standing off shore and guiding vessels inland. We stayed in that area, off the beaches, more or less on police duty for some three months. Whilst standing off shore the ship was hit by bombs. Dockyard repairs were carried out at Chatham. Then the Nith, with its crew, were sent to the Far East, first in Indian waters, later on to the sea bordering Burma. The bombs on Japan saw an end to the fighting. However, it wasn't the end of duty there for us. The war might be officially over but we had to patrol the waters surrounding the many small islands which had been occupied by the Japanese. Then came more action with the outbreak of the Korean War".

Published in her book:

Stretham Wartime Memories, 1939-1945

"Home and Abroad".

Bill, Sally, Chris, Paddy and baby Martin

Buckingham Palace: Bill, Sally and cousin, Jean Roberts

Buckingham Palace: Bill, Sally and Cousin Jean Roberts

Bill, Sally and Paddy at the VC/GC Association 'do'
Mansion House, London

Buckingham Palace: Bill, sister Mollie and husband Douglas Marchant

Naval Record — William Goad RN.

1937-1953

Ganges	Nov 1937 – Sept 1938
Pembroke	Sept 1938 - Nov 1938
Dragon	Nov 1938 – Mar 1939
Pembroke	Mar 1939 – Apr 1939
Pembroke (Mashona)	Apr 1939 – Mar 1941
Tyne (Mashona)	Apr 1941 – May 1941
Pembroke	May 1941 – July 1941
Tyne (Ashanti)	July 1941 – Dec 1942
Cormarant	Jan 1943 – May 1943
Pembroke	June 1943- Sept 1943
Vernon	Sept 1943 – Nov 1943
Pembroke	Nov 1943 – Feb 1944
Spartack (Nith)	Mar 1944 – Mar 1945
Broganza (Nith)	Mar 1945 – Feb 1946
Badger (Nith)	July 1946 – Oct 1946
Duncansby Head (Nith)	July 1946 – Oct 1946
Pembroke	Oct 1946 – Feb 1947
Tyne	Feb 1947 – Jan 1949
Woolwich	Jan 1949 – May 1949
Bulawayo (Victory)	May 1949- June 1950
Jupiter	July 1950- Feb 1951
Plantagenet	Feb 1951- June 1951
Pembroke	June 1951 – July 1951
Mounts Bay	Aug 1951 – May 1953
Pembroke	May 1953 – Oct 1953
Arctic Convoys	1939- 1943

Rank Details

1937	Boy
1940	Ordinary Seaman
Nov 1940	Able Seamanship
Oct 1941	Acting Leading Seaman
Oct 1942	Leading Seaman
Mar 1943	Acting Petty Officer
Mar 1944	Petty Officer
Mar 1953	Chief Petty Officer

Medals

Albert Medal   Sept 1942   Saving   Life   at   Sea
Presented June 1943, became The George Cross in 1971

Atlantic Star   African Star   Burma Star   Korean Star

39 / 45 Campaign Medal   UN Medal   Arctic Star*

1953 Coronation Medal   Jubilee Medal 1977

Released: October 1953

*awarded posthumously 2013

The Albert Medal

As the Victoria Cross is the first of all British decorations for self- forgetting valour in the face of the enemy, so the Albert Medal is the first of all British decorations for self-sacrifice in the saving , or attempting to save life, by land or sea. The standard of personal heroism which it recognises is the highest possible, the measure of the sacrifice of self is the improbability of individual survival. The Albert Medal, following the precedent of the Victoria Cross, is sometimes awarded posthumously, and is then presented by his majesty to the next -of-kin. A man may die in the winning of it. And always before he can win it, must have looked very closely into the face of Death. The Albert Medal was made of the simple bronze of which is considered appropriate to the supreme war decoration of the Victoria Cross. A bar or clasp may be added to the ribbon of the Albert Medal, for a second act worthy of recommendation, but there appears to be no case on record of such an award having been made – at least not on the recommendation of the Board of Trade.

It has been found necessary in practice to set up certain criteria by which to measure the standard of performance of those whose gallant acts at sea have brought their names under consideration for the award of the Albert Medal.

The chief criterion is this:

That the rescuer of life at sea must not only seriously imperil his own life, but must do so under conditions which make his survival extremely unlikely. His risk of death must be greater than his chances of life. A man who gains the Albert Medal must very nearly and, so far as his own prospects are concerned, absolutely have lain down his life for those he had saved.

Issued by the Board of Trade 1923

The Albert Medal

Your Sincerely
M Caslow Boyd M
Captain Boyd M

H.M.S. "Osprey"
19th July 1943.

Dear Goad.

My Heartiest congratulations on the very well deserved award of the Albert Medal of which M. de. quincy has told me. I missed it in the A.F.Os; I do not know why, as I was getting worried ~~as you know I put your~~ that they had not recognized your services Earlier. as you know I put your name forward for award. or mention on three Seperate occasions,

The Albert Medal is indeed a Decoration to be proud of, but I cannot help wishing they had given you a D.S.M. as well, However nobody can complain when they get the highest award for gallantry in saving life. I am really delighted, as also will be Commander Maud when I tell him,

I expect you are sorry that the Ships company has had to be broken up. I shall never have the luck to serve with such a grand crowd again.

Good Luck in your next ship and any congratulation on your advancement to Petty Officer

Letter of Congratulation for Bill from Captain Boyd.
HMS Osprey 19th July, 1943

Transcript:

'My heartiest congratulations on the very well deserved award of the Albert Medal of which Mr. de Quincy has told me. I missed it in the AFOs; I do not know why as I was getting worried that they had not recognised your services earlier.

As you know I put your name forward for award or mention on three separate occasions. The Albert Medal is indeed a decoration to be proud of, but I cannot help wishing they had given you the DSM as well. However nobody can complain when they get the highest award for gallantry in saving life. I am really delighted, as also will be the Commander when I tell him.

I expect you are sorry that the ship's company has had to be broken up. I shall never have the luck to serve with such a grand crowd again.

Good Luck in your next ship and my congratulations on your advancement to Petty Officer.

Yours Sincerely

Boyd,

Captain Royal Navy.

Petty Officer W Goad, AM,

Official no: C/JX.156149.

HMS "ASHANTI"

c/o G.P.O.

London.'

William (Bill) Goad—Naval Appendix

Bill first knew about being awarded The Albert Medal in a letter he received from his mother, Ida Goad. His reply has been included as it gives an insight into Bill's reaction and his thoughts of the incident when it happened and his conclusion as to the acceptance of the medal.

W. Goad
HMS Ashanti
c/o G.P.O.
London
24.2.43

Dear Mum,

Was pleased to get your letter last night, was very surprised to read the news it contained, this being the first I have heard of it. Before I talk of this though I want you to send me a telegram straight away—right now—before you finish reading this letter, and tell me the latest news you have about Freddy. If you can't send a telegram see Mrs Clark (Stretham Post Office) *and get her to send a cablegram or some such thing – only please do it now, so that I can know that by now he is either well on the way to recovery or else he is past recovery. Whichever it is, send and tell me, also his address – if this is in any way practical.*

I could hardly believe my eyes when I read your letter and saw he was wounded, somehow I've always thought of him as one of those chaps who would always keep out of the way of a bullet – what did get him? Was it a bullet or a bomb splinter – not that it makes much difference, neither have much respect for whatever stands in their way. I wonder what he was doing when he caught it. For a silly reason of mine I like to think he was holding a pint of beer in his hand, I don't suppose he was!! – and have a strange feeling he will recover, why I don't know, perhaps because he always had plenty of luck – even if it did desert him for a time. I'm confident it will return and be sure the day will come when he will once more be making us laugh with his yarns of landladies and other women. Only let me know as soon as possible.

This news took whatever shine there was away from the other surprising news you told me. When I started reading your letter I couldn't think for the life of me what you were talking about, it wasn't until I got to the P.S. that I found out.

I had forgotten all about the incident, it seems to have happened in another world, long, long ago, and I didn't want that night revived, it was unpleasant – it was indeed one of the most miserable nights I have ever had, whatever I did was without thought of consequences, if I had stopped to think I would probably never have done it. The memory has faded, now it has been dragged up again, and I feel uncomfortable, because people will think that I would do the same again at any time. Maybe I would but then again maybe I wouldn't.

Thanks for the congratulations though – whereas the congrats from Sally are much more to me than the award is. As long as I can get appreciation from either of you, I know I shan't be far off the beaten track---or is it the straight and narrow!

I have no further news of leave, keep your chin up, though it can't be very far away – am keeping well, very fit with all this sunshine and swimming, but am longing to see you all again.

Must close to catch the mail – this is the first A-Mail for a long time and we only had short notice.

Do let me know about Freddy.

Love Bill

As can be seen, right from the beginning Bill's modesty over the Somali/Ashanti incident was there. He regarded he was just doing his job amongst many other men. His thoughts for his wounded friend Freddy came first.

The love and respect of his Mum and Sally was all the reward he needed.

We have yet to find out who Freddy was!

To-day we have to conclude his friend Freddy did not survive the war, as Bill was never heard to speak of a friend Freddy and the present generation have no knowledge of him.

Torpedoed HMS Somali. HMS Eskimo standing by, Sept 1942

Molde Fjiord, Norway

Arctic Convoys Map

Iceland to North Cape, Brest to Spitzbergen

Gunner Goad

Bill's Medals

Certificate awarded to Bill after crossing the equator aboard HMS Nith on 24th January, 1946

Bill's Diary of 1940

William 'Bill' Goad

William 'Bill' Goad, had been in the Royal Navy for more than two years by 1940; joining HMS Ganges as a boy sailor in 1937 at the age of fifteen years six months.

In September 1939 he found himself helping his country fight a war against Germany, led by Adolf Hitler. These early days of conflict were called the 'Phoney' war.

At this time he was serving as a gunner on HMS Mashona. Destroyer Class No: 59.

In January 1940 Bill decided to keep a daily diary of events while he was at sea – an account of the life as he saw it, of a young sailor serving on the Arctic Convoys in his eighteenth year. I have since discovered while writing this, that keeping a diary was forbidden, Bill's one lapse of discipline (I will put it down to his youth enthusiasm and naivety of fighting a war). He certainly never wrote another one.

It was very small and written in pencil.

The following pages are this diary transcribed and printed 'as written'; a true personal historical document of the first full year of conflict of WWII, on board a Destroyer in the Arctic Seas. To be on Arctic Convoys, to quote the British Prime Minister at the time, Winston Churchill, was, "the worst journey on earth". Today, the work the Arctic Convoys did guarding our oceans and merchant shipping has been recognised by the British government and a medal called the Artic Star has been awarded to all those who took part. Families can receive this posthumously.

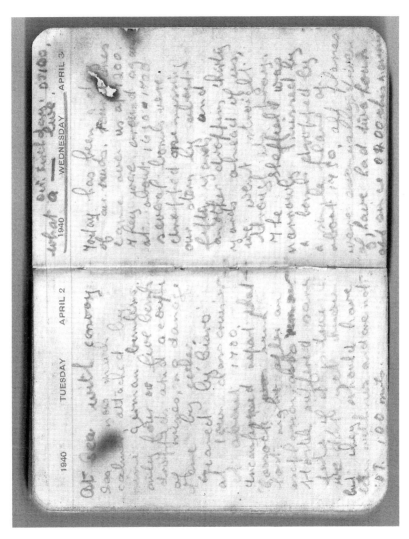

Bill's Diary

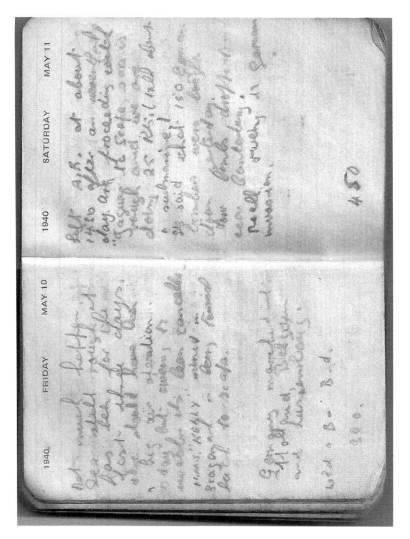

Bill's Diary

Diary of Gunner Bill

Diary of One Year's Experience sailing on Arctic Convoys in 1940 as Gunner on HMS Mashona
Transcribed as written

William (Bill) Goad RN 1922-1994

Ship: HMS Mashona, Destroyer F59 WWII Diary 1940

Age 17 years 7 months

Monday January 1st.

Starting the new year at sea. Left HMS Revenge at Plymouth after escorting her down from Greenock. Are now heading for Chatham where we should arrive tomorrow forenoon. Distance travelled approx:350 miles.

Tuesday January 2nd.

Arrived here at Sheerness at about 10:00. While coming through Dover Straights encountered three mines, all sunk by gunfire. Saw HMS Brilliant explode one mine ahead and one astern. Have been 'de ammo' all day, have finished. 20:00.

We are for Chatham tomorrow at 8:00. Distance Approx: 150 miles

Wednesday January 3rd.

Arrive Chatham dockyard at 10:00 and are now in dry dock. Received letter from home and from Freddy.

Thursday January 4th.

Dry dock. Nothing much doing. First leave? Some men went on leave . Dockyard maties start to pull the ship to pieces. Two letters from Sally, one from Freddy.

Friday January 5th.

Dry dock.

Saturday January 6th.

Dry dock. Went ashore and got measured for suit from Greenhoughs.

Received P.O. From Stretham Bowls Club.

Sunday January 7th.

Dry dock.

Monday January 8th.

Dry dock. Received fags from St. James Church, (Stretham)

Tuesday January 9th.

Dry dock. Are now sleeping and being victualled in R. N. Base.

Friday January 12th.

Went on Friday 'whistle'.

Monday January 15th.

Return at weekend

Friday January 19th.

Went on three weeks leave. Arrive home 5 pm.

Monday February 12th.

Came back of leave. Ship still in dry dock.

Tuesday February 13th.

In dock. Painting. Received letter from Sally.

Wednesday February 14th.

As yesterday. W/E granted.

Thursday February 15th.

As yesterday. Phoned up home.

Friday February 16th.

Went home.

Monday February 19th.

Arrived back on board.

Tuesday February 20th.

Usual.

Wednesday February 21st.

Usual. Received letter from Sally.

Friday February 22nd.

Depart on W/E.

Monday February 28th.

Back on board. Has been a very good month in every respect, especially the weather.

The war is proceeding at about the same pace.

Jim (brother) will be called up 23rd March.

Must not forget I owe father about £6, although I shall be able to pay him back Lord only knows. W/E leave.

Monday March 4th.

Came back on board and our 8 weeks of leave and refitting is over.

May it all soon come round again.

200 miles **Tuesday March 5th.**

Left Chatham and arrived at Sheerness.

Thursday March 7th.

Left Sheerness at 7am for Clyde. Doing speed trials. While going past Deal we see all the Colliers that are causing a controversy. Distance 230 miles.

Friday March 8th.

Arrived Greenock 8pm.

Saturday March 9th.

Left Greenock at 11:30 for gunnery trials. Arrived back 18:00 and go alongside HMS Woolwich and HMS Tarter. Had shock when saw torpedo missed stern by a few feet, but afterwards when recovered from shock found out it was fired in practice by HMS Hotspur.

Distance 60 miles.

Sunday March 10th.

Sheffield had yarn with us on AMD. Left Greenock for Scapa at 11:00 with HMS Tarter, HMS Eskimo and HMS Woolwich. Distance 100 miles.

Monday March 11ᵗʰ.

Arrived Scapa about 16:30. Oil and go to buoy. Seems to be gunfire and the "Gathering of the Clans" here!

P.S. Have just been called up at 23:00 to secure for sea. Distance 120 miles.

Tuesday March 12ᵗʰ.

Proceed to sea at 00:00 and arrive at Greenock 16:30. Are leaving again sometime tonight on a voyage which is expected to take three weeks. Distance 200 miles.

Wednesday March 13ᵗʰ.

Left Greenock at 00:00 with HMS Eskimo and HMS Punjabi and three Merchant ships. If programme isn't changed we are going to the Norwegian coast off Narvik and arriving there in 8 days' time. When there, expect to run into fjords and capture German ships which are hiding there, this will be followed by a week 'sus' patrol, and should arrive back a week later.(if we are still afloat). Distance 100 miles, speed 8 knots.

Thursday March 14ᵗʰ.

All yesterday's plans have been postponed, the reason being America: as we were also taking troops to Q---. are now heading for Scapa with the three Merchant ships at the speed of about 6 knots and going forward at about 1 knot! Sea is rather rough and it is very windy. Distance 110, miles being counted going round and round convoy.

Friday March 15ᵗʰ.

Arrive Scapa 09:00. Tried to go to buoy. Distance 80 miles.

Next 8 lines have been redacted!

Saturday March 16ᵗʰ.

Still at Scapa. Had an air raid, being Jerry's at about 19:30 most of which dived and machined gunned the upper deck of ship in harbour here, we luckily escaped unhurt. HMS Norfolk was damaged and one raider brought down.

Sunday March 17ᵗʰ.

At Scapa. Nothing exciting happened.

Monday March 18th.

Still at Scapa, have nearly sailed twice today so far so I suppose we shall sail after we have all turned in and asleep.

Tuesday March 19th.

At Scapa. Proceeded into Flow to hunt Sub which was supposed to have got through the boat gate. Went to anchor at 01:00, no trace of Sub.

Wednesday March 20th.

Went back to buoy at 09:00. Sailed with HMS Aurora, HMS Galatea, HMS Penelope, HMS Arethusa and 8 destroyers at 23:00 For Stavanger. Distance 20 mile.

Thursday March 21st.

Arrive at Stavanger at about 20:00 and split into 2 forces and hunt for any German merchantmen or warships that might be about. All however is very quiet. Leave the area at about 06:00 and join up with the other squadron. Are trying again tomorrow. Distance 450 miles.

Friday March 22nd.

Patrolled around and along the Norwegian coast, enter Stavanger again. Again no excitement. Distance 300 miles.

Saturday March 23rd.

Started home at about 06:00. Arrive at Scapa at 01:30. Do not go in but hunt for a submarine, depth charges were dropped by us and other destroyers but no sub was seen. Distance 350 miles.

Sunday March 24th.

Enter Scapa at 09:00. Oil and go alongside HMS Woolwich. HMS Firedrake came alongside us. Distance 90 miles.

Monday March 25th.

Alongside HMS Woolwich. Went to pictures on HMS Dunbar Castle.

Tuesday March 26th

Nothing much happened. Still alongside HMS Woolwich. Say goodbye to Luit James.

Wednesday March 27th

Same as yesterday. The weather here is terrible, it has been a severe blizzard all day and snow has covered the hill like it did a month ago.

Thursday March 28th.

Left HMS Woolwich at about 06:30 and go to a buoy. HMS Nubian came alongside and knocked a hole in our bows.

Friday March 29th.

Still at buoy.

Saturday March 30th.

Leave buoy and go back alongside HMS Woolwich to have hole repaired

Sunday March 31st.

Nothing much happened, German plane came over in the forenoon but no bombs were dropped, driven off by accurate firing by shore batteries.

Not a bad month on the whole. Have learned that between outbreak of war and January 1st have had 85 days at sea.

Monday April 1st.

Put to sea with HMS Matabele, HMS Somali and 3 Norwegian merchantmen. Met 3 other destroyers and 18 other Norwegians. We are in the roughest seas we have yet been in, our destination we don't know, but it is rumoured that it is Bergen in Norway. Don't it make you laugh? No! Distance 70 miles.

Tuesday April 2nd.

At sea with convoy, sea much calmer. Attacked by 9 German bombers, only 4 or 5 bombs being dropped and a couple of mines, no damage there either. Unconfirmed report that 2 destroyers were sunk last night after an explosion, if it is true, we don't know yet, but they should have been with us and are not. Distance 100 miles.

Wednesday April 3rd.

Today has been a day of air raids , 4 planes came over us at 12:00. They were around again at 16:30-17:00. Several bombs were dropped, one missing our stern by about 50 yards and another dropping 30yards ahead of us, we went straight through its spray. The Sheffield was narrowly missed by a bomb dropped by a single plane at about 17:50, all planes were eventually driven off. Have had 2 hours off since 04:00 this morning. Distance 100 miles.

Thursday April 4th.

A much quieter day, we left convoy about 09:00 at Bergen. Staying 8 miles outside. Waited about an hour and picked up another convoy of 39 ships, comprising of Norwegian, Danish, Swedish, Finnish and 3 British. Have heard that 2 of the planes that attacked us yesterday crashed over Denmark. Distance 120 miles.

Friday April 5th. Another quiet day, almost like a summer sun burn. Return Shetlands at about 08:00. 6 of our convoy were taken away by a "J" boat. Distance 120miles.

Saturday April 6th.

Quiet day. Weather gone back to its usual roughness. No planes over. Expect to make Rosyth tomorrow night. Distance 120 miles.

Sunday April 7th.

Arrived at Rosyth at 19:00, had news just as we entered Forth that we were proceeding straight out to sea. German fleet is reported to be out of its hole. All ships in here are leaving and preparing to leave. We expect to slip from oiler at midnight or shortly after. Distance 150 miles.

Monday April 8th.

Slipped at 12:30 and proceeded to sea with other destroyers and cruisers. Have been going full speed all day. HMS Gloworm has been reported in action with German destroyer. Reported that British have laid mines in A.T.W. there. Germans sunk by submarine, one of them a troopship.

HMS Kashmir and H.M.S, Kelvin had a collision and are returning home, the Kelvin badly holed aft. Exploded 2 mines. Distance 200 miles.

Tuesday April 9th,

Sticker over first part of writing.

Picked up 6 survivors from H.M.S, Gurka who was sunk by bombs. One has since died. Joined up with the Grand Fleet at 10:30, left them 12:00.

Was attacked by aircraft, 1400 bombs were dropped near cruisers, another attack lasting from 15:00- 17-00 by 20 bombers. HMS Matabele narrowly missed, we were missed by about 20 yards, bombs dropping close to stern. HMS Renown in action. Are expecting to engage. Which one is in Bergen hole? We are now just outside and are watching our bombers attacking them. Distance 320 miles.

Germany has marched on Denmark and is landing troops of Norway.

Wednesday April 10th.

18:00 arrived here at Solheim! 15:30. Left fleet at 12:00 after an uneventful night (apart from the rescue). The dead stoker was buried at 14:30. Expect we shall be leaving tonight. Report from Narvik that HMS Hunter sunk and HMS Hardy badly damaged. HMS Hotspur also damaged. 6 German destroyers were in fjord, 2 believed to be sunk and others seriously damaged. Distance 250 miles. Total to date 4,830 miles.

Thursday April 11th.

22:00. Getting some action. Left Solheim! at 04:20 arrived at Scapa 12:00 Oiled and ammunitioned until 18:00. Navigators came on board to pilot us up the fjords, they came off the tiny Norwegian destroyer which we brought over with us yesterday, Also 14 ratings for extra landing – from HMS Nelson. We are leaving at about 20:00 at full speed ahead. Heard HMS Gloworm was sunk, 3 Jerry cruisers, several destroyers and troop ships have been sunk. Big raid by 60 planes on Scapa.

Friday April 12th.

Left Scapa at 23:45 for arrival off Norwegian coast 01:30. But do not reach fjords because 'Dutchland' and other cruisers and destroyers are reported in the area nearby and we do not want to run into them in a confined space. Are doing a patrol down coast, the sea is very rough. Our boarding party from the 'big ship' are VERY seasick. Distance 240 miles.

Saturday April 13th.

Most beautiful scenery have yet seen. Entered fjord at 05:30 and at 08:30 found 5 Norwegian oilers destined for Germany, hidden away in a small creek. Left this fjord at 12:30 and head north, from then on till 14:30 we were attacked by Junker bombers , many bombs were dropped, most of them directed at us (because we are behind HMS Somali). None however hit. Planes were eventually driven off, 2 of them we have since heard crashed. Enter Morde fjord at 15:00 and are anchoring for the night. Distance 150 miles.

Sunday April 14th.

Left Morde fjord at 04:30 and proceed to sea to rendezvous with HMS Glasgow and HMS Sheffield. Enter the Molde fjord, went alongside HMS Glasgow and took on board about 200 landing party. Left HMS Glasgow and went further up fjord to where we went alongside and landed them, lorry's and bus's took them to their destination inland. Had run ashore in Eidsvag until about 23:00 although practically evacuated we had plenty of fun (snow balling), the snow is still about 4 feet deep. Distance 160 miles.

Monday April 15th.

Left Eidsvag at 01:30 and went on patrol up and down the coast and out to sea. Somali which was left on patrol at Molde was attacked continuously by aircraft. 253 bombs were dropped in about 8 hours, not one of them hit. She had exhausted all her A.A. Ammunition during the attack. Distance 260 miles.

Tuesday April 16th.

Arrived at port! at 07:30 and went alongside HMS Matabele which was alongside an oiler, 09:00. Left oiler and went alongside Polish liner, now a troop carrier, took on board 300 soldiers and 20 tons of provisions and ammunitions. Had just got them on board at 13:50, when we were attacked by aircraft, only one bomb was dropped and it was a 1,000 lb'r (pounder), it did however miss. We were attacked when we got to sea, 4 bombs missing our stern by 20 yards. Landed troops at

Namsos at 20:30. Left and proceeded to sea. Distance 200 miles.

Wednesday April 17th.

Cruised around for most of the day, met troopship at 10:30. Proceeded with it to Namsos where it disembarked its troops. Went alongside HMS Glasgow at 23:50 for oil. HMS Suffolk was bombed today, after an attack which she evaded for an hour. One bomb scored a direct hit, the damage is not yet known, but it is said to have gone down one of her funnels. Distance 250 miles.

Thursday April 18th.

Cruised about for most of the day with the Polish Liner. Took her to Namsos in the evening where she embarked remainder of troops and provisions. Was working until 04:00 getting stores off Liner, and getting ammunition on board. Distance 200 miles.

Friday April 19th.

Left Namsos at 04:00 until attacked by one bomber at 04:30. 10 bombs dropped, no damage. Four destroyers left us to take troops home. Distance 200 miles.

Saturday April 20th.

Heading for home. Heard that Namsos was heavily bombed. Distance 200 miles.

Sunday April 21st.

Arrived at Greenock at 18:30 and go to oiler, get stores on board, are leaving immediately. Distance 200 miles.

Monday April 22nd.

Left Greenock at 04:20 with HMS Ark Royal and 2 other destroyers, are heading for Scapa, expect to arrive tomorrow morning. Distance 200 miles.

Tuesday April 23rd.

Arrived at Scapa at 08:30, go to oiler and then alongside HMS Woolwich, are here for a short boiler clean and expect to leave about Thursday. Distance 100 miles.

Wednesday April 24th.

Boiler cleaning all day alongside HMS Woolwich. Planes came over at 21:00. No bombs dropped near us.

Thursday April 25th.

Went ashore at Kirkwall, arrived back on board 18:00. Left for Rosyth 20:00. Distance 70 miles.

Friday April26th.

Arrived Rosyth at 07:00. Go alongside Wall. Left Rosyth 20:45, with 2 troop ships.

Saturday April 27th.

Arrive at Scapa at 18:00 after a quiet day. Distance 160 miles.

Sunday April 28th.

At Scapa. Nothing happened.

Monday April 29th.

Left Scapa at 12:00 with D6, F45, and 2 Ulster liners.

Are evacuating what's left of our troops, from Norway!

Distance 200 miles.

Tuesday April 30th.

Arrived off ? at about 20:00 with ? and 4 cruisers. Went into the fjord and at 22:00 arrived at a place where we took on board Royal Marines, the few survivors that were left after the terrible time that they have had. Town where we have evacuated them from was ablaze from incendiary bombs dropped by bombers in an 8 hour raid.

Told that only 40 of the 300 Tommies we landed are left. Distance 260 miles.

Wednesday May 1st.

Left fjord at about 13:00 and was attacked by a single bomber 'Junker' which dive bombed HMS Ulster, no damage done. Attacked again in the afternoon, cruisers narrowly missed. We were 'ditto' from the guns fired by them. Went back and took on board 300 soldiers and put them on board HMS Birmingham. Attacked going in, bombs dropped near cruisers, plane brought down in flames by HMS Calcutta who scored a direct hit with third salvo.

Thursday May 2nd.

Left ? fjord at about 08:00. Took on board 20 sailors off the trawler which was sunk by bombers. Also 16 soldiers, survivors of 300. All of them were wounded.

Head for Scapa full speed with HMS Calcutta who, by the way, had 1,000 bombs around her yesterday. Arrive at Scarpa sometime tomorrow. Distance 400 miles.

Friday May 3rd.

At Scapa, are waiting sailing orders and we expect I.T. Leave for a long period. Arrive here and put off the wounded. Distance 180 miles.

Saturday May 4th.

Left Scapa at 16:00 with HMS Ark Royal, HMS Curlew and other destroyers. Are heading for Narvik for a period of 2 or 3 months. Distance 120 miles.

Sunday May 5th.

Quiet day at sea, no sign of trouble at all. Expect to arrive at Narvik sometime Monday morning. Distance 360 miles.

Monday May 6th.

Another quiet day. HMS Ark Royal sent away aircraft through the day. Distance 350 miles.

Tuesday May 7th.

Ditto yesterday. Are patrolling about 30 miles out, 2 destroyers left for Tromso for oil. Three of HMS Ark Royal's aircraft met and drove off 5 Heinkels. Distance 300 miles.

Wednesday May 8th.

Ditto yesterday. Went into Tromso to oil, 23:00. Distance 200 miles.

Thursday May 9th.

Left oiler 04:00 and rejoined HMS Ark Royal. Shot down a Heinkel, one Fairey Swordfish into the sea. We picked up its crew, all ok but the plane sunk.

HMS Africa sunk. Distance 250 miles.

Friday May 10th.

Not much happening. Sea still rough, it has been for the last 3 days. There should have been big air operations today, but owing to weather it's been cancelled.

HMS Kelly (*Lord Mountbatten's ship*) mined in S------! and being towed back to Scapa. Distance 300 miles.

Germany marched into Holland, Belgium and Luxembourg.

What a B--------B.D.   *Bill was 18 today.*

Saturday May 11th.

Left HMS Ark Royal at about 14:50 after an eventful day. Are proceeding with HMS Jaguar to Scapa, sea is rough and we are doing 25 knots (talk about a submarine!). It's said that 150 German bombers were shot down yesterday.

4 Bombs Dropped Near Canterbury!! German Invasion??

Distance 450 miles.

Sunday May 12th.

Arrived at Scapa after a very rough and uncomfortable trip at 19:00. We went alongside oiler. No mail for us.

Monday May 13th.

Programme is not yet known but according to buzz we shouldn't have returned. Signal wasn't read properly!

Tuesday May 14th.

At buoy. Nothing much doing.

Wednesday May 15th.

Ditto yesterday, have been fitting new anti-mine gear. Are probably proceeding to sea tomorrow.

HMS Valentine bombed and afterwards beached on the Belgium coast.

Thursday 16th.

Proceed to sea at 03:00 are heading for Greenock with liner HMS Orient which has just returned from Narvik. Expect to bring a convoy back. HMS Somali damaged off Norway, proceeding off Scapa at about 12 knots.

Dutch Army surrendered after losing 100,000 men.

Distance 350 miles.

Friday May 17th.

Left Orient at midnight after taking her out to sea. She is now on the way to Canada. Arrive Greenock 15:00. Are taking a convoy on Sunday. Can see from where we are lying the French destroyer which was sunk by sabotage, only her funnels and masts protrude out of the water. Distance 300 miles.

Saturday May 18th.

Had O.S. granted during forenoon. Was going to Glasgow to see Sally, had got all night leave, but had sudden sailing orders at 15:15. and are now sailing to Scapa (Land of Dreams). Passed HMS Isis and HMS Bandit, also HMS Somali who was proceeding slowly, she was damaged stern side. Expect to arrive Scapa 06:45. Distance 110 miles.

Sunday May 19th.

Arrived Scapa at 11:30 after being delayed by doing an A.S. sweep in the Reaches. Probable reason for coming here is that there is no other destroyers here bar HMS Silk aside HMS Woolwich and HMS Fortune. Distance 120 miles.

Monday May 20th.

Scapa was called at 02:00 to prepare for sea or rather search the Flow to find an unidentified vessel that had got in. After raising steam found out it was HMS Fury. HMS Whitby bombed and afterwards beached.

Tuesday May 21st.

At Scapa. Nothing much happened. HMS Effingham sunk by hitting a rock.

Wednesday May 22nd.

Left buoy and went alongside HMS Woolwich where minor defects are being repaired.

Thursday May 23rd.

Left HMS Woolwich 08:00. Went to buoy. Left buoy at 13:15 and went along HMS Repulse where we were oiled. Went back to buoy 22:00 Are still waiting for mail from Narvik. 1 French destroyer and 1 merchant ship sunk.

Germans Take Boulogne, France.

Friday May 24th.

At buoy, nothing happened. Expect our mail went down with HMS Effingham!

Saturday May 25th.

Slipped at 10:30 expecting to go to sea but went to oiler. Back to buoy.

Sunday May 26th.

At Scapa, nothing happened. HMS Wessex sunk.

Monday May 27th.

Proceed to sea at 10:00 with air raid siren sounding as we left. Are meeting a convoy and taking a ship to Scapa. Visibility very bad and we are several hours overdue in meeting convoy. Distance 200 miles. HMS Wescot sunk.

Tuesday May 28th.

Arrived at Scapa at 16:00, bringing in 2 merchant ships which we picked up at 02:00 .Distance 100 miles.

Wednesday May 29th.

At Scapa. Nothing happened. HMS Wakefield sunk.

Thursday May 30th.

At Scapa, ditto yesterday. HMS Grenade, HMS Bindish, HMS Curlew sunk.

Friday May 31st.

Left Scapa at 04:45 with 2 ships carrying HMS Effingham survivors. Escorted and left them at Thurso. Arrived back at Scapa at 10:30 and met HMS Sussex and HMS Bedouin and screened former while she had a shot, we had a shot. Left HMS

Sussex at 16:00 and went with Bedouin to patrol off Shetlands. Distance 200 miles.

Saturday June 1st.

Arrived back in Scapa at noon after an uneventful patrol. Go to buoy.

Sunday June 2nd.

Left Scapa at 02:00 and proceed to south off Moray Firth where SS ----- ? had been sunk by torpedo, she finally disappeared at 05:00. Many defence boom buoys which were evidently her cargo left floating. Hunt sub all day with HMS Kelvin, no trace as yet.

Am realising its scene of sinking, to screen salvage vessels. Distance 300 miles.

Monday June 3rd.

Returned to Scapa midday and went alongside Ashanti.

Ashanti went to sea at 18.00. Distance 180 miles.

Tuesday June 4th.

Left Scapa at noon with D6 and H10 for A.S. Patrol. Joined HMS Electra, HMS Escort and HMS Forrester and do large scale sweep. Nothing however 'prized'. Distance 180 miles.

Wednesday June 5th.

On A.S. patrol until 18:00 when D6 left for Scapa, received signal to return ourselves. Speed 35 knots, arrive 20:30. Go to oiler and later buoy. Work all night changing Pom! Pom! Ammunition. Distance 250 miles.

Thursday June 6th.

Left Scapa at 21:00 with D6, F51, F67 and HMS Valiant. Don't know yet where we are going but it is rumoured Norway. Distance 50 miles.

Friday June 7th.

Still heading north, are meeting a convoy at about 01:30 tomorrow and are taking it south. Distance 360 miles.

Saturday June 8th.

Met the convoy at the appointed time, consisting of 7 transport and ----? Head south off Outer Hebrides until 23:00 and turn round north again to pick up another. Hear HMS Glorious has been sunk, don't know yet if it's yet true. Distance 400 miles.

Sunday June 9th.

Heading north until 20:00 when we meet 7 transports A.R. Line cruisers, 20 G.S. and 7 destroyers. Were attacked by aircraft at 15:00. Bombs dropped but all missed. German D.C. Sharnhorst and 2 pocket B.S. are somewhere in the vicinity, SS Aurora was sunk by Sharnhorst yesterday. Our exact position we know, which is about 300 miles NNE of the Faroes. Received information of German forces from H.S. which passed us at 01.00 and who saw SS Aurora sunk. Distance 570 miles.

Monday June 10th.

Were attacked by bombers at 00.30 who managed to drop several bombs before being beaten off by A.R. Skuas. Continue South with convoy (which like yesterday carries troops and supply from evacuated Narvik). Met HMS Renoun and HMS Rodney at 10.00, left convoy with HMS Ark Royal and joined up with them. Proceed towards Trondheim fjord where German Forces are but however met HMS Campbell whose only surviving destroyers were to escort HMS Campbell who can only do 12 knots, to Faroes, leaving Fleet at 20.00, leaving all others heading to Trondheim. Distance 400 miles.

Italy Entering War at Midnight.

Tuesday June 11th.

Arrived in the Faroes at 18.00 after quiet voyage across the North Sea. HMS Campbell came alongside us and oiled (She was almost completely out). Left Faroes at 22.00 and head for Solheim!. Distance 200 miles.

Wednesday June 12th.

Arrived Solhiem at 09.00. Went to oiler and then to anchor. HMS Veteran came alongside for water. Distance 400 miles.

Germans are 30 miles from Paris and attacking with about 2,000,000 men.

Thursday June 13th.

Left Solheim! at 06.00 and proceeded north in company with HMS Veteran, HMS Campbell and found later by HMS Forrester. Are patrolling near Faroes waiting for the Fleet. Heard that two destroyers of C in C screen were in collision and are heading towards us at 7 knots. Distance 350 miles.

Friday June 14th.

Patrol up and down until 17.00 when was found by C in C HMS Renoun and destroyers, don't know as yet what we are doing or where we are going. German D.S. Sharnhorst bombed in Trondheim. Distance 300 miles.

Germans Enter Paris.

Saturday June 15th.

Arrived in Scapa at 18.00. Went to oiler and afterwards to buoy. HMS Calypso sunk by Stalin U boat. Distance 250 miles.

Sunday June 16th.

At Scapa. Nothing happened.

Monday June 17th.

Still at Scapa.

French Army capitulate

Tuesday June 18th.

Went out to Scapa Sound for full calibre shoot. Returned to harbour and anchored near boom.

Wednesday June 19th.

Screened HMS Renoun for a full calibre shoot and H.A. shoot at sleeve target. Return to harbour, left again immediately to intercept 4 Swedish destroyers in Faroes. Distance 300 miles.

Thursday June 20th.

Arrived at Faroes at 08.00 and wait outside fjord after ordering sailors to leave their ships. Went alongside S.D. Psilader at 01.00 and oiled her, left her 02.00. Went alongside HMS Drake and oiled her too. Put steering parts aboard S.D. Psilader. Expect to leave them tomorrow. Distance 200 miles.

Friday June 21st.

Left for Scapa at 06.00. Speed 30 knots, left after removing our steaming party from S.D. Psilader and HMS Nemo. Arrive at Scapa and take up Scapa Defence Ship under Boom. Distance 260 miles.

Saturday June 22nd.

Left Scapa at 08.30 and head for Faroes. Arrive there at 20.00 and anchor off. Wait to receive orders from C in C. Left about an hour later and went to where destroyers are. Went alongside S.D. Psilader. Distance 260 miles.

Sunday June 23rd.

Oil S.D. Psilader again and went alongside HMS Romulus and oiled her. Steaming party arrived from Scapa to man them.

France sign armistice.

Monday June 24th.

Oiled HMS Romulus and S.D. Psilader. HMS Romulus came alongside and left again shortly afterwards. Saw S.D. Psilader to jetty.

Tuesday June 25th.

Left Faroes at 18.00 with S.D. Psilader* and HMS Romulus after they had both broken down two or three times in about one hour. Distance 100 hours.

* S.D. Psilader: Captured Swedish destroyer.

Wednesday June 26th.

Arrived at Scapa 18.00, left immediately after getting more oil, are heading for Rosyth for boiler clean. Leave?!?!

Thursday June 27th.

Arrive at Rosyth 05.00 and went alongside wall.

Went on leave to Glasgow at noon. Went to Sally's home.

Friday June 28th.

Had a lovely day. Shopping and pictures with Sally.

Saturday June 29th.

Returned on board 20.00. Best leave I've ever had.

Sunday June 30th.

Went on leave again. Arrived back on board midnight.

Monday July 1st.

Still alongside wall, nothing much doing.

Think my mind's still in G--!

Tuesday July 2nd.

Left Rosyth at 15.00 for ? where we are picking up a convoy at 19.00 consisting of A.S. Yeovil and small M.S. Are taking them to Scapa. Distance 150 miles.

Wednesday July 3rd.

Proceed north, attacked by bombers (Dorniers) at 17.00. One salvo of bombs dropped from great height, but it was about 100 yards off from the target. Distance 250 miles.

Thursday July 4th.

Arrived at Scapa at 01.30. Left immediately to intercept Swedish fishing vessel. Intercepted and took her to Wick. Arrived back at Scapa at 07.00. Left for H.A. shoot at 11.30. Shoot cancelled at 15.00 and proceeded with D6, F51, F67, on A.S. patrol 100 miles North of Scapa. Distance 300 miles.

French D82 cruiser and other vessels sunk by our Navy when they were trying to turn them over to Jerrys.

Friday July 5th.

Arrived back at Scapa at 18.00 after dropping D.C. in afternoon. Plenty of bubbles. Went alongside HMS Zulu who is alongside HMS Woolwich. Distance 200 miles.

Saturday July 6th.

At Scapa, nothing much happened. Left HMS Woolwich in evening and went to buoy.

Sunday July 7th.

Still at Scapa, nothing doing.

Monday July 8th.

At Scapa, went into Flow for A.S. practice and for torpedo shoot in the afternoon. Went to boom as Defence Boat. HMS Whirlwind sunk.

Tuesday July 9th.

Went to buoy. Ship was searched by officers and men of HMS Repulse for gear missing off Swedish destroyers!

Main part of French fleet taken and destroyed by us.

Wednesday July 10th.

Went into Flow for torpedo exercises. Should have had Sub calibre firing in the afternoon but proceeded to sea at 16.00 to hunt sub which had torpedoed Dutch Steamer. Search around and dropped D.C. at 19.00. Merchant ship finally sunk at 21.30 going down by the stern. Distance 200 miles.

Thursday July 11th.

Patrolled with F67 until 14.00. Intercepted 2 Dutch fishing boats in forenoon. Searched them and sent them to Wick. Picked up with a convoy at 15.00, escorted until off Ross Point. Turned back for Scapa, arrived in 21.00. Distance 200 miles.

Friday July 12th.

At Scapa. Nothing happened.

Saturday July 13th.

Big Court of Enquiry on HMS Woolwich. Re-claim by Swedish Destroyers.

Sunday July 14th.

At Scapa.

Monday July 15th.

At Scapa. Left to escort HMS Barham while she does H.A. shoot. At 16.00 brought her in and took HMS Nelson out at 20.30. Thick fog fell and shoot was cancelled and we lost HMS Nelson. Found HMS Nelson at 11.30 and are now staying out at sea all night. Distance 90 miles.

Tuesday July 16th.

At sea with Nelson who carried out shooting, lost Nelson several times during night owing to fog. Arrived back in Scapa at 17.00. HMS Glasgow in collision with HMS Imogen in fog. HMS Imogen sunk.

Wednesday July 17th.

Proceeded to sea at 11.30 with HMS Ashanti, are going on H.S. patrol. 10 Subs were yesterday seen near Norway heading for England. Distance 300 miles. HMS Vandyke sunk, crew taken prisoner.

Thursday July 18th.

In thick fog all night and all day today visibility about 100 yards at best. Distance 250 miles.

Friday July 19th.

Still thick fog, arrived Scapa 12.00. Oil and go to buoy. Left Scapa at 17.00 and escorted HMS Glasgow as far as Cape Roth. Distance 250 miles.

Saturday July 20th.

Arrived at Scapa 01.00, went to buoy.

Sunday July 21st.

At Scapa.

Monday July 22nd.

Left Scapa at 06.00 with HMS Furious. Manoeuvres. Carried out trials. Arrive back at Scapa 17.00. Distance 200 miles.

Tuesday July 23rd.

At Scapa.

Wednesday July 24th.

Slipped out 11.30. Screened HMS Furious for shoot. Returned harbour 17.00.

Thursday July 25th.

At Scapa.

Friday July 26th.

Destroyer exercises in Flow. Returned to buoy at 17.00.

Saturday July 27th.

Proceed to sea with 4 cruisers and 10 destroyers at 18.00. Distance 140 miles.

Sunday July 28th.

Searching for German battleship all day. Return to Scapa. Distance 400 miles.

Monday July 29th.

Searching. Arrive Scapa 00.03. Went to buoy. Distance 100 miles.

Tuesday July 30th

At Scapa.

Wednesday July 31st.

Proceed to sea. Long range shoot practice, and A.S. practice. Returned to harbour. Distance 150 miles.

Thursday August 1st.

Slipped at 07.00 with F67 and F21. Screened HMS Furious for exercises. One plane crashed on deck. Returned to harbour at 20.00. Distance 180 miles.

Friday August 2nd.

Left at 07.00 in company with HMS Maori and troopships to Shetland. Proceeded north off Shetlands for A.S. patrol. Attacked U Boat which was spotted by HMS Maroi at 21.00. No sign of it after depth charges were dropped. Distance 250 miles.

Saturday August 3rd.

On patrol. Nothing happened.

Sunday August 4th.

On patrol until 20.00, attacked by Dornier (Flying Peril) during forenoon. Three bombs dropped near HMS Maori. Returned to Scapa 22.00.

Monday August 5th. HMS Barham and went to Shetland. Distance 300 miles.

Tuesday August 6th.

Arrived off Aberdeen and left T.S. at 11.00. Left for Scapa. Arrived Scapa 16.00 and carry out A.S exercises and sub calibre shooting. Went into Scapa 18.00.

Wednesday August 7th.

At Scapa all day, nothing much happened. Changed our Pennants from F to G.

Thursday August 8th.

Left Scapa at 07.00 met HMS Furious at 10.00. Picked up 5 torpedoes fired by her torpedo bombers. Took them back to Scapa, anchored there until 11.00 and then went to D5 Range. Left Scapa 14.00 and met HMS Barham. Barham carried out shoot. Returning to harbour tomorrow morning. Distance 150 miles.

Friday August 9th.

Arrived back in harbour 02.00 went to oil, left oiler 07.00. Went to buoy.

Saturday August 10th.

Went to sea with destroyers and carried out shoot and A.S. exercises. Went alongside oiler. 18.00 alongside HMS Furious. Went to concert on HMS Furious but had to leave because of rough weather making it unsafe to remain alongside. Went to anchor in Scapa Bay. Distance 180 miles.

Sunday August 11th.

At anchor all day.

Monday August 12th.

Went to buoy at 07.00.

Tuesday August 13th.

Left Scapa at 16.00 with G67, G21and D6, are screening HMS Renoun. Where we are bound for we are yet to know.

Wednesday August 14th.

At sea with HMS Renoun. We are out in the Atlantic and nothing is yet known of HMS Renoun's destination.

Left HMS Renoun at 12.00 are patrolling back to Scapa.

Thursday August 15th.

Arrive at Scapa 07.00. Went to oiler, later buoy. Remained in harbour all day.

Friday August 16th.

At Scapa.

Saturday August 17th.

Left Scapa at 10.00 for Kirkwall Bay. Arrived 12.00 and anchored there for D.F. exercises.

Sunday August 18th.

At anchor Kirkwall. Went ashore.

Monday August 19th.

Left Kirkwall Bay at 21.00 arrive Scapa 01.30.

Tuesday August 20th.

At anchor at Scapa.

Wednesday August 21st.

Left Scapa with HMS Illustrious, cruisers and destroyers. Were taking oil and turned back because of rough weather.

Arrived back at Scapa at 16.00. Went to anchor, left to go on oiler and then to buoy. Our A.S. gear is out of order, owing to hard going today.

Thursday August 22nd.

Left buoy at 05.00 and went into the Flow with HMS Barnham. Barnham doing some exercises with us. Left the Flow and try to go alongside HMS Greenwich but it was too rough and HMS Greenwich is in too awkward position. Went to buoy.

Friday August 23rd.

Left buoy and went alongside HMS Greenwich.

Saturday August 24th.

Left HMS Greenwich at 16.00. Went to buoy. Left buoy 18.00. Bound for Liverpool and LEAVE.

Sunday August 25th.

Arrive Liverpool at 18.00. Tie up at Bidston Dock. It is about 19.30.

Monday August 26th.

Went on leave at 09.00. Arrived home 22.00.

4 WEEKS LEAVE.

Tuesday October 3rd.

Left Cammell Laird and go to Bidston Dock.

Tuesday October 8th.

Left Bidston Dock at 14.00 and stay in docks until 17.00 then proceed to sea. Are going to Scapa (as if we could go anywhere else). Shall probably have a month or so 'rubbing up' as there are 50 new ratings on board.

Wednesday October 9th.

Arrive at Scapa at about 17.00 and go to anchor.

Thursday October 10th.

Left anchor at 01.00 and go to oiler, and later to buoy.

Friday October 11th.

In harbour.

Saturday October 12th.

Went to sea with HMS Furious, and 2 cruisers and other destroyers. Don't as yet know where we are bound for.

Sunday October 13th.

At sea with HMS Furious, are taking her partway up to Norway. Are now going round in circles in the hope that sea will calm and allow aircraft to take off. Left HMS Furious at 18.00 when being relieved by HMS Matabele and HMS Elijah.

Monday October 14th.

Arrived at Scapa at 18.00 and so to oiler and afterwards buoy.

Tuesday October 15th.

Left buoy at 12.00 have Sub calibre shoot and at 16.00 meet HMS Hood, and D6, HMS Eskimo and HMS Duncan. Are going to form covering for HMS Furious should she be attacked on her way back after raids.

Wednesday October 16th.

At sea, visibility very bad.

Thursday October 17th.

At sea. Fog. Have been going north practically all the time. As well as fog it is very cold.

Friday October 18th.

Turned south during the night and at midday fog cleared and we are making good speed to Scapa.

Saturday October 19th.

Arrived Scapa forenoon, oiler then buoy.

Sunday October 20th.

Left Scapa 11.30 with other destroyers, head south until 17.00 when we meet HMS Repulse. Relieve destroyers of her screen and then turn back with HMS Repulse to Scapa arriving 21.30. Go to oiler.

Monday October 21st.

Left oiler and went to boom at 19.00.

Tuesday October 22nd.

Left oiler at 08.00 and went into Flow at Narvik and had several shots. Returned to oil at 22.00.

Wednesday October 23rd.

Left oiler 08.00, go into Flow for A.S. exercises. Left Flow at 12.00 for Thurso where we were picking up RAD. Recalled to Scapa at 13.15 arriving at 14.30. Go to oiler, and later to buoy at 18.00 and in the company of HMS Hood, HMS Repulse, 2 cruisers and destroyers leave Scapa. Are doing a sweep of S---!

Thursday October 24th.

At sea. HMS Somali and HMS Matebele (part of this unit) sunk 4 transporters during the night.

Friday October 25th.

Arrive back in Scapa at about 12.00 and had to wait until 17.00 while channel had been swept for suspected mines. Go to oiler later buoy.

Saturday October 26th.

In harbour all day.

Sunday October 27th.

In harbour all day, went to boom at 19.00 as B.D.

Monday October 28th.

Left Scapa 08.00. Had shots during forenoon, also screened HMS Repulse for shots. Was joined by HMS Hood, HMS Furious, 3 cruisers and more destroyers. At 16.00 turn NW and are hoping to intercept enemy A.M.S.

Tuesday October 29th.

At sea, nothing much happening. Sea started to crack-up during the latter part of the day.

Wednesday October 30th.

At sea. Weather very rough, are now getting some of those 80 degree waves have heard so much about but have never seen before.

Thursday October 31st.

Arrived back in Scapa at 14.00 after a rough and uncomfortable night and day. Went to oiler and later buoy. Number 2 hold floods and bulkhead bent.

Friday November 1st.

Harbour all day.

Saturday November 2nd.

Left Scapa at 00.00 with HMS Keppel. Met Empress of Australia and 2 A.M.C. Are taking them to Greenock.

Sunday November 3rd.

Arrive Greenock 07.00. Went to oiler. Left Greenock at 13.00, are probably heading for Scapa.

Monday November 4th.

Arrive Scapa 07.30. To oiler then to buoy.

Tuesday November 5th.

Left buoy at 13.00 and proceed to sea for H.A. shoot with HMS Phoebe. Returned to harbour at 18.00. Go to oiler, later to buoy. Left buoy at 23.00 and leave Scapa with HMS Hood, HMS Repulse and 3 cruisers and destroyers. Reported that German raider attacked homecoming convoy. How many ships have been sunk has not been disclosed.

Wednesday November 6th.

Sailed until 11.00, when HMS Hood and 2 cruisers break off and head south to cut off raider should he try to reach Breast. We then, and still, are going with HMS Repulse SW straight towards where convoy was attacked, unconfirmed report that AMC is actual? Raider which was reported of Admiral Sheen class. Weather and conditions for once are perfect and barring no unforeseen circumstances, we should with luck catch up with him sometime tomorrow. "Good Old Repulse".

Thursday November 7th.

At sea. Nothing happened. Still going West but have no further reports since early this morning on position of raider, which was then about 300 miles away. Thought that unless we meet it by tomorrow night, we are turning back.

Friday November 8th.

Left HMS Repulse in convoy of HMS Boneventure (possibly HMS Bonaventure). Are sweeping area where convoy was sunk looking for survivors. Don't know when we are turning back, but unless we oil from HMS Repulse we shall have to turn back soon, as our speed has been pretty high. There has been no further news of raider. Sea is rather rough.

Saturday November 9th.

Searching for survivors all night with aid of searchlight and star shell. Turned around for Scapa about midday. Sea still rough.

Sunday November 10th.

Heading for Scapa, should have met HMS Repulse at 09.00 but owing to weather we are 200 miles off course, as we are unable to head into the seas. Number 2 hold and lower Mess Deck sheared up and there is doubt if they will hold out.

Monday November 11th.

Arrived Scapa at 12.00. Go to oiler. Have only 40 tons of oil left out of 500 tons – about another 4 hours steaming. Left oiler and went to buoy at 16.00.

Tuesday November 12th.

Left Scapa at 12.00 with HMS Repulse and destroyers. Are going NW so probably the same job as before.

Wednesday November 13th.

With HMS Repulse until 17.00 when we turn round and head for Scapa, reason is that the ship is literally falling to pieces. The bows have cracked, and holds are flooded.

Thursday November 14th.

Arrived in Scapa at 10.00 and go to buoy. At 16,00 the C.O. comes on board to inspect damage. 22.00 Have been told we are proceeding to Rosyth for repairs. LEAVE??

Friday November 15th.

Arrive Rosyth 12.00, go to anchor. Ammunition all day. Are going on leave tomorrow. Length of leave as yet in doubt.

Friday November 16th.

Went home on 7 days leave.

Saturday November 23rd.

Came back off leave. Ship now in dry dock.

Wednesday November 27th.

Went to Glasgow had a grand time, I don't quite know why, but it must be something to do with G that makes me want 2B with S forever more (Bill's in Love).

Thursday November 28th.

Came back from Glasgow.

Saturday November 30[h].

Left dry dock at 15.00, went alongside jetty.

Sunday December 1st.

Went to buoy. Ammunitioned ship. Left buoy 18.00 and anchor other side of bridge as emergency destroyer.

Monday December 2nd.

Went back to buoy, completed ammunition. Left buoy at 14.00 and proceeded to sea. Patrolled until 16.00 and then picked up K.G.V. and probably taking her to Scapa.

Tuesday December 3rd.

Arrive Scapa 04.00. Go to oiler, go to buoy at 08.30. Left buoy 12.00 and proceed to sea with 2 cruisers and destroyers. Are going off the coast of Norway on the lookout for German convoy.

Wednesday December 4th.

Patrol coast from midnight until 02.00, at only 2 miles from coast, turn back at 07.00. Arrive at Scapa 13.00. Go to oiler and buoy.

Thursday December 5th.

Left Scapa at 16.30. Are with HMS Repulse and destroyers. Don't know what we are doing.

Friday December 6th.

At sea. Still do not know what's happening but we seem to be covering forces for a big convoy of mine layers. Where they are going to lay mines isn't known as we are well out into the Atlantic sea. A blizzard is raging and it's about 10 below.

Saturday December 7th.

Still out in a now calm sea. Are somewhere near Iceland, we could see the tops of the mountains this afternoon.

Sunday December 8th.

At sea. Sea very rough again. Visibility very bad. Had a mad dash for about 20 miles to 'engage' a warship, got there and found it to be one of the Yankee boats.

Monday December 9th.

At sea . Conditions the same as yesterday, are probably getting in tomorrow.

Tuesday December 10th.

Arrived Scapa.

Wednesday December 11th.

In harbour.

Thursday December 12th.

In harbour. Went to buoy as D.S.

Friday December 13th.

Screened HMS Hood for shoot, returned to harbour.

Saturday December 14th.

At anchor owing to bad weather.

Sunday December 15th.

Went to buoy 00.00. In harbour all day.

Monday December 16th.

Screened HMS Formidable for shoot, had shoot ourselves, returned to Boom as D.C. at 19.00.

Tuesday December 17th.

Went to Flow for exercises until 11.00 and then went to buoy.

Our troops are doing well in Egypt. They have already taken 31,000 prisoners and have advanced into Libya.

Wednesday December 18th.

At buoy until 16.30 when we went to sea with HMS Formidable, do not know where we are going but it's rumoured that we are turning back on the 22nd arriving back on Christmas Day.

Thursday December 19th.

At sea. HMS Formidable flew off aircraft until around 14.00 when sea became too rough. Four of her aircraft crashed on deck while landing. Are taking HMS Formidable and HMS

Sussex clear of sub area, they are on their way to the Straights. (Gibraltar).

Friday December 20th.

At sea. It's too rough for any air approach. Our position is known to enemy. Admiralty says that we are almost surrounded by U Boats. Not a very comfortable thought with the aircraft carriers along with us. Had narrow escape during the night when HMS Matabele missed our stern, only quick manoeuvring saved us.

Saturday December 21st.

At sea. Left HMS Formidable and HMS Sussex at 21.00 last night to proceed on their way to the Mediterranean. Were on our way back and A.C.C. aircraft spotted U Boat some distance away. So have turned around and are remaining at sea on A.S. patrol until we have only enough fuel to take us home.

Christmas Dinner looking a bit 'Shaky'.

Sunday December 22nd.

At sea on patrol. Nothing much happened, but should very much like to have a calm sea now and then!

Monday December 23rd.

At sea. Are now patrolling our way back to Scapa and should arrive tomorrow morning.

Tuesday December 24th.

Arrive Scapa at 05.00. Go to anchor until 09.30 when we went alongside oiler, stayed at oiler until 15.30 and then went to buoy.

Wednesday December 25th.

Started the day well. Had just started dinner when sailing orders were received, slipped at 15.00 and proceeded to sea, this was bad enough but just when we were about to start Christmas tea the alarm went for aircraft attack. Attack didn't develop but were alarmed up until dark. Are out with HMS Repulse, believe we are screening a convoy and then bringing it back in. That's just to cheer us up.

Thursday December 26th.

At sea. All quiet until 18.00 when we investigated a ship which turned out to be a New Zealand merchantman. Returned to normal course and at 19.30 had distress call from merchantman who had been torpedoed. We turned round at 21.00 to search for now sinking ship. Took on board 78 survivors from 4 boats (4 women), this was completed by 22.30. Only one man was dead and nobody else was injured. Ship was bound for Glasgow from New Zealand with mixed cargo, she was stuffed full of tinned fish.

Friday December 27th.

Hunted around in case of more survivors and in search of sub. Skipper and crew went on board their damaged ship to see state of salvage. Her engine room was awash and her pumps wouldn't work, after getting Mails from her she was abandoned. At 19.30, 3 of the small boats were found again and all gear removed. Are now on our way to Greenock to land survivors. Learned that yesterday speed at times was 30 knots.

Saturday December 28th.

Arrived at Greenock at 09.00 and went alongside jetty, landed survivors. Stayed alongside until 13.50. Got leave from 17.50 – 23.50. So went to G to see S! Had a lovely time. Arrived back on board 23.50. Secured for sea. Ship now alongside oiler. Are proceeding to sea 00.30.

Sunday December 29th.

Slipped 07.00 and proceeded to sea. Had high speed trials during forenoon and arrived at Scapa at 17.00. Went to oiler then to buoy at 18.30.

Monday December 30th.

In harbour all day. Went ashore and saw Will Fyffe and Robert Wilson in personal appearances.

Tuesday December 31st.

In harbour all day.

And so ends one year in the life of HMS during this war.

MAY THE NEXT YEAR BRING PEACE.

William (Bill) Goad, HMS Mashona

1940

Bill and sister Betty

Transcript of Bill's Letter to His Mother Ida Goad

Bill, still only 17 years of age, describing 17 Days of Action at Sea, April 1st – 17th 1940 – the same year as his diary.

A. Mess
HMS Mashona
c/o G.P.O.
LONDON

20.4.40

Dear Mum,

I suppose you have been waiting for a letter from me to tell you of our doings of the last fortnight, although I ought to say three weeks, as we shall finish three weeks consecutive sea time tomorrow night, bar for two very brief visits to harbour, both about two hours.

I may as well start at the beginning.

On Sunday April 1st, we put to sea with a large convoy of Norwegians and British ships, twenty five in all. Monday was a quiet day, but Tuesday brought the first of many air raids, this one however was not a very ferocious one, only about ten bombs and three mines were dropped, none of them doing any damage.

Wednesday was a day when we all learnt to appreciate our Captain, at about 12.00 we were off course, still heading for Norway (It took eight days), Four Dornier bombers came over at a great height and then disappeared.

Two hours later they were back again with three more, and then the fun started; three of them attacked a cruiser (I hadn't better mention any names). About ten bombs were dropped, but only one of them was anywhere near its target, and they decided Mashona would make a good target.

Three of them appeared very high directly astern of us, one of them started to power dive, it's not what you might call a time to stand and gape when a damn great Dornier is roaring down on you at about four hundred miles an hour.

He levelled at about three thousand yards and we saw five bombs drop from under it, and then the Captain acted, with full speed ahead and the wheel hard over, it was only his good timing saved us, for a few seconds later the bombs hit the water about twenty yards astern, just where we would have been had the Captain not have acted when he did.

This was repeated twice more, the Captain's swift actions saved us, but it was a bit close once when one bomb fell directly ahead of us and we ploughed through the spray. They were eventually driven off and we afterwards heard that three of them had crashed in the sea on their way home.

Thursday 4th, we left the convoy outside the three mile limit of Bergen (Norway) and hung around until another one came out, this one comprised of forty ships of all nationalities and we turned for home, the sea which had been very rough had calmed down. Friday and Saturday we were going peacefully along.

Sunday 7th, we arrived back in English port, expecting when we got there to have a few days in, but we were there for exactly three hours.

At midnight we were off again at full speed for the Norwegian coast. We had of course learnt what was happening so we were all looking forward to some action.

We were still ploughing along on Monday. Tuesday 9th, met the Grand Fleet and were with them until midday when we left with three cruisers and five destroyers to intercept a German light force off Bergen.

At 14.00 we were attacked by fifteen German bombers, several bombs were dropped around the cruisers, but they didn't stop long as they were on their way, it seems, to attack the battle fleet.

About an hour later twenty Dorniers appeared over the horizon, and you can't imagine what it's like unless you actually have experienced it, what it feels like to see twenty bombers coming at you. Of course we scattered and the fray commenced. Forty bombs were dropped around us alone, but only about ten in two lots of five were anywhere near us. This time the bomber didn't power dive onto us but dropped its eggs from a great height, the chances of them hitting are not very good and with the great work of the Captain we managed to escape unscathed, although once I thought and so did everyone else that they had dropped one with F59 on it.

It was towards the end of the raid that a Dornier appeared out of the clouds high above us, it was only visible for about a minute, I was on the bridge look out at the time and I thought the Skipper was never going to dodge out of the way.

As though from that height you couldn't see the bombs falling, you had a feeling that they were coming straight down and hit you amid ships. Anyhow the Skipper acted as before, just at the right moment, just as the stern swung round and the engines were throbbing out their forty knots, there was a high pitched whine of the bombs falling through the air and then the explosions as they almost dropped under the stern, making the old girl shake all over.

But at 11.30 that night we learned that all of them hadn't been as lucky as us. HMS Gurkha which was operating fifty miles away, was as you now know, hit by a bomb.

We were heading south to do a sweep of Scargarth! when a whaler (rowing boat) was spotted drifting in the water, of course we hove to, but there was nobody in it.

We didn't know at the time anyone had been sunk, but following the whaler there were bits of wreckage and lots of oil on the water and then a raft came into sight, or rather we heard somebody shout and when the searchlight was switched on, we could see the raft with four or five men on it.

We had a terrible job getting them on board, as it was pretty rough and they were practically frozen stiff (they had been in the water for about seven hours), but with a lot of clever manoeuvres by the Skipper, we got them alongside. But it was another hour before we managed to get them inboard.

One of them died a few minutes after we got them in, and the others were unconscious until the next morning.

After seeing those poor devils you can imagine how most of us felt; it was like waving a red flag before a bull, but it seemed that the bull was doomed to be tied back.

Wednesday 10th was a quiet day and we put back to Sollen! for ammunition and oil (nearly all of our A.A. Ammunition was gone).

At midnight we left again with an extra landing party on board and two Norwegian sailors to act as interpreters. We are going to "mop up" the fjords in the vicinity of Narvik.

Friday 12th. We expected to enter Trondheim fjord but just as we were about to enter, a report came through that there were a couple of cruisers, almost four 8 inch shore Batteries and lord knows how many mines waiting for us. As there were only three other destroyers with us, it would have been suicide, so we patrolled outside waiting for the next dawn.

At dawn on Saturday 13th we entered one of the large fjords and searched all the small creeks, we only came upon two ships, both of which we grabbed and put a prize crew on board.

We left there about midday and headed North, we had just got clear of the shallow water when overcame the bombers. Twenty two of the devils this time, they attacked us in couples continuously for about four hours, we counted about ninety bombs but as before we dodged out of harm's way. Once three bombs fell either side of us, both at the same time, eventually they left us, three of them with black smoke trails.

They all crashed into the sea, and were picked up by one of our cruisers several miles away.

We anchored in a small fjord for the night and next morning Sunday 14th we left at ten that night, we met two of our cruisers and entered another fjord. We went alongside one of them and took on board about 200 sailors and marines, we took these right up the fjord to a landing jetty at (better not say) after landing them and their provisions, we were allowed ashore to stretch our legs.

It was only a small place and most of the people had evacuated, but we had a good snowball fight with our flotilla leader, the snow is still about four foot deep. I think the natives thought we were lunatics, but it gets you that way after being at sea for a long time.

We left there next morning and went on patrol, heading South, we learned later in the day that our leader which had left us early that morning had been attacked by bombers and that fifty eight bombs had been dropped.

On Monday 16th we arrived at a place with a fairy tale name (Archangel) and went alongside a big troop carrier that was there, we took on board 300 troops and tons of ammunition.

And then we had our narrowest escape so far, we had just got the last man on board when the bombers appeared out of the blue, we were still tied alongside when one of the lookouts happened, by a great bit of luck, to see a bomb leave a plane almost above us. It was a split second after his report that the securing wires were slipped or cut and we were leaving the liner, going at full speed (She nearly took off).

We were a hundred yards away when the bomb hit the exact spot we had been.

The liner was damaged, but as it was a 1500lb bomb, she was lucky she wasn't damaged more.

We were attacked on and off all day, but none however fell very close.

We landed troops without mishap (bar a lot of sea sickness).

Then we were at sea again.

Wednesday 17th. We were cruising around waiting for dark. When it fell, we met a troopship and took her up a fjord where she landed her troops.

From the 17th, until time of writing we have been at sea, where we are going nobody knows, nobody cares. But unless we soon make port for more than two hours, we shall be chewing our cords. We hope before long we shall manage to get a couple of days in, so that we can get some mail, we haven't had any for three weeks, excepting one small lot.

Let Jim read this and see what he thinks and whether he still would like to be in the "three day a week navy".

For ten days we never had a minute to ourselves, we were eating and sleeping (such as it was) at our action stations, and after being bombed once it loses its excitement.

I think I shall have to close now as I can just about write after this lot.

So Bye for now, All My Love Bill

P.S. Have left a lot out. If I was allowed to write it all down, it would take another 20 pages.

Petty Officer William 'Bill' Goad

GUNNERY HISTORY SHEET.

To be attached to the rating's Service Certificate until final discharge from the Service, when this History Sheet is to be given to the man, together with his Service Certificate.

Name....W. GOAD....
(Surname in BLOCK LETTERS).

Official No. C/JX 156149

Port Division....CHATHAM....

RECORD OF GUNNERY STATIONS IN SHIPS AT SEA.

To be filled in, in H.M. Ships at sea, when duties are performed **for not less than six months.**

Where a rating is found unsuited for any particular Gunnery duty, a notation to that effect is to be made in RED. Should any man be subject to severe seasickness, and therefore unsuitable for employment in ships smaller than cruisers, this fact is to be reported to the Commodore of the man's Depôt, and a notation made on Page 1. If trained as spare number, note the duty in columns 5 and 6, and insert the word "spare" in column 7.

Date	SHIP	Rate		Station		Ability	Initials of Gunnery Officer
		Seaman	Gunnery	Gun and Mounting	Duty		
1	2	3	4	5	6	7	8
Aug: 1938	CURLEW.	Boy	TM	4"	N° 4		
29.iii.40	MASHONA	Boy OB	TM	4.7"	N° 3.		
26.v.41.	do.	+AB	TM	4.7"	N° 3		
4.7.41.– H.v.4?	ASHANTI	AB	TM	4.7"	N° 3	V.G.	M
1.V.42 –	AJHANTI	L/S.	TM	Cordite	N° 1.	V.G.	M

Gunnery History Sheet

S.—1245 b. (Revised—October, 1937.)

TORPEDO HISTORY SHEET.

(See K.R. & A.I., Article 609.)

To be attached to the rating's Service Certificate until final discharge from the Service, when this History Sheet is to be given to the man, together with his Service...

Surname............. Christian Names }......... Port Division }......... Official Number }

Record of Torpedo Examinations.

Information is to be inserted when a rating qualifies in torpedo for A.B. and as regards examinations for acting as well as confirmed torpedo ratings.

Marks obtained in each subject are to be shown as a fraction of the possible total, thus 115/160

Date	Ship or School	Rating held	Torpedo Rating examined	Q.R. or P.F.	Examination Marks												REMARKS
					School	Whitehead	Mining and P.V.s	High Power	Low Power	Gyro Compass	Torpedo Control	Seaman's Electrical	Electrics and Accounts			Total Percentage	
1	2	3	4	5	6	7	8	9	10	11	12	13	14	15	16	17	18

Sta. 118/37

(4817) W1.4374/D636 80m 2/11 B1
S.—12

Torpedo History Sheet

S.460A. (Established October, 1945).

INTERIM TRADE CERTIFICATE *

During his service in the Royal Navy William (EOA) c/JX 156149 ....has been employed on duties appertaining to the Trade of Petty Officer,
with the various aspects of which he was shown himself fully conversant, either through his prior experience in the Trade, or by training in the work, and employment thereon, which he has had since his entry into the Navy, 29th November, 1937, including 13 years Sea Service since September, 1939.

His general efficiency in carrying out such duties was
Superior

His efficiency on discharge was
Superior

His character during his Service was Very Good.

Signed.

Commanding Officer.

Date................................   H.M.S.................................

(To be issued in the absence of other documents not immediately available on the rating's discharge.)*

N.S.1675/45

Wt. 34181 11/45 Gp. 38/3

Interim Trade Certificate

4.

Name *William Goad*

Conduct.

Second Class for Conduct (inclusive dates)		Character and Efficiency on 31st December yearly, on final discharge, and other occasions prescribed by regulation. If qualified by service and recommended for Re-engagement or for Medal and Gratuity, " R.R." or " R.M.G." to be awarded on 31st December and final discharge, if not, a line to be drawn across column.
From	To	**Note as to method of assessing Efficiency.**

Superior—above average efficiency.
Satisfactory—average efficiency.
Moderate—less than average efficiency.
Inferior—inefficient.

in substantive rating,- without regard to fitness for advancement.

Variations in efficiency are often explained by the fact that the man had recently been promoted—see pages 2 and 3—and had not gained sufficient experience in his new position to justify a higher award than that actually assessed.

Good Conduct Badges			Character	Efficiency in Rating, noting substantive rating in brackets	Whether R.R. R.M.G. or not	Date	Captain's Signature
Date	1st, 2nd, 3rd	Granted, Deprived, Restored					
May 43	*1st*	*Granted*	V.G.	Sat.			
May 48	*2nd*	*Granted*	V.G.	Supr.	(Boy/a)	9 May 46	
May 53	*3rd*	*Granted*	V.G.	Supr.			
			V.G.	Supr.	(A.B.)	31 Dec 40	
			V.G.	Supr.	(A.B.)	31 Dec	
			V.G.	Supr.	(L. Sea)	31 Dec 42	
			V.G.	Supr.	(A.B.) (H)	31 Dec 43	
			V.G.	Supr.	(P.O.)	31 Dec 44	
			V.G.		(P.O.)	31 Dec 45	
			V.G.	Supr.	(P.O.)	31 Dec 46	
			V.G.	Supr.		R.R.	
			V.G.	Supr.	(P.O.)	R.R.	31 Dec 48
			V.G.	Sat	(- -)	R.R.	31 Dec 49
			V.G.	Sat	(P.O.)	R.R.	31 Dec 50
			V.G.	Supr.	(P.O.)	R.R.	31 Dec 51
			V.G.	Supr.	(P.O.)	R.R.	31 Dec 52
			V.G.	Sup.	(C.P.O.)		6 Oct 53

Time forfeited		
Date	P.,D., C., C.P. W.T.	Number of days Award-ed Served

William (Bill) Goad. RN AM./GC

Conduct Record 1937—1953

Tribute to Bill, written and read by his son Paddy at his funeral, January 11th, 1995

"Loving, Honest, Industrious, Realistic, Open Minded, Orderly and Reliable.

He sounds almost too good to be true, doesn't he?

He was a man of great integrity.

Above all---To Me,

He was my friend.

He was My Best Friend.

We shared years of happy hours, not in each other's pockets by any means.

But both knowing the other was there, just in case.

He loved to talk and argue, especially round the table. Meal times were an event for Dad, not just a necessity.

He was always interested in everyone; Family and friends whom he shared his life with. Milked them all for news and opinion, better still to get a friendly argument going if he could.

If he was eating at my home or yours he would have more than a casual interest in the menu. If it was OK. he would more than likely take the recipe home.

He was a fair old cook as well!!

Many years ago while working in Iran, I had been through a period of being unable to speak or read any English while working on remote farms. Strolling one evening when back in Esfehan I paused at a pavement book stall, gazed over the various publications in the vain hope I'd find something in English.

There it was! At last! One book. A book of poetry by Rudyard Kipling.

With my need to read English overcoming my prior indifference to poetry, I bought the book.

For the remainder of my stay in Iran the book and many of its characters became good friends, and it was also then when I discovered the poem "If".

I have read and reread the poem and digested it over the years and it has become a sort of 'rule book' which I try to live my life by.

However the qualities it illustrates seem too great for me and most men.

But the one person I genuinely believe lived his life as this was Dad.

And I would like to read you this poem as a tribute to him."

'IF'

If you can keep your head when all about you

Are losing theirs and blaming it on you,

If you can trust yourself when all men doubt you,

But make allowance for their doubting too:

If you can wait and not be tired by waiting,

Or being lied about, don't deal in lies,

Or being hated, don't give way to hating.

And yet don't look too good, nor talk too wise:

If you can dream- and not make dreams your master:

If you can think- and not make thoughts your aim:

If you can meet Triumph and Disaster

And treat those two imposters just the same:

If you can bear to hear the truth youv'e spoken

Twisted by knaves to make a trap for fools,

Or watch the things you gave your life to, broken,

And stoop and build 'em up with worn-out tools:

If you can make one heap of all your winnings

And risk it all on one turn of pitch-and-toss,

And lose, and start again at your beginnings

And never breathe a word about your loss:

If you can force your heart and nerve and sinew

To serve your turn long after they are gone

And so hold on when there is nothing in you

Except the Will which says to them "Hold On!

If you can walk with crowds and keep your virtue,

Or walk with Kings- nor lose the common touch,

If neither foes nor loving friends can hurt you,

If all men count with you, but none too much:

If you can fill the unforgiving minute

With sixty seconds' worth of distance run,

Your's is the Earth and everything that's in it,

And- which is more- you'll be a Man, my son!

Rudyard Kipling 1865—1936

Mementoes

When sorting out Bill's home Millway, Stretham, after his death in 1994, the family found some naval mementos, carefully packed away by his wife Sally many years before. There was his old battered naval suitcase, inside was a 'whites uniform'.

Also a small tin box containing his row of medals, woven badges cut from his final uniform and the wood-cut inked name stamp, W. GOAD, well used and his Naval Pay book.

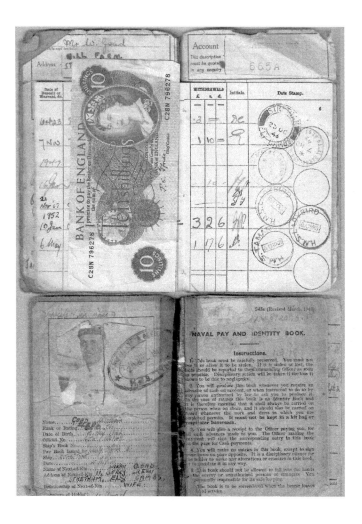

Naval pay book

ROYAL NAVAL COVERS GROUP

Organiser: Chris Hockaday

44 Fisher Road,
Milehouse,
PLYMOUTH
Devon PL2 3BB
Tel. 0752 558541

Date: 24th January 1994.

Mr W Goad, Esq GC.
Millway,
Ely Road,
STRETHAM,
Cambridgeshire.

Dear Mr Goad,

Please find enclosed, with our very great thanks, the finished
article, you kindly agreed to sign from our Battle of the
Atlantic Commemorative issue.

My thanks go along with that of Jim Burnhams who is the corner
stone of our Group, and the covers were very much appreciated
by our membership. A collectors item for sure.

We have sent a donation of £50, from this cover alone, to the
VC GC Association.

My thanks once again, and may I on behalf of the group wish you
and your family al the best of health and happiness.

Yours sincerely,

FIFTIETH ANNIVERSARY OF THE

BATTLE FOR THE ATLANTIC

By the spring of 1943 it became evident that the tide was
turning in favour of the Allies. More convoys were getting
through with fewer losses. Escort carriers and their aircraft
were successful in protecting shipping from the menacing U-
Boats. This, combined with the active involvement of RAF
Coastal Command, caused Admiral Dönitz at the end of May to order his
remaining U-Boats to southern waters.

HMS Biter, with 811 Sqdn on board, a typical escort carrier which helped
secure the seas and make the invasion of Europe possible.

Royal Naval Covers. Series One No. 3

C. F. Hockaday,
44 Fisher Rd,
PL2 3BB

Our aim is to record the history of the Royal Navy, past and present, on Philatelic Covers,
and to foster good relations with the Royal Navy by raising funds for Naval Charities.

First Day Stamp Cover commemorating the Battle for the Atlantic,
signed by Bill

There were also two embroideries sewn by Bill, done to while away the off-duty hours of long trips at sea. All sailors had to sew and maintain their uniforms and traditionally some men became very creative in this craft, one of these is now a cushion, the other a framed picture.

Bill's Embroidery Picture

WILLIAM GOAD, GC

William Goad, GC, who won the Albert Medal (later translated to George Cross) while on wartime Arctic convoys, died on Christmas Day aged 72. He was born on May 10, 1922.

IT WAS while serving in the destroyer *Ashanti* on Murmansk convoys in the winter of 1942 that William Goad won his Albert Medal for a rescue which he carried out in conditions of extreme hazard. At that time a Leading Seaman, he volunteered to go over the ship's side on a line after a senior officer, Commander Colin Maud, had fallen overboard.

The weather was appalling; a full gale was blowing, whipping up gigantic seas which incessantly flung the destroyer on her beam ends. To go overboard on a line in such conditions carried with it the near certainty that the would-be rescuer would be slammed against the steel plating of the ship's side every time she rolled or, indeed, be swept right under the bilge keel.

In addition, the temperature of the sea in those northern waters was well below freezing at that time of the year. Drenched through as he was from the very outset of his rescue attempt, Goad's hands might quickly have lost all blood circulation, rendering them completely useless. Indeed, in those latitudes death from hypothermia could happen in a matter of minutes.

Remarkably, Goad overcame all these hazards and succeeded in locating the officer in the murk of an Arctic winter's day. In spite of the numbing cold which threatened at every moment to paralyse his hands, he laid hold on Commander Maud and brought him to the safety of *Ashanti's* deck.

The Albert Medal which Goad was awarded for this rescue was gazetted on January 26, 1943, and he received his decoration from King George VI at Buckingham Palace in July of that year. At the time his former commanding officer in *Ashanti* (the ship's company having been by then dispersed) told him in a letter that he deserved to have been awarded the Distinguished Service Medal, as well.

Born into a farming family in Cambridgeshire, William Goad went to school at Stretham near Ely and joined the Royal Navy at the age of 15 in 1937. During the war he served in all the principal naval theatres, including the Atlantic and the Far East, gaining the campaign medals associated with them and several times having ships sunk under him.

When the Korean War broke out he saw service there, too, retiring from the Navy at the end of that conflict as a chief petty officer in 1953. Going back to his native Cambridgeshire he joined his brother working on his father's farm, where at the age of 30 he had to learn the business from scratch.

The brothers ran the farm after their father's retirement eight years later, William concentrating on the management of the 300-head herd of beef cattle, while his brother Jack looked after the arable side.

Bill Goad finally retired in 1987, but after the death of his wife following an attack of meningitis in 1988 he enrolled as a volunteer driver with the local social services. In this capacity he was able to do valuable work for his community.

On November 21, 1956, when a new naval housing estate had been opened at Chatham by the Duchess of Kent, five Victoria Cross winners and four Albert Medal holders had streets named after them, one being Goad Avenue.

A gentle, retiring man, Goad never thrust himself forward, although his tall, slim figure and good looks ensured that he could never be overlooked at reunions of the VC and GC Association.

When in 1971 the Albert Medal was translated into the George Cross and holders of the AM were invited to exchange the insignia for that of the GC, Goad declined. "The King put that on my chest and I'm keeping it", he said.

Goad was not the only member of his family to hold the George Cross. His brother-in-law Joseph Hughes won the GC posthumously when, while serving with the Royal Army Service Corps in Hong Kong in 1946, he attempted single-handed to extinguish a fire which had broken out in the back of a three-ton munitions lorry he was driving. Hughes's brave efforts and his shouted warnings to everyone else in the vicinity to get clear of the blazing vehicle undoubtedly prevented severe loss of life when the explosives suddenly blew up, fatally wounding him.

William Goad's wife Sally, whom he had met in Scotland during the war, had been a longtime sufferer from Parkinson's disease, and it was hoped by him that any money that might be raised by the sale of his decoration would be donated to research into the condition. He is survived by

---

William Goad

WILLIAM GOAD, who has died aged 72, was awarded the Albert Medal for his gallantry in 1942, when he was serving in the Arctic convoys as a Leading Seaman on *Ashanti*.

"Leading Seaman Goad went over his ship's side," the citation recorded, "on a line well below freezing point, and rescued an unconscious man. It was blowing a full gale and there was a very great risk that he would either be washed away by the breaking seas, or swept under the bilge keel of his ship, which was rolling heavily."

William Goad was born in Cambridgeshire on May 10 1922, and educated at Stretham, near Ely. At 15 he joined the Royal Navy and served for 16 years, retiring in 1953 as Chief Petty Officer. He then became a farmer in Cambridgeshire.

Together with 13 other crew members of the *Ashanti* he was invested with the Albert Medal in July 1943 by King George VI. At various times he was also awarded the 1939-45 Star, the Atlantic Star, the Burma Star, the Africa Star, the War Medal, the Korea Medal, the Naval Long Service and Good Conduct Medal and the Queen's Silver Jubilee Medal.

In 1956 Goad Avenue, on the naval housing estate at Darget's Wood, Chatham, was named after him.

In 1971 a Royal Warrant relating to the Albert Medal revoked all existing Royal Warrants and provided for the optional exchange for the George Cross — though from then on all Albert Medal holders, whether they exchanged or not, were regarded as recipients of the George Cross. Goad elected to retain his original award.

His wife predeceased him. They had three sons.

Goad (1946): gallant

The Times and The Daily Telegraph Obituaries

(received from Cambridge Library, May 2014)

Wonderful World

I see trees of green, Red roses too
I see them bloom, for me and you
 And I think to myself, What a wonderful world.

I see skies of blue, And clouds of white.
Bright blessed days, Warm sacred nights.
 And I think to myself, What a wonderful world.

The colours of the rainbow, So pretty in the sky,
Are also on the faces Of people passing by.
 I see friends shaking hands, Saying, "How do you do".
They're really saying, I love you.

I hear babies cry, I watch them grow.
They'll learn so much more Than I'll ever know.
 And I think to myself, What a wonderful world.
Yes, I think to myself, What A Wonderful World.

(Song written by Bob Thiele and George David Weiss)

Millway New Rose Garden

Bill off duty in Korea, 1951

Conclusion

After this two year long journey of discovery I have been on, with often the strange feeling in my mind at times that I have been living in two worlds, I reflect how little we all knew of our Goad family ancestors when I began. Just snippets of stories and a few letters from the past.

There were two criteria I had to fulfil in the beginning.

One: To discover who the mother was of our great grandfather James Stuart Goad, to trace his unknown father and give our present day Goad family a lineage.

Two: To find where the farming heritage came from, when only knowing of three Goad generations tilling the soil.

Combined with the knowledge from cousin John Howes and a few Canadian cousin letters and intensive internet research, I came across William Trickett Reilly Goad.

James Stuart's father and Elizabeth Overton, his mother.

The surprising fact to me of William Trickett's birth in India, and his short time in the British Army, gave me a life worthy of any detective story.

With many more hours of research, I have pieced together that Elizabeth and her step-family, the Marshalls brought farming and dairy skills to our first Goad farmer James Stuart as well as our Jacobs ancestors – I have traced them back to 1605, all connected to the land. It was a surprise to find our three Jacobs brothers (Shadrach, Meshach and Abednego), it caused a smile and more thoughts of our interesting heritage of so many generations of Jacobs ancestors living off the land. By discovering the intermarriage of these three families of Marshall, Goad and Jacobs, I have given us our farming family heritage and am so glad to be able answer my husband Paddy's original question.

Now to explore your Goad family, and touch on some interesting facts going back to 1601 as I feel they deserve a mention in the overall picture.

Our 18th and 19th Goad line is colonial and military, extensive and colourful.

Three generations with The East India Company.

James Stuart's father William Trickett Reilly Goad was born in 1834 in Calcutta, India.

His father Charles Elliot Goad had been born 1812 in Madras, India, and his grandfather Samuel Thomas Goad was born 1779 in Middlesex, London.

Samuel Thomas was the first Goad of this family to seek his fortune in India.

His son, Samuel Boileau Goad (William Trickett's uncle) born Madras, India. 1806, was a Major in the 1st Bengal European Light Infantry. After his Army success, he became a Judicial Judge in India, also becoming a principle property owner in the prime Hill Station of Simla, owning on his death thirty three properties.

Samuel Boileau Goad was also the grandfather of Sir Frederick Treves (James Stuart's cousin) born London 1853. The Royal Surgeon, who befriended and helped Joseph Merrick, whose story is so touchingly told in the 1980s film "The Elephant Man" – Frederick Treves being played by Sir Anthony Hopkins and Joseph Merrick, magnificently portrayed by actor John Hurt.

Samuel Boileau's son, Horatio Boileau Goad born India, 1839, cousin to our X2 Great Grandfather William Trickett Goad, was Chief of Police in Simla and rose to be the Secretary of the Municipal Corporation of Simla, British India.

He had an extraordinary knowledge of local languages and customs and was a 'master of disguise'.

Rudyard Kipling based the character of 'Strickland' in his book, 'Plain Tales from the Hills', on his friend Horatio Goad.

There were also three Goad brothers in The Charge of The Light Brigade, at the Crimea, Thomas Howard, George and Charles.

Three letters linking them all are held in the British Library, London. One edged in black, containing purple flowers gathered from the battlefield where two brothers had died. Flowers picked by a friend and sent to their brother Charles, who survived for three more months after that fateful day.

They were all serving in the 13th Light Dragoons.

These three generations of Goads were travelling prolifically between India and London, all educated and of the ruling professions, so obviously of the affluent upper middle classes.

After research I have found four more direct grandfather generations of Goads back to 1601; William b1741, Joseph b1673, John b1632 to Christopher b1601.

This Christopher, our X8 great grandfather, is mentioned in the House of Commons Journal, Volume 6 on 22nd May 1649, just four months after the execution of King Charles I. He was close to The Commonwealth Government in the tumultuous time of the Civil War; an auspicious time of English political history.

He was a Fellow of King's College Cambridge, and a Bachelor of Divinity, also a Presbyterian priest in London where he had been born. He married a Ruth Pottes at St,Giles', Cripplegate, London in 1622 and they had two sons Christopher and John – John being our X7 great grandfather.

The House of Commons Journal states he has been appointed to the 'Committee for Reformation of the Universities of Oxford and Cambridge.'

To organise and regulate the setting up of a 'Commonwealth Government Lecture for the Exposition Of Scriptures'. This was in a drive to reform the nation's morals and later, he was to report back to Parliament.

As a London Presbyterian Minister he wrote a sermon titled "Refreshing Drops and Scorching Vials", based on the Book of Revelations in the Bible, which was printed and published in 1653, the year after his death. The introduction in it was written by Major General Charles Worsley, Oliver Cromwell's most trusted advisor and the Commander of the ruling Parliamentary Army.

An original copy of his book can today be found in Harvard University Library, America.

Christopher Goad was at the heart of seventeenth century government and truly a 'man of his time'.

This is just to touch on the lives of our Goad past, but it has been a pleasure to place the Goad links so far back in time. More research for the future perhaps!

For me, writing and researching as a woman, I can't help but admire our 20th century pioneering nurse, great Aunt Nance, walking in the footsteps of Florence Nightingale and Edith Cavell, at the time of suffragettes and the emancipation of women.

After my basic research, I concluded that James Stuart's life was shaped by strong women. The early women had a tale to tell in the shaping of James Stuart's successes, hence I wrote profiles of Sarah Curtis-Overton-Marshall, his grandmother, Elizabeth-Overton-Goad, his mother, Phoebe Marshall-Tibbitt, his aunt; all caring for him at different times of his life, and wrote a cameo love biography of him and the all-important Mary Jane Jacobs.

His son Thomas Goad had wife Ida Clark-Goad for support.

William (Bill) Goad had Sarah (Sally) Hughes-Goad to 'hold the fort' while he was away at war.

Latterly, Thomas Goad and William Goad's stories took precedence, but it could be said Ida and Sally were certainly 'the power behind the throne'; Strong in their own way. I think the old adage of 'Behind every successful man is a good woman' appears so true in this family story and as I suspect for most.

I'm thinking too, of lives of the past. Before the 20th century, for women, marriage meant unlimited childbirth, with all the dangers it entailed and possibly death. Life and mortality was so precarious for women – no antibiotics and hygiene was not properly understood. No umbrella of our wonderful NHS that we have today.

In times past it was such a blessing to be born with a strong constitution. What a different world we live in today and how lucky we are that the health aspect of life has been transformed in the 20th century.

But basically, no matter what century we have lived in, our lives are just the same, as are our expectations. Always for health, family and happiness.

From the family knowing so little in 2012, it has been a pleasure to paint these pictures for you, of all our past known and unknown ancestors, all of them important in the span of our history, all contributing a few genes to make us as we are today as a family.

I write only as a Goad in name, but I am so glad you have all touched my life and together we can do nothing better as a family than continue the ideal of 'Goadfest'.

Family Homes in Stretham

20th Century Goad-Jacobs

James Stuart and Mary Jane Jacobs-Goad
Grove House, Newmarket Road.
Above in 1930s, below 2014

Jonathan, Mary Elizabeth Hazel-Jacobs and Family
Cambridge House, Wilburton Road in 1920s

Cambridge House in 2014

Tommy and Rachael Crisp-Jacobs and Family
Oakley Farm House, Top Street in 1930s

Oakley Farm House, Top Street in 2014

Reuben and Alice Longford-Wright Jacobs and Family

The Chequers Inn, Front Street

The Chequers, Front Street in 2014

Thomas Jacobs and Family.

Laburnum Farm House, Read Street

His last home

Laburnum Farm House and Baptist Chapel, 2014

Thomas and Ida Clark-Goad and Family

Hill Farm House, Ely Road

Thomas and Ida moved to the farm in 1937

Hill Farm House, 2014

Sarah (Sally), Christopher and Paddy Goad

Millview House, Ely Road

Lived here in 1947 while Bill was away at sea

Millview House, Ely Road, 2014

William (Bill), Sarah (Sally) and Family

Millway, 11 Ely Road

Built by Bill and Sally 1965-66

Millway, 2014

Russell and Constance May Goad-Routledge
The Routledge Bakery, Cage Lane in 2014
Russ and Con lived here in the 1930s. Now known as The Old Bakery

James (Jim) Owen and Bess King-Goad
Aikeman House, High Street, Stretham in 2014
Jim and Bess lived here in 1960s

Acknowledgements

To My Husband Paddy, for his inspiration, support and patience.

Brother Chris Bettinson, for reading my first handwritten draft and encouragement to carry on.

My son, Mark Smith for help with photographs.

Cousin John Howes, for X2 Great Grandmother Elizabeth's mementoes, and information of the lives of his Grandparents Maud and Walter Hepher.

Cousin Cathryn Goad-Haylock, for the first basic Goad family tree and family photographs.

Cousin Gillian Goad-Johnson, for the loan of Berry Wayman Tibbitt's letters and photographs.

Canadian Cousin Joanne Robb, Berry Wayman Tibbitt's Great Granddaughter, for current Canadian family history and news.

Cousin Richard Goad, for information of his father James Owen Goad's wartime history.

Cousin David Marchant, for his mother Mollie Goad Marchant's wartime history.

Debbie Goad, American Cousin-in-Law, for Stuart Goad's family information.

The late Beatrice Stevens, BEM, for the details of the Jacobs family, from her books, 'Stretham, A Feast of Memories', and 'Stretham Wartime Memories', helping with the life of Betty Goad.

Mike and Pat Petty, for advice and help with historical photographs of ancestors' homes.

The Ellis Family of Ted Ellis, Wheatfen, Surlingham, Norfolk for allowing me to use his poem, Fulfilment.

John Shepperson, Swavesey historian, for helping with the early 20th century Goad life in Swavesey, and use of excerpts from his book 'A Village During the Great War', and photographs.

Major Hugo White, of Cornwall's Regimental Museum Archive, Bodmin, for help in verifying William Trickett's life and service.

Clint and Luke Edwards, for their photographic skills.

Thanks to Chris and Jane Thomas of Milton Contact Ltd for their help to bring this book to publication.

Ancestry.co.uk, for being there!

Last, but not least, thank you, Rob Hammond, of Computer Wizards, Littleport, who during the course of writing this has become a friend. Thank you for sharing your skills and patience over the years with a novice "Silver-Surfer"!

Epilogue

'The Elephant In the Room' – 2012-2014

When nearing the completion of this book I pondered how when writing, how it has dominated my life. It has become like the proverbial 'elephant in the room'! Sitting in the corner, dictating my days. Reaching out from my laptop, the blank white manuscript pages are demanding to be fed with the thoughts and words which have been obsessing my mind for the past two years.

When beginning I would have hardly believed this gestation period would have taken as long as for an elephant to give birth. But who knows! Two years, as one gets older, certainly passes a lot quicker than when a child.

Thinking as a woman and mother, I feel that creating a book, with all its emotions, is quite on par with giving birth: Experiencing the joy of the idea in its conception; the excitement of the highs and the emotional lows of the months of research and writing; conquering an apprehensiveness of technology to express my words in the new world of computers and latterly to endure the nervous anticipation and trepidation of publication.

Also the surprise in feeling the pain of regret of letting go of the new friends which you have brought alive from the past, after creating their reality and embracing them into your own existence.

But hopefully on the day when I see my completed creation, crisp, colourful and new, I will have the proud feelings of that as a mother, watching her grown child (or baby elephant even) leaving the room. Seeing it now confident and ready to face the uncertainty of its future in the unknown wide world of books.

Goad – Jacobs – Marshall – Tibbitt Family Tree

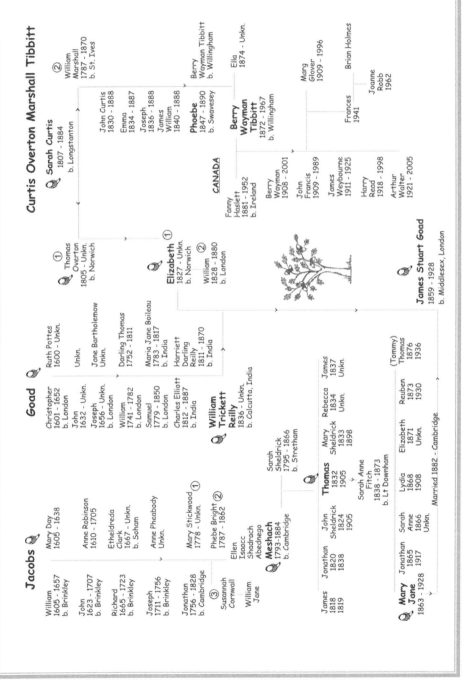

Curtis Overton Marshall Tibbitt

Sarah Curtis
1807 - 1884
b. Longstanton

② William Marshall
1787 - 1870
b. St. Ives

John Curtis
1830 - 1888

Emma
1834 - 1887

Joseph
1836 - 1888

James
William
1840 - 1888

Phoebe
1847 - 1890
b. Swavesey

Berry
Wayman Tibbitt
b. Willingham

Ella
1874 - Unkn.

Marg
Glover
1909 - 1996

Berry
Wayman
Tibbitt
1872 - 1967
b. Willingham

Frances
1941

Joanne
Robb
1962

Brian Holmes

CANADA

Fanny
Haslett
1881 - 1952
b. Ireland

Berry
Wayman
1908 - 2001

John
Francis
1909 - 1989

James
Weybourne
1911 - 1925

Harry
Read
1918 - 1998

Arthur
Walter
1921 - 2005

Goad

Ruth Pottes
1600 - Unkn.

Christopher
1601 - 1652
b. London

John
1632 - Unkn.

Unkn.

Joseph
1656 - Unkn.
b. London

Jane Bartholemow
Unkn.

William
1741 - 1782
b. London

Darling Thomas
1752 - 1811

Samuel
1779 - 1850
b. London

Maria Jane Boileau
1783 - 1817
b. India

Charles Elliott
1812 - 1887
b. India

Harriett
Darling
Reilly
1811 - 1870
b. India

① Thomas
Overton
1805 - Unkn.
b. Norwich

① Elizabeth
1827 - Unkn.
b. Norwich

② William
1828 - 1880
b. London

William Trickett Reilly
1836 - Unkn.
b. Calcutta, India

James Stuart Goad
1859 - 1928
b. Middlesex, London

Jacobs

William
1605 - 1657
b. Brinkley

Mary Day
1605 -1638

John
1623 - 1707
b. Brinkley

Anne Robinson
1610 - 1705

Richard
1665 - 1723
b. Brinkley

Etheldreda
Clark
1667 - Unkn.
b. Soham

Joseph
1711 - 1756
b. Brinkley

Anne Pheabody
Unkn.

Jonathan
1756 - 1828
b. Cambridge

① Mary Stickwood
1778 - Unkn.

② Phebe Bright
1787 - 1862

Ellen
Isaac
Shadrach
Abednego

③ Susannah
Cornwall

William
Jane

Meshach
1793-1884
b. Cambridge

Sarah
Sheldrick
1795 - 1866
b. Stretham

Thomas
1832
1905

Sarah Anne
Fitch
1838 - 1873
b. Lt Downham

Jonathan
1820
1838

John
Sheldrick
1824
1905

James
1818
1819

Mary
Sheldrick
1833
1898

Rebecca
1834
Unkn.

James
1837
Unkn.

(Tommy)
Thomas
1876
1936

Lydia
1868
1908

Elizabeth
1871
Unkn.

Reuben
1873
1930

Sarah
Anne
1866
Unkn.

Mary
Jane
1863 - 1928

Married 1882 - Cambridge

Mary Jane Jacobs — The Swavesey Children — James Stuart Good

Maud 1883 1965 m. 1906 Walter Hepher
Sarah Anne 1884 1940
Thomas 1886 1961 m. 1914 Ida Clark
James William 1890 1918
Stuart 1891 1935 — AMERICA
George York 1893 1979 (1) Maude Willetts (2) Winifrid Lower
Constance May 1894 1945 m. Russell Routledge
Mabel 1896 1977 m. Horace Ashby
Lilian 1899 1937 m. Arthur Peacock

Marjorie 1907
Daphne 1927

Ella Porath
John 1917
Viva Lent
Mary 1927

Mabel 1922 1964 m. Roger Fredrikson
James Francis 1923 1950
Harold Wesley 1925 1992
Christine 1929 1958

John 1944

Carol (1) — Bonnie Benjamin
(2) Jean Rae Katzenberg — Larry Rae, Mary Christine, Barry Scot, Debra Sue

John Stuart 1914 - 1988 m. 1946 Joan Fisher
James Owen 1916 - 1990 m. Bess King
Betty 1918 - 1985
William 1922 - 1994 m. Sarah Hughes
Mollie 1924 - 2000 m. 1949 Douglas Marchant

Gillian 1948 m. Robert Johnson
Cathryn 1950 m. David Haylock
John 1952 - 2003 (1) Fiona Makay Rae (2) Alison Scaife
Christopher James

Joanne m. Andrew Blazey
Darren m. Hannah Watts
Ben & Sinead
Emma
Kathleen Mary (2014)

Robert 1941 2010 m. Francoise Rey
Richard 1946 m. Pauline Bass

Christine m. Mark
Natalie m. Manolo
Emma
Oliver

Nick m. Cathrine
Jason Kerry
Laura Jamie Ben
Lisa Jane Ted Owen
Ettienne

David 1953 m. Sally Mumford
Timothy 1956 Stella (1) Morgan
(2) Jax — Alison Simeon Romy Calvin
Louise Georgina m. Christopher Hodsman
Elizabeth

Christopher 1944
(1) Carol
(2) Kim
(3) Carol Yen Han

Joan 1961 m. Paul Godfrey
Jane 1964 m. Glen Brown
Lynn 1966
Tom 1968
Kate 1985 m. John Troupe

Susan Steven Hannah
Amber Rome Christopher
John Christopher

Poppy Sally m. Daniel Lewin

Patrick John 1947 m. (1) Meloy Burke 1998 Lesley Bettinson Smith (2)
Martin 1955 m. 1995 Cathrine Tobin

Patrick 1970 m. Vanessa Brooks
Sarah 1971
Helen 1973

Joshua Thomas George Grace

Polly 1996
Alice 1998

Oak tree grown by Paddy from a Hill Farm acorn

The Swavesey Children

Mary Jane Jacobs   James Stuart Goad

Maud 1883 1965
m. 1906 Walter Hepher

Marjorie 1907

Sarah Anne 1884 1940

🌰 Thomas 1886 1961
m. 1914 Ida Clark

James William 1890 1918

Stuart 1891 1935
AMERICA

Ella Porath
John 1917

Viva Lent

George York 1893 1979 ②
① Maude Willetts
Mary 1927
Winifrid Lower

Constance May 1894 1945
m. Russell Routledge

Mollie 1924 - 2000
m. 1949 Douglas Marchant

Mabel 1896 1977
m. Horace Ashby

Daphne 1927

Lilian 1899 1937
m. Arthur Peacock

Mabel 1922 1964
m. Roger Fredrikson

James Francis 1923 1950

Harold Wesley 1925 1992

Christine 1929 1958

Carol ①
Bonnie Benjamin

② Jean Rae Katzenberg
Larry Rae   Mary Christine

Barry Scot
m. Debra Sue

William 1922 - 1994
m. Sarah Hughes

James Owen 1916 - 1990
m. Bess King

Betty 1918 - 1985

David 1953
m. Sally Mumford
Louise Georgina
m. Christopher Hodsman

Timothy 1956

Stella ①
Alison   Morgan
② Jax
Alison Simeon
Romy Calvin
Elizabeth

John 1944

John Stuart 1914 - 1988
m. 1946 Joan Fisher

Robert 1941 2010
m. Froncoise Rey

Richard 1946
m. Pauline Bass

Christine
m. Mark
Natalie
m. Manolo
Emma Oliver
Ettienne

Nick   Cathrine
Jason   Kerry

Laura Jamie Ben

Lisa Jane Ted Owen

Patrick John 1947
m.
① Meloy Burke

Sarah 1971
Helen 1973

Patrick 1970
m. Vanessa Brooks

Joshua Thomas George Grace

1998 Lesley Bettinson Smith ②

Martin 1955
m. 1995 Cathrine Tobin

Polly 1996
Alice 1998

Gillian 1948
m. Robert Johnson

Cathryn 1950
m. David Haylock

John 1952-2003
m.
① Fiona Makay Rae Scaife
② Alison

Christopher James

Christopher 1944

① Carol

② Kim
③ Carol Yen Han

Poppy
Sally
m. Daniel Lewin

Joanne
m.
Andrew Blazey

Darren
&
Hannah Sinead

Ben Emma

Kathleen Mary (2014)

Joan 1961

Jane 1964
m. Paul Godfry

Lynn 1966
Glen 1971

Tom 1968
Kate 1985
m. John Troupe

John
Rome Christopher

Susan Steven Hannah

Amber

🌰 327 🌰

Oak tree grown by Paddy from a Hill Farm acorn